AN INTRODUCTION TO FRANCHISING

A. Robert Webber

Leicester Business School, De Montfort University, UK

palgrave
macmillan

First published 2013 by
PALGRAVE MACMILLAN

Palgrave Macmillan in the UK is an imprint of Macmillan Publishers Limited,
registered in England, company number 785998, of Houndmills, Basingstoke,
Hampshire RG21 6XS.

Palgrave Macmillan in the US is a division of St Martin's Press LLC,
175 Fifth Avenue, New York, NY 10010.

Palgrave Macmillan is the global academic imprint of the above companies
and has companies and representatives throughout the world.

Palgrave® and Macmillan® are registered trademarks in the United States,
the United Kingdom, Europe and other countries

ISBN 978–0–230–36164–5

This book is printed on paper suitable for recycling and made from fully
managed and sustained forest sources. Logging, pulping and manufacturing
processes are expected to conform to the environmental regulations of the
country of origin.

A catalogue record for this book is available from the British Library.

Library of Congress Cataloging-in-Publication Data

Webber, Robert, 1956?–
  An introduction to franchising / by Robert Webber.
      p. cm.
  Includes bibliographical references and index.
  ISBN 978-0-230-36164-5
  1. Franchises (Retail trade) I. Title.
  HF5429.23.W43 2013
  658.8'708--dc23   2012036830

10   9   8   7   6   5   4   3   2   1
22   21   20   19   18   17   16   15   14   13

Printed and bound in Great Britain by
the MPG Books Group

I have tried not to make the dedication sound like a theatrical award acceptance speech, but there are several people who must be mentioned without whose support this book would not have been written.

First, my dearest wife Alla, and son Nicolai, who have had to endure my squirrelling myself away while researching and writing this book, often when we have been on family holidays. My eternal love and gratitude for their forbearance. Second, to Alfredo, for his inspiration throughout my business life. And finally, and by no means least, to my father, Tony, and my mother, Barbara, who supported me ceaselessly through the highs and lows of life and who, sadly, did not survive to see this book in print.

Thank you all!

CONTENTS

FIGURES

CASE STUDIES

ACKNOWLEDGEMENTS

The author and publishers would like to thank the following for permission to reproduce copyright material: British Franchise Association for Appendix 1; International Franchise Association for Case Study 8.1 from 'Transition: From Military Service to Civilian Life', *Franchising World*, March 2009, and Appendix 3; *The Economist* for Figure 10.1 from 'The Big Mac Index', *The Economist*, 24 January 2012; Rosenberg International Franchise Center for Figure 3.1 and Figure 10.2; World Franchise Council for Appendix 2; Well Kneaded Food for Case Study 6.2. Every effort has been made to contact all copyright-holders, but if any have been inadvertently omitted the publishers will be pleased to make the necessary arrangements at the earliest opportunity.

PREFACE

Franchising is fascinating business area and one that has served those well who have been involved with ethical and responsible franchise operations.

In deciding to write this book, I looked at the available texts on the subject and found most of them to be extremely technical, many written by lawyers as texts for those who are fluent in the language of law, while others written for a specific geographical region, which may or may not have relevance to a more global audience. Virtually none of the texts sought to unravel the mysteries of the art of franchising in a generalist manner focused on those who were coming to franchising for the first time and who did not know the technical terms that many authors hid behind.

As the leader of a course at a major British university for undergraduate students on the subject of franchising, and as a director of a group of companies that has previously used franchising as a business expansion method, I quickly identified that a simpler, more understandable text was desirable, and this book is my contribution. It is not intended to be purely a textbook for my students (though it is hoped that some might buy copies), nor is it intended as a practitioner's handbook, but rather a simpler, light-hearted but in-depth analysis of the franchise industry, which can be read and which will offer guidance equally to students, those wishing to buy a franchise, and those wishing to franchise their business.

There is a need to look at some technical aspects – for example, the technicalities of franchise agreements – but wherever possible I have attempted to avoid using too much technical terminology.

My philosophy on franchising is that it is a fantastic method whereby those who have experienced and been successful in a structured business environment, and who would love to satisfy the dream of self-employment, are able to do so but with the safety net of having the organizational structure of the franchisor behind them to give advice and guidance as they realize the dream and move forward to self-employed success. I do not necessarily consider franchising to be a halfway house between employed status and full-blown self-employment, though there will be some readers who will use franchising in this manner. Franchising is a fabulous opportunity for both franchisor and franchisee to benefit from a system that has been developed to maximize the business prospects for both parties, and as such should be regarded as a unique and exceptional opportunity for those involved.

In reading this book, you may be ready to embark on a different phase of your career so, as you plan your campaign, use this book as your guide through the exciting times ahead and be on your guard against the unexpected pitfalls that may trap the unwary traveller on the path to success.

A. ROBERT WEBBER

1 THE ORIGINS AND HISTORY OF FRANCHISING

INTRODUCTION AND LEARNING OUTCOMES

The purpose of this chapter is to give the reader an understanding of the history of franchising, looking back to the origins of the word and discovering how franchising has developed into the business expansion system we have come to associate with the term in current usage.
    The reader will be able to:

- Understand how franchising was conceived and how it has been modified.
- Understand the importance of the concept throughout history and its importance in today's business world.

Franchising is not a new concept! However, its origins are a matter of much debate and discussion. Some authors would have readers believe that it is a wholly American concept, devised in the mid-1800s to help American businesses establish an efficient distributor network. As we shall see over the next few pages, this notion does have some limited foundation and it was certainly the origins of business-format franchising, but the concept of franchising was undoubtedly in existence considerably earlier than when Christopher Columbus first set foot on the American continent!

The foundation of the franchising system probably lies closer to the Roman Empire as it existed in the early years of the New Testament than the commercial empires of businesses that have utilized this phenomenally successful business development model. Even the word franchise has its roots in the languages of central Europe, rather than the English language, though its precise origins are unclear.

FRANCHISING – THE EARLY YEARS

In ancient times, there was a Germanic tribe called the Franks, who derived their name from their weapon of choice – a spear. These Germanic warriors were given their name by their immediate neighbours, because this tribe was renowned for standing up for its rights in a vigorous manner (usually in battle, and using their trusty spears) so their name came to mean 'free' or 'the defenders of freedom', from which we get the phrase 'to speak frankly, or freely'. The country name France comes from the same root, meaning the place where one can be free. Indeed, prior to the French Revolution, the currency of France was the *écu d'or* in Louis IX's time (*écu* means 'shield', which featured on the coins, bearing a coat of arms, though it may be a reason why the French were firmly in favour of calling the currency currently called 'the euro', the European Currency Unit, or ecu for short), or the *Louis d'or*, which was first minted in 1640 during Louis XIII's time. In 1795, having removed the aristocracy, the French Revolutionary Council introduced the silver decimal franc, meaning 'free money' or coinage minted after the freedom from the oppressive monarchy.

In the Middle Ages in England, the word franchise had come to be associated with citizenship and the freedoms that being a citizen brought, specifically the right to vote, and this is where the word disenfranchised enters the language, meaning those who have lost their citizenship rights, particularly the right to vote. Therefore, some would argue that, in deriving from the old French word *'franc'*, meaning 'free', we can assume that the original concept of franchising is the granting of certain rights to those who deserve (or can afford) a specific right to be granted, which in a positive sense is precisely what franchising does; the word franchise actually means freeness.

Nevertheless if one goes back to the early Roman Empire, where the lingua franca was Latin, there was the verb *'frango'*, meaning 'to break into pieces', and it may be that the roots of the word 'franchise' can be traced back to here.

Originally, when the legions of Rome colonized what has become known as the continent of Europe, the senate appointed a Governor to control the newly acquired settlement. The Governor had the responsibility of protecting the land and the people that inhabited it, to introduce Roman law, and to establish a level of governance that was intended to establish both freedom and a level of authority in the conquered land.

The cost of establishing a protectorate was to be met by the imposition of taxes, which were collected by the Governor from the inhabitants of the state. Any expenses were deducted from the taxes collected, including a percentage which the Governor retained as his remuneration, and the balance was sent to Rome to swell the Roman treasury. So we can see that the Roman Empire was comprised of many semi-autonomous states, each holding allegiance to Rome, and controlled by an appointee of the Senate in Rome, whose task was to gather revenue (taxes) from the populace and after defraying costs of providing services (governance), would send the balance to the Rome.

When transposed over the business format model, we can see many similarities: the Roman Senate (franchisor) appoints a Governor (franchisee) to a dependent state (territory) where his task is to maximize potential and revenue and, after deducting his expenses, submit the balance to the Roman treasury (fees). Consequently, the concept of franchising potentially has its roots more in the task of collecting taxes than in any commercial enterprise, but the step forward to a mercantile arrangement was both simple and rational.

On a commercial footing, the Governors of Rome's far-flung dependent states quickly identified that sourcing all the needs for their local governance directly from Italy was both cumbersome and time-consuming, so they appointed local craftsmen and tradesmen to supply the needs of their administration – from chariots and weapons for the legions, to food and other provisions for their administration, each was sourced locally. The suppliers of these essential needs received their patronage from the Governor; they were licensed to supply their goods and services, and in return for their licences, they would pay the Governor a fee.

Using the previous analogy to interpret the actions of various parties, we can now see that, as well as holding the franchise from the Roman senate, the local Governor was now acting more in the role of franchisor in handing out licences to local tradesmen, and so we can also see where the concept of the master franchisee was born; that is, the franchisee who has the authority to issue licences to sub-franchisees.

This system of tax collection under franchise was so successful that it was adopted by most of the victorious powers down the ages. Certainly, when William the Conqueror arrived in England in 1066, he imposed a similar system of tax collection and created the role for local governors, though in William's administration, these were more localized, often being restricted to the area of a county or large city. William called his governors Sheriffs (coming from *scir* and *gerefa*, an ancient word for the royal authority in a shire) and we can therefore see that the much hated Sheriff of Nottingham from the Robin Hood fable was probably one of the first master franchisees in Britain!

One of the ancient rights bestowed by the Sheriff on the population was the privilege of holding fairs in the town, and many of these fairs still exist today (for example, the Nottingham Goose Fair). The fair was held on land owned by the state and controlled by the Sheriff, and in return the tradesmen who set up stalls at the fair paid a percentage of their takings to the Sheriff, often a tenth, or a tithe, as it was called.

The title of Sheriff still exists today as the representative of the monarch in some regions of England, but the role is now only a ceremonial title, as the role of tax collector has since devolved to central government, following the rule of Oliver Cromwell and the rise of Parliament. However, the concept of tithing continued. Gradually, the Church obtained more and more property and land, and those who worked on the Church estates were obliged to tender a tithe to the Church for God's bounty in giving them work. Naturally, the Church could not indulge in commercial activities, residing as it did on a far higher spiritual plane, but in order to meet its expenses, it had to raise capital and tithing was a legitimate route to fund-raising. Even today, in some religions, the expectancy of tithing still exists.

Moving away from matters religious and the funding of the Church, some would lay claim that franchising originated in the twelfth century with the ancient guilds of London. Certainly, there is evidence that a form of franchising was adopted by these august bodies, which would charge members an affiliation fee set by the guild and there would be a large fee payable for membership and annual payments to retain that membership. Some guilds charged a percentage of turnover as their fee, while others a set monetary amount. Membership of the guilds brought wealth and prosperity to the merchant classes – the name 'guild' comes from the ancient Anglo-Saxon word *gilden*, meaning 'to pay'.

THE BREWING CONNECTION

Moving forward to the early part of the nineteenth century, we find ourselves in the time when alcohol was starting to play an increasingly significant role in the lives of Britons and in other European states.

It has been suggested that business format franchising was originally conceived by the German brewer, Späten, who gave the rights to sell their beers to certain taverns, but the emergence of a single German brewer in this field alongside a number of British brewers who at the same time used this approach, might suggest that this form of franchising originated in Britain rather than in Germany, but there is little to support this hypothesis other than the quantity issue.

Wherever it started, at this time, the manufacture of ale was very much a more local affair than it is today; most hostelries made their own ale, and ale houses were spreading throughout the country. These ale houses brought with them other social problems and it soon became clear that some sort of regulation was needed. The government of the time decided that the taxation of ale manufacture would significantly reduce the number of ale houses, and consequently the inherent problems associated with them. Faced with financial ruin, however, the proprietors of these ale houses joined together and formed breweries, where the ale could be

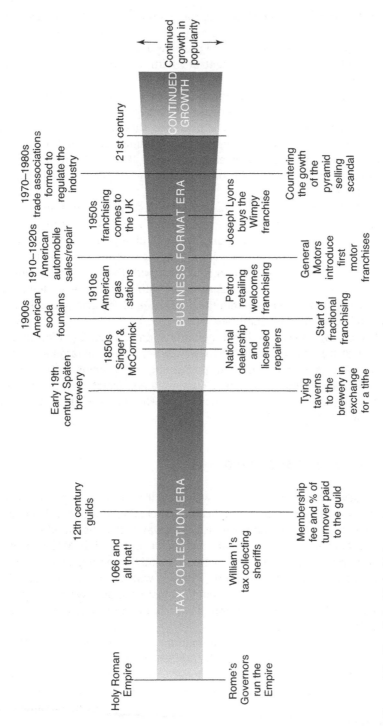

Figure 1.1 Timeline of franchising

brewed centrally and distributed to the ale houses that formed part of the brewing group. The landlords bought their ales from the brewer and in addition paid a tithe which covered the cost of the brewing tax. The brewer collected the tithes and dealt centrally with the tax-collecting arm of the treasury.

So we can see that, even at this late stage, relatively speaking, the franchise issued by the brewer was more concerned with the collection of taxes than being an ongoing commercial business, though the brewer derived its profit from the mark-up on the ale it was selling. The tithed houses soon became known as tied houses, and the term still exists today, where public houses are tied to a particular brewery, to which a percentage of the profits are paid.

The higher level of the franchising concept survives to this day – one will often hear it said that the government has awarded the franchise to do something to a particular company. In effect, charging a commercial operation for the right to carry out some task in exchange for revenue (or tax) paid to the Treasury. This notion is at odds with the definition of business format franchising, as we shall see, but within the general definition of franchising, and certainly within the guidelines of the original understanding of franchising, it is legitimate.

Readers will have noted that a qualification has just been introduced in respect of franchising to which they may be, as yet, unfamiliar. *Business format franchising* is the method of adapting the franchising model to the version to which most of us are accustomed and which we associate most frequently with the idiom 'franchising'. The history of franchising is summarized in Figure 1.1.

BUSINESS FORMAT FRANCHISING

It has never been entirely clear who was the originator of the business system that grew into business format franchising, but general consensus suggests that it happened in America and was either the founder of Singer Sewing Machines, Isaac Merritt Singer, or Cyrus Hall McCormick, the inspirational father of mechanical reaping and harvesting, as both systems appeared at about the same time, 1850–1, way before the American Civil War; but whichever got past the winning post first, both were instigators of a great tradition that has developed and changed the world of business in the following 160-odd years.

Looking at the case put by the founder of the Singer Sewing Machine Company, we learn that Isaac Merritt Singer was producing a range of highly popular sewing machines. Singer's sales force travelled the length and breadth of the country selling these marvellous machines to families and businesses that, until this time, had been sewing by hand. Singer soon became the victim of his own success, however, because while he was able to sell vast quantities of the new machines, bringing them back to the head office for service and repair was both costly and highly cumbersome; moreover, it was occupying too much of his representatives' time and consequently sales were starting to fall.

Singer devised a plan whereby he would develop a network of licensed engineers, who would carry stocks of the most common components and repair the machines locally. The engineers were all self-employed and were paid directly by the customer, but could legitimately call themselves 'official licensed repairers' of Singer's machines; the engineer would buy component stock from Singer and would also pay Singer a small percentage of the invoice price as a fee for being allowed to operate as an authorized repairer. This concept freed up the representatives' time to expand sales and gave their customers a local point of contact for a more efficiently handled repair or service.

Soon these repair engineers began selling replacement machines as the originally purchased machines wore out, and the concept of a true franchised dealer was born. These first franchisees held stocks of the latest Singer machines, which they would sell and repair locally, and they were expected to pay Singer a percentage of their sales turnover as a franchise fee. Consequently, the Singer Sewing Machine Company became the first business format franchisor. As Singer's business grew, it soon became apparent that the franchisees were making a solid living out of their relationship with the company, and Singer was inundated with applicants to become a licensed dealer. It became clear that some sort of selection process was required and the easiest one to implement was a financial entry barrier; if one could not afford to buy into the system, one could not join. Despite this payment being only a few dollars, it quickly sorted the genuine from the opportunistic applicants and allowed for a management structure with adequate training for the franchisee network to be funded independently of Singer's core profit margin. The business was so successful that others looked at the model as a method of expanding their own businesses.

CASE STUDY 1.1

McCormick Harvesting Machine Company – a pioneer franchisor

Cyrus Hall McCormick was an outstanding early American mechanic; he was a man of vision with a passion, and a genius at business development and marketing.

Even though McCormick manufactured reapers for sale as early as 1834, he did not sell any for the next six years, but was undaunted by

→

CASE STUDY 1.1 *continued*

this. Eventually, he sold two machines in 1840, seven in 1842, and fifty in 1844. The reaper was not suited to the hills of Virginia, where McCormick was based, and the conservative farmers were uncertain about buying expensive new machinery that needed to be repaired by a skilled mechanic.

When McCormick made a trip to America's Mid-West, however, things changed rapidly. He saw his opportunity in the endless and verdant prairies, with hundreds of miles of good rich soil with few trees and fewer rocks. When his fierce rival, Obed Hussey, moved east, Cyrus McCormick moved west and established himself in Chicago in 1847. At that time, Chicago was a small town of little more than 10,000 citizens, but McCormick built a factory there, and manufactured 500 machines in time for the harvest of 1848.

McCormick's skill in marketing resulted in him creating a complex business plan. He sold his machines at a fixed price, and if farmers could not afford the capital cost, they could pay by instalments, and he gave a guarantee of satisfaction.

Recognizing that his machines would be sold throughout the USA, McCormick quickly identified a major problem. His machines were used during the harvest period and if a farmer's machine needed spare parts from the Chicago factory, the crop would be ruined before they could be delivered and fitted. So McCormick set up a system of agencies which would sell his machines, give instruction to the buyers and supply spare parts. This was during the infancy of business format franchising, but it is clear that Cyrus McCormick's innovative approach to business helped to develop its current form.

This industrial revolution set up an arrangement whereby a business system would allow the latest technology to be distributed, sold and serviced over a vast physical area, without the costs of developing a fully owned and operated infrastructure. This system became known as 'business format franchising'.

The next big influence in the development of business format franchising arrived with the big soft-drinks manufacturers in the USA – Coca-Cola, 7-Up and Dr Pepper's Root Beer – when it was quickly discovered that shipping bottles of what was essentially carbonated sweet water around the continent was a phenomenally expensive operation. What was needed was a system whereby water, sugar and carbonation could be added at source to the vital ingredients of these popular drinks. The drinks companies started to produce syrups that could be added to locally sourced water and then carbonated at point of sale, giving rise to the famed American soda fountains. The proprietors of the soda fountains became fractional franchisees, paying a percentage of their soda sales to the drinks companies who were supplying their base syrups. The concept of the fractional franchise arose because most soda fountains were in stores that sold other commodities – from hardware to ice-cream. The proprietors bought their syrups and equipment from the drinks companies and gave a percentage of their soda sales as a franchise fee.

Again, soda fountains became popular, and soon there were more applicants than there were 'territories' available, so the system of paying for a franchise was implemented, to include equipment, uniforms, training and a marketing package. Very soon, soda fountains moved into the mainstream and dedicated stores began to operate.

This was all around the time of the expansion of America's love of the motor-car, and with motor-cars came the need for petroleum spirit on which to run them. Owning vast numbers of petrol retailing outlets was prohibitively expensive, even for the wealthy American oil giants, so a system of franchised operators was introduced. A garage operator would buy the franchise for Standard Oil (Esso), or Texaco, or one of the other numerous oil producers, and the operators were supplied with petrol pumps in the oil company's livery, a sign to hang on their forecourt and other dedicated products from their chosen supplier. The franchising concept allowed for exceptional growth of outlets at minimal cost to the oil companies, and the race was on to get the widest coverage in the quickest time.

Similarly, as more and more cars appeared on American highways, so the need for competent local salesmen and repairers grew; after several motor manufacturers joined forces in 1910 under the banner of General Motors, so the concept of franchising extended to vehicle sales and repairs. Some say that General Motors emulated the Singer model of franchising; while others will suggest that they looked to Belgium and the rival business of Adam Opel (who, incidentally, came under the GM banner in 1929) for their inspiration. Opel, before manufacturing cars, had made sewing machines and it is said that Opel had adopted Singer's model and refined it for the European market; whichever story is true, General Motors set up hundreds of franchised automobile dealerships in a very short period of time and left the rest of the industry playing 'catch-up'.

The franchising model of business development proved so successful that it became the preferred method of retail expansion in America in the early part of the twentieth century; and despite wars, recessions and the mob, franchising flourished.

Following the success of the wartime cartoons featuring a muscular, spinach-eating sailor by the name of Popeye, and his friend, Wimpy, Joseph Lyons in England identified a strong American trademark and niche product and subsequently bought the non-US global rights to the Wimpy brand of hamburger restaurants, and with the rights to the brand brought the concept of business format franchising to mainstream fast food in the UK. Growing the business through franchising was so successful that Lyons very quickly applied the model to his other business divisions, and the jingle of the Lyons Maid ice cream franchise was soon to be heard throughout the nation.

Many other businesses followed Lyons' franchising model and now the world has a vast number of franchised businesses, but success did not come without some problems. In the 1970s the commercial world was rocked by the shame of the pyramid selling scandal; unsuspecting 'pyramiders' were offered the opportunity of vast wealth merely by introducing friends to the pyramid. As the new pyramiders paid their entry fees to the person who introduced them, the fee was passed up the line, being diluted increasingly until the organizer of the pyramid scam received a vast quantity of small remunerations, making him or her exceedingly wealthy.

> **Pyramid selling**: *a practice adopted by some manufacturers of advertising for distributors, and selling them batches of goods. The first distributors then advertise for more distributors, who are sold subdivisions of the original batches at an increased price. This process continues until the final distributors are left with a stock that is unsaleable except at a loss.*

Like most scams, this had no real basis for success, but there were some slight similarities to business format franchising, and consequently the franchise industry was tainted by the scam. It was clear that there needed to be some control over the industry, and in many countries regulatory legislation was introduced. Following the British tradition of self-regulation, several franchisors joined forces to create the forerunner of the British Franchise Association, and in the USA a similar organization was formed, with global aspirations, under the banner of the International Franchise Association.

With the growth of the European Union, the BFA and other European national franchising bodies affiliated under the European Franchising Federation, each retaining its own identity but all subscribing to a European set of principles and a code of ethics that would create a level playing field for franchising throughout Europe.

Therefore, we can see that what started life as an efficient method of collecting taxes from the distant corners of empires has developed into a highly successful business expansion model and as business opportunities evolve, one can be sure that franchising will develop in more refined forms to meet the needs of commercial evolution.

WHAT DO YOU THINK?

On the face of it, franchising can be adapted to suit just about any business, from service centres through to retail businesses; indeed, some might argue that governance could even be franchised, which would rather take the concept back to its roots.

It could be argued that business operators who collect sales tax (or value added tax – VAT) are franchisees of the government in the original role of tax collector, and their reward is being allowed to reclaim the portion of tax they have spent on goods and services. Is this really comparable?

In some countries, governments have already supposedly entered into franchise agreements with suppliers and operators of infrastructural services, such as rail operating companies. But are these really franchises?

Further reading

Dicke, Thomas S., *Franchising in America: The Development of a Business Method, 1840–1980* (University of North Carolina Press 1992).

Icon Group International, *Franchising: Webster's Timeline History, 1232–2007* (ICON Group International, Inc. 2010).

Ritzer, George, *The McDonaldization of Society: 20th Anniversary Edition* (Sage 2012).

2 DEFINING FRANCHISING

INTRODUCTION AND LEARNING OUTCOMES

The purpose of this chapter is to give the reader a good understanding of the legal definition of franchising as appreciated by the leading franchise organizations and associations across the world. We explore whether the definition goes far enough, or whether there is a better definition that can be applied. We understand the four 'cornerstones' of franchising as well as the 'seven pillars of successful franchising'.

The reader will be able to:

- Appreciate the need for some level of regulation to protect both the franchisor and franchisee.
- Understand whether there are any types of business that cannot be franchised.
- Understand that franchising offers a true level playing field for both men and women to be successful.

There have been many and varied definitions of franchising through the ages and throughout the world; and most have been determined to set legal boundaries within the industry. The biggest problem with legal definitions is that they are intended merely to set limitations and guide the reader as to which law should be applied in dealing with the concept. Consequently, these legal definitions go some way towards identifying the most important elements of the transaction, but fail miserably in the inclusion of the inherent aspects that define the industry.

In attempting any definition of franchising, it would be as well to identify the various players on the field of battle. A generally accepted definition of a *'franchisor'* is a person or company that has established a successful commercial system

> *A **franchisor** is a person or company that has created a commercial business and who wishes to allow other persons or companies to operate a business under their brand.*

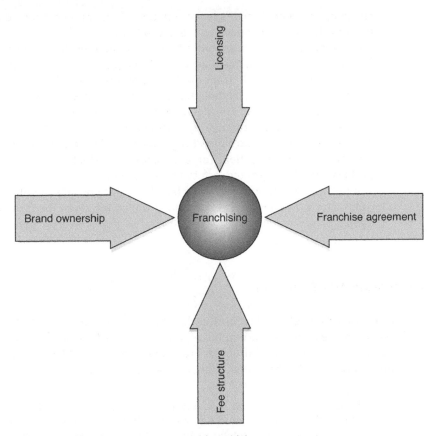

Figure 2.1   The four cornerstones of franchising

and business model through experience, and is willing to allow other persons or companies a licence to carry on an independent business under the auspices of the franchisor's brand or trade mark. Similarly, a *fran-chisee'* is typically defined as a person or company who participates in a franchise agreement as the purchaser of the right to carry on an autonomous business using the know-how and privileged trade secrets of the franchisor.

Any franchise system should be based on the four cornerstones shown in Figure 2.1, and it can be taken for granted that these would be fundamental to any definition of a franchise system:

- The ownership by the franchisor of a brand, or a trade mark, or a secret process, or a

> *A* **franchisee** *is a person or company that agrees to purchase the rights to operate an independent business using the franchisor's specialist know-how and brand in exchange for a financial consideration.*

concept, or a patent, or a specialized item of equipment, coupled with the knowledge and goodwill connected with it.
- The willingness of the franchisor to grant to an individual or business (the franchisee) a licence allowing the development and exploitation of the franchisor's brand, trademark, secret process, idea, patent or equipment, comprising confidential and privileged information, and the associated goodwill and knowledge to maximize advancement.
- The inclusion and acceptance by both parties to the franchise agreement or licence, of controls and regulations under which the contractual rights and obligations of a business in which the franchisee exploits the rights granted, are to be managed.
- The payment by the franchisee of fees (or other consideration) for the rights and privileges that are obtained under the agreement, and for ongoing services and assistance provided by the franchisor during the term of the contract.

THE EUROPEAN DEFINITION

A good example of a definition that has been written by lawyers trying to meet the needs and requirements of many interested parties is that which has been issued by the European Franchise Federation (EFF) and subsequently adopted by the British Franchise Association (BFA):

> ❝ Franchising is a system of marketing goods and/or technology, which is based upon a close and ongoing collaboration between legally and financially separate and independent undertakings, the Franchisor and its Individual Franchisees, whereby the Franchisor grants its Individual Franchisees the right, and imposes the obligation, to conduct a business in accordance with the Franchisor's concept. The right entitles and compels the Individual Franchisee, in exchange for direct or indirect financial consideration, to use the Franchisor's trade name, and/or trade mark and/or service mark, know-how, business and technical methods, procedural system, and other industrial and/or intellectual property rights, supported by continuing provision of commercial and technical assistance, within the framework and for the term of a written franchise agreement, concluded between the parties for this purpose.
>
> (*European Code of Ethics for Franchising*, part II, section IV, para. 1, 12/2003)

The language adopted by the EFF's lawyers was obviously intended to provide a technical definition for legal purposes rather than a clear definition for the layperson; however, we shall try to identify and analyse the most significant points.

The definition appears wide enough to cover just about every conceivable level of franchising, but in trying to find a compromise that would satisfy the requirements of a broad and diverse set of stakeholders the definition has left some gaping holes in accurate explanation.

The opening statement: 'franchising is a system of marketing goods and/or technology' rather sets the tone and relegates franchising to the mere functional role of a marketing device employed by the franchisor. By the end of this chapter it is hoped that the reader will understand that franchising is an entire lifestyle change for both the franchisor and franchisee, which involves a huge level of commitment over many years.

On a more positive note, the next phrase is quite accurate: 'a close and ongoing collaboration between legally and financially separate and independent undertakings', as it identifies that the franchisor's and franchisee's businesses are entirely separate entities, and one is not merely a subsidiary of the other. This principle of independence is enshrined in the second cornerstone on which the concept of franchising is founded (see Figure 2.1).

It is also true that 'the Franchisor grants its Individual Franchisees the right, and imposes the obligation, to conduct a business in accordance with the Franchisor's concept', and, without a mention of the explicit and implicit obligations of the franchisor to its franchisees, rattles on to identify the elements that *compel* the Franchisee to operate in a certain manner before acknowledging the franchisees' rights and expectations in the penultimate nine-word statement: 'supported by continuing provision of commercial and technical assistance'!

Finally, and almost as an afterthought, it is recognized that one party is contracted to the other through a written franchise agreement.

To say that the EFF's definition is not fit for purpose would be inaccurate: so far as it goes, the definition is convoluted but accurate. The definition does ignore the principle of territorial rights, and whereas the subject of territory is company specific, franchisees can and do expect some element of exclusivity in a given territory so that that they are protected against over-saturation of their geographical area of operation.

Equally, the reference to a franchise agreement rather than binding the definition to the legal restrictions of a contract, might account for the fact that in many European countries there are specific laws on the subject of franchising, whereas in the UK the agreement is subject to general contract law.

The legal characteristic of the franchise agreement is extremely important within franchising (possibly more than in any other contractual agreement) and does not deserve to be relegated to an afterthought. It is imperative that each and every term on which agreement has been established is included in the franchise agreement; after all, this contract is going to be in existence for some considerable time. From the franchisee's point of view, this contract is likely to form the source of all income over the duration of the term, so any negligent omission is likely to have a major impact on the franchisee's financial success.

> *The **franchise agreement** is the contract that exists between the franchisor and franchisee, setting out the terms and scope of the agreement that exists between the parties.*

Without doubt, the EFF definition is franchisor-centric; it does much to identify what franchisees must do for the franchisor, but lacks the balance of the rights and expectations of the franchisee network upon which the franchisor relies to support and provide revenue for his or her business.

The word *partnership* in respect of franchise operations is an unfortunate choice as, at best, it is a unequal partnership, but the reading of the EFF definition seems to ignore the fact that both parties to a franchise agreement rely on each other for the success of their individual businesses, and as such there has to be some element of joint venture. If the franchisee does not perform to expectations, then the franchisor is not maximizing his/her opportunity in that territory, and if sufficient numbers of franchisees fail to meet performance criteria, then the franchisor is unlikely to be able to survive financially. Successful franchisees make for successful franchisors, so it is incumbent on every responsible franchisor to ensure that their individual franchisees meet and surpass expectations; in franchising, it is the only way to ensure financial stability for all parties.

THE AMERICAN DEFINITION

Having established the positives and negatives of the EFF's definition, let us proceed to examine the definition of franchising that the International Franchise Association (IFA) uses to describe franchising theory, and see if that fares any better:

> **"** A franchise operation is a contractual relationship between Franchisor and Franchisee in which the Franchisor offers or is obliged to maintain a continuing interest in the business of the Franchisee in such areas as know-how and training; wherein the Franchisee operates under a common trade name, format and/or procedure owned or controlled by the Franchisor and in which the Franchisee has or will have a substantial capital investment in his business from his own resources.
>
> (International Franchise Association website)

On the face of it, this again appears to be an adequate definition, but on closer examination we can see that, once more, it leaves much to be desired; it implies much and asserts little. For example, one of the four cornerstones of franchising is that there is consideration paid from franchisee to franchisor by means of ongoing fees or royalties, and sadly this is missing from the IFA's definition.

Another elementary omission features the principle of independence whereby the franchisee *owns* his/her business; it does feature by implication in the phrase 'will make a substantial capital investment in his business', but as this is a fundamental requirement of franchising, it ought to be stated rather than inferred. Again, the principle of exclusivity within a territory is completely ignored.

Nevertheless, the IFA definition does better in considering some elements that are crucial to understanding franchising. The definition states boldly in the first line that the relationship is based on a contract and the reader may conclude from this that the appropriate law in dealing with franchising must be general contract law.

Continuing our analysis of the better points raised in this definition, we come next to the obligation of the franchisor to 'maintain a continuing interest in the Franchisee's business'. Without a doubt, it is fundamental to the success of both the franchisee and the franchisor that interest is retained, as the franchisor is expecting the franchisee to develop sufficient turnover to enable sufficient royalties or fees to be paid by the franchisee in order to keep the franchisor's business afloat! Nevertheless, effective as this clause might be, it does not begin to define the depth of the relationship that needs to be established.

Like the EFF definition, the IFA definition fails to state that it is incumbent on the franchisor to ensure that the franchisee will fit well into the former's system; it is essential that the right franchisees are identified, as a bad or lazy franchisee will undoubtedly cause more disruption than they are worth!

The definition does identify the training requirement, which again is a key element of any successful franchise operation. Training the prospective franchisee in the know-how, conduct and operation of the business format ensures similarity of operation across the whole business.

The concept of 'know-how' is not only industry-specific, but is also company-specific. The know-how involved in one cleaning company is likely to be vastly different from the know-how used by another – both reach a similar result, but the methodology in achieving cleanliness applied in each company is the specific know-how unique to that franchise system.

Not only must this know-how be passed on to the franchisee prior to the start of his/her operation, but an ongoing system of continuous

> **Commonality** *is the key to a successful franchise operation; each franchisee should operate its business in the same manner as every other franchisee in the system.*

training must also be implemented, both as refresher/update training for the franchisee, but also in a system for effective training of his/her staff.

Know-how *is the intangible element of the franchisor's intellectual property that relates to the methodology needed to carry out his/her business, which cannot be legally protected.*

The third praiseworthy element of the description is the reference to operating under a under 'a common trade name, format and/or procedure owned or controlled by the Franchisor'. This aspect of franchising is the core element. In every franchise there must be a universal trade mark or trade name which commonly identifies the identical character of the businesses operated by every franchisee, wherever they may be located.

It goes further, however, than merely a common name or trade mark; in retail franchises, customers would expect to see common elements in how the outlet is designed, decorated and laid out. In van-based franchises, customers would expect to see identical vans equipped identically with operators uniformly dressed. In office-based or service-oriented franchises there may be fewer identifying elements, but there will be commonality in paperwork and procedural systems or protocols of operation.

What the definition fails to state is that all franchisees depend on the goodwill and honesty of their colleagues to ensure the success of the operation. If a fast-food franchised outlet tries to cut corners and reduce costs by not adhering to the high levels of quality control expected by the franchisor, the headlines in the following day's press will not state that Mr John Smith, operating a fast-food outlet in Never-Neverland, had caused several of his customers some distress and digestive discomfort; the next day's headlines would read 'Woppa Dogburger Poisons 7-year-old' and the reputation of the entire franchise operation would be called into doubt, and the financial security of every single franchisee jeopardized.

In short, should one choose to visit a globalized fast food outlet in Detroit, London, Moscow or Beijing, one should appreciate a certain similarity in operation across the different continents, and one's expectations of service should equally be met.

Despite having identified the strengths and weaknesses in the definition regarding ownership of the franchise business, commendably the definition does acknowledge the fact that 'the Franchisee has or will have a substantial capital investment in his business from his own resources'. Remembering that the franchisee owns his/her business (albeit implied by definition) and all the capital equipment that the business uses to operate, it becomes important that the need for personal investment by the franchisee is underlined. There is a proverb that says 'A free gift has no value', and this is just as true in business. If a franchisee has invested his/her own resources in the business and can see that s/he has the ability to control his/her future by correct operation and conscientious attention to the business's affairs, s/he is far more likely to work hard to ensure the success of the business than if s/he had been handed everything on a plate! This is the defining difference between an owner-operator and a manager; managers tend to be reckless with their employer's wealth, whereas owner-operators tend to be more efficient and cost-effective.

THE BRITISH ADAPTATION

A better definition than those examined above comes from the British Franchise Association who, while being members of the EFF, have retained their own definition for domestic purposes:

> " Business format franchising is the granting of a licence by one person (the Franchisor) to another (the Franchisee), which entitles the Franchisee to trade under the trade mark/trade name of the Franchisor and to make use of an entire package, comprising all the elements necessary to establish a previously untrained person in the business and to run it with continual assistance on a predetermined basis.
>
> (British Franchise Association website)

While this is better, the definition still falls short on a few crucial issues: namely, failing to mention the *legal* relationship that exists between the franchisor and the franchisee; neglecting to recognize that the franchisee will be committed to paying the franchisor fees both initially and throughout the duration of the contract; and not acknowledging the independence of the franchisee. Nevertheless, on a more positive note, it does allow for the fact that the majority of franchisees begin their businesses with little or no knowledge of the industry, and commits a franchisor to offering sufficient training to allow such a person to run their business successfully. The major improvement in the BFA definition is that it is understandable to the layman, and this is one of the benchmarks of the British Franchise Association, by which they seek to produce their literature in an understandable and forthright manner.

THE AUSTRALIAN DEFINITION

Probably the simplest definition comes from the Franchise Council of Australia (FCA), which defines franchising in this way:

> " Franchising is a business relationship in which the Franchisor (the owner of the business providing the product or service) assigns to

independent people (the Franchisees) the right to market and distribute the Franchisor's goods or service, and to use the business name for a fixed period of time.

(Franchise Council of Australia website)

This definition is undeniably true, but it does appear to be somewhat superficial and without the depth that prospective franchisees might expect. Again, little is mentioned of the contractual relationship and there is no reference to the necessity for fees to be paid, but at least the word 'independent' creeps into the description.

However, in saying that the definition is weak, Australia has some of the most effective Federal legislation on the subject, and it is true to say that the legal definition contained within the Australian Competition & Consumer Commission's *Trade Practices (Industry Codes – Franchising) Regulations of 1998 (as amended)* is considerably more comprehensive and goes on to enshrine in law the Franchising Code of Conduct, being the Australian franchising ethical principles.

AN ALTERNATIVE DEFINITION

Having identified that the EFF, IFA and the FCA's definitions of franchising fall some way short of the mark, despite each including some redeeming elements, I propose throwing my own hat into the ring by suggesting an accurate and more encompassing definition of franchising:

> ❝ Franchising is a contractual agreement by and between two parties, whereby one party (the Franchisor) extends the right to the other party (the Franchisee) to carry on an independent business under the trade mark or trade name or brand of the Franchisor and to receive sufficient privileged know-how, derived through the Franchisor's experience in operating such a business, throughout the term of the agreement, consisting of all components as to enable a previously inexperienced person to establish a successful business under the Franchisor's brand. In consideration for the initial and ongoing assistance from the Franchisor, the Franchisee commits to substantially invest in his own business and to a scheme of payments in the form of initial and ongoing fees. The Franchisee further undertakes to use his best endeavours to ensure the success of the Franchisor's brand and to adhere to the Franchise system, following the guidance of the Franchisor to mutual benefit.

This definition encompasses the four cornerstones illustrated in Figure 2.1, on which any successful franchise system is established. Moreover, the definition also meets the requirements of the seven rules for ethical franchising (see also Figure 2.2):

1   Franchise relationships are established through *contractual agreements*, which should comprise all terms and conditions agreed upon.
2   Franchisors must establish successful and *replicable business models or formats* (the system) that can be and are identified by unique brand names, trade marks, service marks and/or trade names.
3   The franchisee must be *instructed and trained in all aspects of the franchisor's system* prior to the commencement of the franchisee's business operation, so that the franchisee is equipped to operate the business efficiently, effectively and successfully; and the franchisor must commit to assisting the franchisee in the successful launch of his/her business venture.
4   Following the successful launch of the franchisee's business, the franchisor must undertake to *maintain an ongoing business relationship* with the franchisee, providing support in all aspects of the successful operation of the business.
5   The franchisee must be permitted (under guidance and control of the franchisor) to operate under the franchisor's brand and with the franchisor's trade marks, service marks, or trade name, as well as the business systems that have been developed and are owned by the franchisor, and *be permitted to benefit from the associated goodwill.*
6   The franchisee must *own his/her own business* and must make a substantial investment in that business from his/her own resources.
7   The *franchisee must agree to pay the franchisor a consideration* for the rights obtained under the franchise agreement and for the continuing

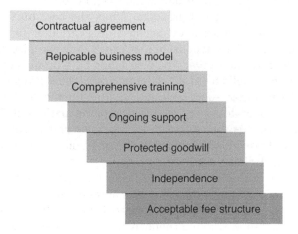

Figure 2.2   Rules for ethical franchising

support and services with which s/he will be provided during the course of the contract.

In defining franchising, it would be remiss not to make passing comment about a few cousins of the concept; some perfectly legitimate, and others, perhaps not so.

First, we should consider the concept of agency, as it is often thought that franchisees are agents of the franchisor (which is not the case), and the two concepts are often confused. A good definition of an agent is: 'A business or person who has the express authority of another to act on their behalf'. So, an agent is somebody who might buy or sell articles on behalf of their principal, but they do not act on their own behalf. The contract that exists is between the principal and the client, for which the agent usually receives a commission from the principal. Whatever is said by the agent is completely binding on the principal. Good examples of agency are auctions and property sales; when one buys and sells in either of these circumstances, the auction house or the estate agent acts as a facilitator between the buyer and seller, bringing the two together, and assists in the creation of the contract that will exist between the two entities. In the case of franchises, the contract exists between the franchisee and the client, and in all conscience when negotiating to purchase a franchise, the prospective franchisee goes to great lengths to ensure that there is no element of agency between him/her and the franchisor.

> *Agents and franchisees are not the same, though they may be distantly related!*

Another confusing concept is that of distributorship. A distributor is usually a wholly independent wholesale operation that has been granted some level of distribution rights for a product or a range of products. Often, the distributor will carry several competitive product lines, acting as a distributor for several competing companies. The relationship that exists between distributor and client is that of buyer and seller. The distributor buys products from the manufacturer and resells them at a different price, generating his/her own profit by the level of mark-up s/he is able to attach to the products. The distributor typically operates under his/her own name and brand. One of the defining differences between a franchised operation and a dealership arrangement is that there is usually minimal ongoing support for distributors, virtually no initial training and no fee structure.

Know-how agreements and licensing agreements are also related to this concept. In general, know-how agreements are specific to a particular invention or patent, whereby the user is allowed to operate with the particular know-how within a confined area of business. Licensing agreements similarly exist to allow one party to carry out some task which would be an infringement of the rights of the licensor had a licence not existed. A good example exists in the music industry, whereby a band would license a venue to play its music; if the licence did not exist, the copyright of the band would be infringed.

How does franchising compare with these concepts? Well, the franchisee certainly is not an agent as s/he does not act for and on behalf of the franchisor, and nor do his/her words bind the franchisor to a particular course of action.

The franchisee is part of the franchisor's distribution network, so to some extent s/he can be described as a distributor, in the loosest possible way. The key difference is that a franchisee is operating as a principal and at the same time under the franchisor's brand, and offers the franchisor's product lines exclusively. In many cases, franchisees are operating at a retail level, whereas distributors are operating in the world of wholesale.

Know-how and licensing agreements are closer relations still. It can be said that the franchisee uses the specific know-how of the franchisor, and this is what the franchisee is paying for through his/her fees, but in a traditional know-how agreement the parties trade under their own brand name and the only tie between the owner of the know-how and the user is that the user is applying the know-how in some element of his business, but it is rarely the whole business. Certainly, a licence exists between the franchisor and franchisee to use the brand and the know-how of the franchisor to carry out a business, but in the traditional licence agreement it might be presumed that the licensee has some knowledge of the business at the granting of the licence, whereas in the franchising agreement, the franchisee does not have the skills and knowledge to operate the licence at the inception, and expects to receive sufficient and necessary training as and when it is required. To some extent, a traditional licensee will expect the licensor to offer support with some degree of marketing and promotional activities, but at the franchise level a complete and wholehearted continuing interest in the franchisee's business would be an expectation, and participation in the franchisor's marketing and promotional activity is part and parcel of the franchise agreement.

> *Pyramid selling and multi-level marketing are cousins of franchising, but no self-respecting franchisor would ever use such methods.*

Next, we should consider a distant cousin from the 'other side of the blanket'. In the previous chapter, we saw that pyramid selling caused numerous problems to franchising in the 1970s, but it can be seen that pyramid selling, or multi-level marketing, or network marketing, might be a cousin of franchising, but one that has its roots in short-termism and is not much interested in forging a long-term business arrangement.

Essentially, the system works on the basis that the scheme member is encouraged not only to sell the products of the principal, but also to recruit new scheme members, who are then also encouraged to recruit new members *ad infinitum*. The member (at whatever level) receives a commission on products that they sell themselves, but they also receive an overriding commission on the sales generated by those members whom they have directly or indirectly recruited to the scheme. As the network expands beneath the pyramider, so the level of commissions received from the sales of others increases to a level where it is many times the value of the commissions derived from the pyramider's own sales.

The single most important and delineating difference between franchising and network marketing is that the franchisee will not receive any commissions derived from the sales made by other franchisees (except in the rare occasion of one being a 'master franchisee'). Franchisees might be rewarded with a *bounty* or *incentive* for introducing potential new franchisees to the business, but would not expect to receive ongoing overriding commissions on their sales. In short, the franchisee's main source of income is derived from the business they have conducted directly. It is doubtful whether *any* responsible franchise body would condone any franchisor that operates through a network scheme, and as these pyramid schemes have been identified as containing aspects that are at best dishonest and at worst fraudulent, one would not expect reputable bodies to be associated with this type of operation.

> There are very few businesses that cannot be franchised in some way, though low-margin businesses, or short-term businesses would be difficult to franchise effectively.

There are many reputable franchise operations in the marketplace that offer participants an extremely good living without having to resort to underhand and deceitful methods. At the same time, there are many pyramid-type businesses in the marketplace that have cost unsuspecting investors a considerable amount of money. Consequently, the best advice one can offer is that if a prospective franchisee is offered an ongoing reward for doing something other than that related to the sale and promotion of the basic product, then the prospective franchisee ought to be suspicious and should walk away from the deal … no, s/he should run away from the deal!

UNDERSTANDING WHAT CAN AND CANNOT BE FRANCHISED

Traditionally speaking, it is often said that there are some businesses that it is 'impossible' to franchise. It is said, for example, that 'creative' businesses cannot be franchised, because the whole business is based on and focused on the vision of the creative or inventive genius who conceived the business idea: fashion designers, chefs, artists and so on would be examples of businesses that are difficult to franchise. Add to this low-margin businesses (such as greengrocery), or businesses that cannot be replicated, or short-term, 'trendy' businesses, and it would appear that there is a massive pool of businesses that, it is said, just cannot be franchised. I very much take the view that these preconceptions are not to be considered as insurmountable obstacles – merely factors that make franchising more difficult.

When Gianni Versace was killed, did the whole Versace business collapse after the inspirational genius died? No – the business moved forward with the design team continuing to produce clothes in the style of Versace. This seems to belie the notion that when the creative genius dies, so must the business. Chefs, often considered to be the most tempera-mental of artists, are expanding their business empires into ferries, trains and airports. It can be doubted that the award-winning, Michelin-starred celebrity chef spends his time flitting between ferry crossings, or supervis-ing the all-day breakfast service at railway termini, or even gallivanting around the country dropping in on the far-flung outlets of his or her busi-ness empire! Chefs have become a brand, and as such have generated a replicable business where people can be trained to work in the style of the genius. Consequently, there are some elements of the creative business that can be replicated and franchised.

Whereas concessions may have to be made that low-margin businesses are difficult to franchise, as there must be sufficient financial incentives to attract the franchisee to the business and to make it viable for the poten-tial franchisor; so traditional low-margin businesses might, on the face of it, make for challenging franchising opportunities. The answer may lie in the repositioning of the business to generate a greater profit margin, perhaps by becoming a more sophisticated and specialized business in a more focused niche market. Instead of trying to franchise a low-margin greengrocery business where the average customer wants to buy a kilo of potatoes, reposition the business to offer high-quality, high-profit produce to the more discerning buyer, or to the specialist trade market, thereby generating sufficient margins to satisfy the needs of all parties.

Trendy short-term business opportunities may be an even more difficult challenge, unless one accepts the fact that, as market trends change, so the focus of the business needs to change. The successful video hire busi-nesses of the 1980s now rent DVDs and games for the multitude of differ-ent gaming formats. Crazes or fads are perfectly franchisable provided that the franchisor has the experience and the vision (plus the willingness to listen to grass-roots intelligence) to move the business forward into a new fad or craze as and when the previous whim starts to wane, and the fran-chisee has the foresight to accept that the business into which s/he is buying on day one may be a vastly different business by the end of the fran-chise contract. Of course, these market shifts within trends will make the franchise model considerably riskier, but invariably the higher the risk, the higher the profit margins, and provided these are shared equitably between the franchisor and franchisee, then the risk factor of an unsuccessful market shift may be acceptable to a more dynamic franchisee.

CASE STUDY 2.1

Dabbah Wallah – food delivery Indian style

It all began in 1999, when Sunil Kumar had just finished the final exam of his business degree from a British University. To celebrate, he decided to order a pizza from his local pizzeria. After fifteen minutes, the hot pizza was delivered by a smiling young man who had arrived on a small motorcycle.

Following the completion of his studies, Sunil had already wondered what to do, and was worried that returning to his family's restaurant business in London would not be sufficient to stretch the newly found entrepreneurial craving that four years at University had fine-tuned to perfection. Sunil knew it would be disappointing to his father, who had hoped his son would rejoin the business and take it over when he retired, but Sunil had grown up with the business and he was worried that it would be far too confining.

Sunil had a 'road to Damascus' moment as the pizza delivery man was walking away. He remembered family holidays from his childhood, visiting relations in what is now Mumbai. Sunil recalled the variously named dabba wallahs or tiffin wallahs taking home-prepared food to the workers; there must have been thousands of these delivery guys, delivering tens of thousands of meals every day. 'Why can't I build a business that takes freshly cooked home-style food to people's work and homes?'

As the whole ethos of the dabbah wallah was the delivery of fresh, home-cooked food, Sunil did not discuss his ideas with his father. Instead, he talked his idea over with his mother, who was responsible for making the food that was eaten at home – how easy would it be to scale up in order to make a viable business? Sunil's mother indulged her son with the patience of a parent pandering to a childish dream, but he was not disheartened.

Having developed a comprehensive and convincing business plan with the help of his former tutors, the local business advisory service and even a commercial bank, Sunil steeled himself to discuss his plans with his father. Surprisingly, his father was enthusiastic and even offered to invest in his son's business: so Dabbah Wallah, the home-cooked tiffin delivery service, was born.

Over the course of the next year, premises were rented and fully equipped to the highest health and safety and food hygiene standards, and soon Sunil's fleet of small motorcycle delivery Dabbah Wallahs were seen buzzing around the city of Manchester, UK. The business developed and then, in 2004, Sunil happened to visit the local franchise

→

CASE STUDY 2.1 *continued*

exhibition where he met Trevor, who was working as a consultant for a locally based franchise consultancy.

Already a customer of Dabbah Wallah, Trevor could easily see how the business might be franchised and began negotiations with Sunil on how he could help to develop the business. It was decided to open a pilot operation in another city to test whether the concept could be replicated. Harish Joshi, a former University friend, joined the business to pilot the concept in the city of Leeds, and he later became Director of Franchising.

Over the next two years, Sunil and Harish, with Trevor's help, developed a comprehensive Operations Manual and put in place sound business practices to ensure that the business was able to be franchised elsewhere. In 2006, two more franchises, one in Sheffield and the other in Nottingham, were opened. The target of five further outlets in 2007 was not achieved, but three were opened and then towards the end of the year Sunil was awarded provisional membership of the British Franchise Association.

With the BFA's help, the business model was refined and a further five outlets opened in 2008, even though by then the UK had been engulfed in the biggest financial downturn since the 1930s.

Currently, the business has 36 franchises in major towns and cities throughout the UK, and when asked what led to the success of his business, Sunil readily answers:

" We were lucky; we arrived at the right time with the right product. We identified a market niche which could be filled and we set about filling it. Even in these terrible economic times, when the catering industry is really suffering, the informal dining market is expanding.

We developed a strong brand image and ensured that we had a sustainable business model that can be easily replicated and without having to pay expensive rents for High Street premises; all of our outlets operate out of small industrial units and the original outlet in Manchester (which has now been franchised) still operates out of a converted railway arch! We ensured that, before we embarked on franchising, we made sure that the mother business was financially stable. We take our responsibility towards our franchisees very seriously.

When recruiting new franchisees, we have a very tough and arduous selection process; we do not cut corners to build numbers. All of our franchisees have to meet *our* standards, but at the same time we are willing to work with a talented prospect to help them reach those standards. We believe that fairness is the only way to go in franchising and have substantially reduced

→

CASE STUDY 2.1 *continued*

our franchisees' input costs by practising strict economies of scale. By passing on these savings, it makes our franchisees more profitable and strengthens our relationship with our team; we both have to run profitable businesses!

Talking of the future, Sunil says with a glint in his eye, 'My dream is to have a Dabbah Wallah franchise in every major town or city in the UK ... and when we've achieved that, there's always Europe!'

Note: While this case study is based on a true story, the names of the franchisor and his business have been changed, at his request. The Dabbah Wallah franchise used for this illustration is a fictitious business and does not reflect on any existing business, whether franchised or otherwise.

Who would have thought that the fast food craze that swept through the post-war Western civilization might go down in history as a 'fad', but with the trend towards a healthier lifestyle, the globalized fast-food companies are being forced to reposition their offerings towards a healthier, less calorific and more ecological range of products to satisfy the requirements of a consumer base that has different interpretations of quality, and different values, from the consumers of 10 or 20 years ago.

Technical businesses are also said to be impossible to franchise, as the training time needed to take novices and train them makes the concept unachievable, but in saying this we are seeing a form of franchising appear in, for example, the profession of dentistry. Dentists have, by law, to undergo considerable medical training, and one can no longer ride into town and hang a sign outside a shop and start practising dentistry, as the pioneers of the profession did in the Wild West. In order to gain the benefits of franchising, such as centralized purchasing economies of scale, and brand recognition, some dentists are franchising their surgeries to specialist companies who are happy to undertake the administrative duties of the dentist in exchange for a percentage of the turnover. Opticians, who also have to be formally trained, and pharmacists likewise are also attracted to the benefits of franchising. The difference with this type of franchising is that the franchisee is trained in the system of running the business, and s/he employs the necessary qualified technicians, or else the person who already holds the qualification becomes the franchisee and is trained in the method of running the business.

Therefore, the notion that there are businesses that cannot be franchised is flawed. Whereas it is accepted that there are businesses that may be more difficult to franchise, to say that it is impossible to franchise a particular business, or element of a business, is nonsense. The defining characteristic of any business opportunity is whether the risks are outweighed by the potential financial rewards, and if the franchisor has responsibly conducted a successful trial of the business model and can demonstrate that s/he has minimized the risks involved, franchising will almost certainly be justifiable.

There are very few businesses that fall into the category of 'no advantage' businesses, but they do exist and this is really the only category where it might be justified in saying that franchising is impractical.

WHAT DO YOU THINK?

We have seen that there are few businesses that cannot be franchised, but we have identified a few. Can you think of ways that elements of these businesses might be franchisable?

Do you feel that the higher qualifications required when taking on a particular franchise (for example, dentistry) might give the franchisee a greater amount of leverage when negotiating franchise terms? How might franchisors combat this danger?

Further reading

Birkeland, Peter M., *Franchising Dreams: The Lure of Entrepreneurship in America* (University of Chicago Press 2004).

Hero, Marco, *International Franchising: A Practitioner's Guide* (Globe Law & Business 2010).

Hoy, Frank (ed.), *Franchising: An International Perspective* (Routledge 2002).

3 THE PROS AND CONS OF FRANCHISING

INTRODUCTION AND LEARNING OUTCOMES

The purpose of this chapter is to deconstruct the concept of franchising and identify areas that are beneficial to both the franchisor and franchisee, as well as to identify those areas that are less advantageous to both parties.

Towards the end of the chapter, analysis will be carried out of the features and benefits of opportunities at each end of the franchising scale: home-based franchises and taking a well-known franchise.

The reader will be able to:

- Identify the advantages and disadvantages to buying a franchise.
- Identify the advantages and disadvantages of franchising a business.
- Appreciate the positives and negatives of operating a home-based franchise.
- Realize the positive and negatives of buying a well-known, High Street brand franchise.

To decide with which to start might be an excuse for critics to decide that this is a book for franchisors, or for franchisees, which is specifically not my intention, as I prefer a more balanced view. Consequently, when writing this book, I asked the question (in the manner of eggs and chickens): which came first? This is the only reason why the pros and cons from the franchisor's aspect will be considered first.

ADVANTAGES FOR THE FRANCHISOR

Usually, the single most important reason why franchisors seek to franchise their business is the growth potential, which is offset by the belief that it is a low-cost option. Expansion is an

> *Franchising can represent a very cost-effective way of expanding a business, but the typical belief that it is 'low-cost' is inaccurate.*

expensive option for any business, and to fund the expansion in-house puts pressure on the balance sheet. Often, when quite substantial companies seek to expand, the growth potential is impeded by the finance available to fund the growth. The huge advantage of franchising is that expansion is largely funded by external financial sources, namely by the franchisees' capital. Franchisees provide the capital for growth. and assuming that they have been selected thoughtfully and are committed to the success of the business, will ensure a faster market penetration than the franchisor could hope to achieve if funding were to be found internally.

This is particularly true of new product development or a new business concept, because being first to market is fine, but if one cannot guarantee rapid and widespread coverage, the competition, who have not had to fund the development costs, will find it relatively easy to secure a market share. The use of franchising gets a product or business to market first, with the pilot operation and fast geographical expansion making it difficult for the competition to secure a substantial market share.

However, seizing market share and rapid expansion is fine, but they must never be at the expense of quality; a franchisee network takes time to develop, and if the only recruitment criterion is having sufficient capital to 'buy-in', it is likely that the quality of the franchise network will be inferior, all a result of the franchisor's greed and short-sightedness.

The next benefit to the franchisor is that it is quite typical that franchisees will seek to operate in their own locality, meaning that they are also bringing to the table a wealth of local knowledge that it would otherwise be difficult or expensive to acquire. The franchisee will undoubtedly also bring local contacts and possibly even a few potential customers, despite their industry knowledge still being embryonic.

Local knowledge is highly important in developing a local business, which is what franchising is all about, and while regional and even national diversity is nowhere as significant as it used to be in the multicultural society in which we live, the fact remains that somebody living and operating in a region will have a better understanding of that region's customers than will somebody coming from outside, so we can identify this availability of local knowledge as another benefit.

The element of control is a thorny problem in franchising; the franchisor must control his/her network, but must also recognize that franchisees are running their own independent businesses and consequently must be allowed some element of freedom. Typically, the franchise agreement (which we shall discuss at greater length later) will specify in great detail the level of control that the franchisor will exert over the network, and the operations manual will go into even greater detail of how the franchise will function.

To maximize similarity of offerings across the brand, these controls are necessary and must be rigidly enforced, but similarity of brand offering is only one aspect of the need for strict control; by maintaining strict control on both product and equipment purchasing, a greater level of profit margin can be achieved, offering greater rewards for both franchisor and franchisee.

Some franchisors will even become involved with the administrative duties of the franchisee, running their accounts, debt collection and even payroll, to allow the total effort of the franchisee to be focused on business development and satisfying their customers' needs. Care must be taken that the franchisee does not feel as though s/he is becoming a manager or, worse still, nothing more than an agent; franchisees are running their own businesses independently of the franchisor and there must be clear water dividing the two camps.

Finally, when considering the advantages to the franchisor, we come to the subject of human endeavour. Most of us, at some point in our lives, have been employees and have been guilty of exerting only the minimum amount of effort we feel is necessary to achieve the results expected by our employers. This attitude changes, however, when we cross the line between an employee and self-employed. Doctors have been known to support the view that the best cure for the minor complaints that clog up their surgery hours – the sneezes, snuffles, bad backs and so on, would be a dose of self-employment. The self-employed do not ring in sick, or stay in bed unless they are physically unable to work, and even if they are genuinely unable to work at any time, they will spend their recuperation time booking appointments and dealing with administrative tasks, so that they do not lose a single day of profit-making.

The fact is that the self-employed are more industrious, work longer hours, deliver better performance, increase market share more rapidly, maximize efficiency and reduce costs, and consequently improve profit margins. This dedication to the success of their business also has a positive impact on the success of the franchisor's business.

CASE STUDY 3.1

Cape Town Fish Market Restaurant

Douw Krugmann is unique in the sense that he has truly done it all. Having started his working life as a schoolteacher, he eventually left the profession to realize his dream of becoming an entrepreneur. He eased himself into this new role by acquiring a Spur franchise in Klerksdorp. The restaurant did extremely well, but after a few years as a franchisee, Douw was ready to move on, in more ways than one.

He sold his restaurant and relocated to Cape Town, where he bought a fish store located on the V&A Waterfront. After studying the market

→

CASE STUDY 3.1 *continued*

carefully, he decided to extend the concept of his business by combining the retail store with a restaurant that would focus on fish dishes. After much hard work, and a substantial investment, the first Cape Town Fish Market (CTFM) opened its doors in 1997.

From that day forward, Douw kept his finger on the pulse of his customers. He had realized early on that, when visiting restaurants, people don't just want to consume large chunks of fish, but want to venture into more exotic offerings, such as sushi. Adventurous spirits aside, people's growing awareness of the need to eat healthily provided a further impetus for the success of the CTFM concept.

Douw's vision was to create a restaurant that would attract a mix of local and international customers, eager to sample the best South African and Asian cooking imaginable. To this end, his restaurant offers an à la carte menu and a conveyor belt sushi bar (which, at the time of its installation, was a first in South Africa). The fresh fish market was retained.

The combination of restaurant and fish retail store made it possible to offer an unprecedented range of fish dishes, both for consumption at the restaurant and for customers who wanted to cook meals themselves. An exquisite wine list added to the restaurant's attraction.

The CTFM's success did not remain unnoticed for long. Soon, would-be entrepreneurs keen to emulate Douw's success approached him with requests for a franchise and today, a total of 16 franchises are in operation in South Africa and another in London, England. There are plans to expand into Tanzania shortly.

Operating the CTFM has turned out to be Douw's real calling, and he continues to be involved in a hands-on fashion to this day. He retains overall oversight of every project, but also travels the world in search of the latest trends in cuisine and restaurant equipment. Among the novelties diners rave about, and which were introduced as a result of this are *robata* and *teppanyaki* (charcoal grills on which food is prepared for customers seated around the cooking area) – Japanese delights that connoisseurs rave about.

When asked what advice he would give to aspiring entrepreneurs, Douw warns that the most important thing is introspection: 'Many people think that they want to be entrepreneurs but once they are in this situation, they can't cope with the stress and the hassle that comes with it. However, by the time they have figured that out, they have committed their life's savings and would face financial ruin if they were to turn back.'

Douw also advises that, once you are sure that entrepreneurship is what you really want, formulate a vision and work hard towards making it a reality. There will be obstacles along the way, but the important thing is never to give up: 'Keep going, no matter how impossible things

→

> **CASE STUDY 3.1** *continued*
>
> may seem. There is always a solution to every problem. But remember that, to succeed, you have to be a born leader. As the owner of a business, you are responsible not just for your own future, but also for the future of everyone who works for you.'
>
> © *Which Franchise (South Africa) 2009*

DISADVANTAGES FOR THE FRANCHISOR

This utopian existence, described over the past few pages, does not come without some drawbacks, however, and one of the biggest is the aspect of 'ownership'. Despite the considerable advantages of having owner-operators running the outposts of the franchised empire, they are not employees and cannot be treated as such. One can dismiss and discipline salaried staff, but because of the existence of the franchise agreement, franchisees have to be handled differently. It is as well that I mention the franchise agreement at this point, as this is usually the document that details how conflict is resolved, and a franchisor will be extremely lucky if disagreement does not exist at some point within his network, so having clear guidelines regarding conflict management is essential. Ideally, the perfect franchisee will have sufficient enterprise to be able to recognize a business opportunity, and the scope to be able to take advantage of it.

Despite all the warnings, there will be occasions where a franchisor will have recruited a franchisee who does not fit the system: s/he might be lazy, or just plain disruptive. In the worst case scenario, a franchisor will be faced with a franchisee who is sufficiently disruptive as to cause interference, but not sufficiently so to breach their franchise agreement, and in this case there remains little option but to buy out the franchisee and probably pay an inflated premium to do so; even so, this is far preferable to having a disruptive franchisee upsetting the balance of an otherwise successful team.

The fact remains that in any franchise relationship there needs to be an element of mutual respect, and this is best achieved by retaining friendly and encouraging contact while dealing with minor grumbles before they become major concerns. The franchisee who believes his/her franchisor is overbearing and intrusive will become disenchanted and bitter and will probably seek to cause as much disruption and discontent as possible.

The franchisee who has a catalogue of disputes or disruptions with their franchisor is less likely to disappear into the wide blue yonder when they have been bought out, and far more likely to use the knowledge and skills they have learned at the franchisor's expense when they develop a business and set it up in direct competition with their former franchisor. It is possible that the original franchise agreement will be considered redundant if a franchisor tries to impose the restrictions that were included to prevent competition by a franchisee leaving the system, especially if the franchisor has terminated the contract by a buy-out. Specific termination contracts or exit contracts that a disgruntled franchisee would be expected to sign as a condition for the buy-out, which reiterate the restrictive clauses of the original franchise agreement, are an obvious choice for franchisors wishing to protect their system against a former franchisee going freelance.

It may seem slightly incongruous and a rather peculiar idea, but in reality the last characteristic that a franchisor seeks in a franchisee is 'entrepreneurship' – it is a strange phenomenon that entrepreneurs tend to try to reinvent the wheel, while what most franchisors call for is a franchisee who is enterprising, but who knows how to follow instructions!

It has already been accepted that profits in a franchise arrangement are split between the franchisor and the franchisee, and the conclusion must therefore be drawn that this means that the franchisor's profits will be less than if s/he were running an in-house managed business. However, we have already seen in the previous section the benefits that a franchisor derives from having dedicated franchisees beavering away to the benefit of his/her business, and so the benefits of franchising often far outweigh the disadvantage of having to accept lower margins.

Lower margins, however, may be exacerbated by the 'dishonest' franchisee who seeks to be economical with the truth when declaring his trading figures, resulting in the franchisor accepting lower management fees for that period. Invariably, this is one of the main reasons for implementing strict controls and maintaining a watching brief over the financial affairs of the individual franchisees. Minor infractions need to be policed as vigorously as major violations, and it is likely to be the terms and conditions of the franchise agreement that will curb the antics of a dishonest franchisee.

At the start of this chapter we considered that the opportunity to grow a business with the help of other people's money was an attractive proposition for the franchisor, but that should not be taken as a euphemism for being able to set up on the cheap! Franchising is not a cheap option, though it certainly may be the least expensive. Whereas growing the business might be funded through franchisees' investments into the system, getting the system in place at the outset is an expensive business in itself. The cost of piloting the venture is not inconsiderable, and neither are the training costs of the new franchisees; and it may also take some time before the first franchisees start to generate management fees. Consequently, the franchisor will still have to find sufficient funding to take the business to break-even, and whereas that will be significantly less than funding a managed expansion, it will still be a quite considerable sum.

ADVANTAGES FOR THE FRANCHISEE

Without doubt, the greatest benefit to any hopeful franchisee is that they will be joining a franchise whose business model and commercial concept has been tried and tested over a generous period of time, which has a recognizable brand and a strong corporate image. The greater the brand recognition, the lower the risk, but that is not to say that joining a system that does not have a recognizable brand is a bad idea; everything has to start somewhere, and the next big globalized brand might be the company that a prospective franchisee is considering. In addition, franchisees can often get a better deal by going in at the ground floor than joining a more established franchised brand. It might be thought that, the higher the risk, the lower the buy-in, and that is invariably true, but so is the reverse.

Even accepting that there may be some element of risk in franchising, that risk is reduced quite considerably when the franchisor's business model has already been well established and shown to be commercially effective. The London School of Economics has carried out research showing clearly that four out of every five businesses started from scratch will cease trading within five years – an 80 per cent failure rate! In the most recent survey carried out by the British Franchise Association in co-operation with NatWest Bank (BFA/Natwest Survey 2011), shows that the same figures in respect of franchising are currently about 8 per cent, of which nearly 2 per cent are through so-called forced retirements (death, serious illness and so on).

Looking more globally, the University of New Hampshire's Rosenberg International Center of Franchising, named after William Rosenberg, the founder of the international chain, Dunkin' Donuts, has created an authoritative index that follows and monitors the top 50 US public franchises. It is a staggering fact that these top 50 franchisors in America account for a massive 98 per cent of the market capitalization of all Business Format Franchisors in the USA. By using a method that is similar to that used by the S&P500 Index, the Rosenberg Center is able to generate indices that monitor the stock market performance of America's top 50 Business Format Franchisors (see Figure 3.1).

The graph shows how the industry has performed in the period 2000–11 compared to the S&P500 index. Even allowing for the adverse economic conditions that applied in the early twenty-first century, it can be shown clearly that the sector is behaving extremely positively.

The reason why franchising offers such a reduced risk factor lies in the piloting and replication of the franchise model. The franchisor has already proved that the business concept is sound by carrying out a responsible pilot operation; s/he has already ironed out as many of the developmental wrinkles as possible before completing the pilot, before offering clones of the original concept for sale to enterprising franchisees. However, there are still hidden problems that might trap the unwary franchisee: cash-flow

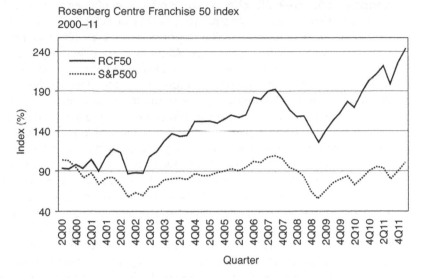

Rosenberg Centre Franchise 50 index
2000–11

Source: © Rosenberg International Franchise Center, UNH (2012).

Figure 3.1 The RCF50 Index, 2000–11

difficulties, for example, but these should be spotted by the franchisor in his/her control of the franchisee, and corrective action implemented before the situation becomes unmanageable.

The strength of the system is also manifest in other areas, particularly that of purchasing power. A franchisee in a successful system can expect to benefit from the purchasing power of the group, and to obtain raw materials or basic products at far more favourable prices than a stand-alone business could ever hope to achieve. Suppliers may not care for the bargaining power of large conglomerates, but they rush to join in the tendering process for new business, because they all enjoy the certainty and lower administrative costs of dealing with a few large customers compared to many small buyers.

> **Piloting the business** *is a great way of ironing out any of the difficulties that franchisees may find in their businesses, and it enables the franchisor to create a truly replicable model.*

In business, the way to increased profit is either to reduce costs or to increase profitability; if both are achievable, then so much the better! The achievability of reduced purchasing costs will drive down the input costs of the business, while the ability to market the products through a recognizable brand adds a factor that allows for premium pricing.

A ruse that has been employed successfully by the less scrupulous franchisor, or even those disreputable companies who call themselves franchisors but are really offering some other sort of licensing, is to tie the unwary franchisee into buying products either directly from them or from their nominated suppliers at inflated prices, when they could source identical products locally for less money. Whereas there is nothing wrong with franchisors supplying franchisees with goods to maintain product consistency, or in nominating preferred suppliers to standardize the offering, doing so at highly inflated input costs to the franchisee flies in the face of ethical franchising, and prospective franchisees who discover this custom should dissociate themselves from the franchisor with minimum delay, and certainly before signing any long-lasting and binding agreement. Heeding the advice of a specialist franchise lawyer and a professional franchise consultant should identify any problems of this nature, but even so franchisees are still being caught out time and again by such unprincipled operators. Generally speaking, economies of scale should be reflected in the prices paid by the franchisee for the purchase of goods to be used in their business. The advice given by one's advisory team should identify whether the prospective franchisor is acting in a deceitful manner, or whether s/he is merely offsetting some of the management fees in a mark-up on goods supplied, which might be an acceptable procedure.

Obtaining finance for a new-start operation may be quite a frustrating mission for the aspiring new businessperson, but generally speaking, banks actually like franchises as they offer lower risks than traditional start-ups. Generally, banks are rather suspicious of the aspiring businessman with his head in the clouds, believing that he will be the next Bill Gates within the coming five years. Talking to the bank about franchising will often reveal a completely different side to the traditional banker – a more approachable and kindlier nature!

Banks are equally aware that the risks attached to franchising are much lower than to any other business start-up, largely because they recognize that the business concept has previously been in operation, and typically there exist many thriving franchisees operating similar businesses throughout the country; thus there is a proven and successful track record. Banks are in the business of offsetting lending against risk, and if the risk is lower, the bank is likely to be much more willing to lend on favourable terms.

Franchisors will undoubtedly have forged strong links with one of the main banking providers in the franchisee's country, and may already have negotiated favourable terms for their operators, but do not get carried away in the hope that banks treat franchising in the same way that benevolent uncles treat favoured nephews: they do not; they will carry out a risk assessment on the other half of the equation, the franchisee, and if there are doubts about the person's motivation or ability to operate a successful franchise, the bank's hard-faced and clenched fist approach will soon become apparent, and that will often put an end to the franchisee's dreams.

Two of the biggest worries when starting up in business is that the business proprietor will be competing in an extremely competitive marketplace; or if they are launching a new and unique product, just how long will they be able to retain exclusivity before competitors enter the marketplace and start to entice their customers away? One of the main advantages of joining a franchised network is that the potential franchisee is buying an exclusive territory with a recognized brand; they understand that this means the franchisor cannot and will not appoint another franchisee within the territory, because the franchisee has exclusivity of territory enshrined in his/her franchise agreement.

Of course, competition will still exist; a franchisee from a rival company may well set up shop next door, and the unlucky franchisee will have to rise to the challenge, but at least s/he knows that the full support of the franchisor is firmly in place behind his/her efforts to see off the usurper, and this support does give franchisees the advantage over a stand-alone business, which does not have a heavyweight ally in the wings ready to swing into action on its behalf.

However, having exclusivity in a territory is only half the battle. Franchisees need to satisfy themselves that the territory in which they plan to operate will generate sufficient business to make their franchise a viable proposition. Having exclusivity in a sparsely populated rural area is fine if the type of business that they are operating is in the high-profit, low-turnover agricultural sector, but generally franchises need a strong customer base of willing buyers, and these are often conspicuous by their absence in rural areas.

The boast of successful franchisors is that they take 'raw material' from many and varied backgrounds, typically with no experience in the industry, and turn them into successful business operators. Franchisors are often considered to be like King Midas, who turned everything he touched into gold. Business format franchising is unique in this role of developing personalities and making improvements to enable them to achieve a high level of self-actualization.

The reason why franchisors are so careful in selecting their franchisees is that the franchisee is the weak link in the equation; the business format is proven, the training and support is first-class, and the only unknown quantity is the franchisee him/herself. Ambition and determination are not enough; there has to be a drive, a passion, a commitment to the success of the brand, plus the willingness to work hard, sound business intuition, and the ability to sell.

So, whereas franchisors are keen to take apprentices and train them in the business, the right skills set is a prerequisite, plus a receptive attitude towards learning how to succeed, and the ability to face the future with an open mind and without preconceptions as to what might be expected.

	Franchisor	Franchisee
Advantages	Growth potential Ability to use local knowledge Control over activities Increased effort to franchise	Established brand Minimalized risk Mutuality Increased purchasing power Easier to finance Exclusive territory
Disadvantages	Reduced ownership Ill-fitting franchisees Split profits Initially expensive	Lack of total control Ongoing fees Long-term relationship Lack of flexibility Risk of brand damage Exit restrictions

Figure 3.2 Grid showing advantages and disadvantages

Remembering that it is enshrined as one of the 'Seven Rules of Ethical Franchising' that the franchisee operates a business that is independent of the franchisor, it is often assumed that independence means that franchisees have the freedom to control their own destiny, to make their own decisions, and to harvest the fruits of their labours. This, however, is the misnomer of franchising; franchisees do have all these freedoms, but within the confines of the franchise system. They are obligated by contract to follow the guidance of the franchisor, and in this it is clear that their independence is being constrained. Similarly, unless their franchisor is running the accounting procedures, the franchise accounts have to be made available for the franchisor to inspect, and this is often perceived to be a fundamental infringement of franchisees' rights of independence.

Though this is starting to sound like a disadvantage, there is one significant advantage to this concept of restricted independence; it takes away the concerns that franchisees may have regarding the viability of their business, and allows them to focus on its development. So franchisees are running an independent business, but within the fellowship of a well-tried and effective system. In a way, they enjoy many of the freedoms of full independence, but retain the safety net and support of their franchisor; it is a kind of half-way house between being an employee and a fully stand-alone business.

DISADVANTAGES FOR THE FRANCHISEE

Before we become too embroiled in the disadvantages to the franchisee, it is fair that we put the opposite side of the independence issue, and it is true to say that the 'fellowship' of the franchise system can at times seem like an iron fetter. The necessary imposition of restrictions as to how the franchisee can run his/her business, and the tight controls necessary to ensure identical offerings across the network can be seen by some as a huge disadvantage to franchising. The solution to this problem is to allow the franchisee some freedom in the running of his/her business and not to discourage the imposing of his/her own personality on the franchise. Successful franchisors allow franchisees to contribute to the development of the franchise system – remember, it was a franchisee that came up with the idea of the Big Mac!

Franchisees will often cite, as a major negative to the franchise system, the constant drain on their resources to pay ongoing management fees to the franchisor. It is doubtful whether there is a franchisee in existence who has not at some point wondered whether s/he could cut the franchisor out of the loop and go it alone; after all, surely it is the franchisee who has developed the successful business unit?

Nevertheless, while it might seem an irritation to continue paying these exorbitant management fees, the wise franchisee will examine exactly what s/he is getting for his/her money, and carry out an analysis of what it would cost to provide these benefits directly, added to the loss of preferential purchasing power, which will usually drive all thoughts of 'bad value' from the franchisee's mind.

In a way, one can liken the development of a franchise unit to the manner in which parents see their children develop; in the beginning, they need the most help, but as they develop, so the need for constant supervision becomes less, until eventually they are mature adults.

Franchisees need to be aware, though, that franchisors are uncommonly keen that franchisees constantly increase turnover, because increased turnover means increased management fees for the franchisor; the franchisee might wish to increase profitability by reducing costs, which (of course) does not benefit the franchisor in any way, and this is a potential disadvantage to the franchisor.

In much the same manner, franchisors will often encourage successful franchisees to buy more franchise units, on the basis that, if a franchisee can be successful with one outlet, s/he can replicate his/her success with two, three, four or even more. This is a bit of a fool's errand, as it dilutes the franchisee's direct involvement with the successful unit and spreads his/her influence over the whole of his/her group, meaning that the franchisee eventually has a series of under-performing franchise units rather than one very successful unit; his/her costs, however, are a multiplication of the fees charged to each franchise unit. This pandering to the franchisee's latent megalomania might mean that the overall profits are increased, but the individual unit profit *ratio* is reduced, making for a potentially dissatisfied franchisor and franchisee alike.

Similar in nature to this point is that the franchisee has no control over the geographical coverage of the system; we have seen that there is an immense advantage in having a dedicated territory where the franchisee enjoys exclusivity rights, but it is the franchisor who decides how large that territory should be, and where to locate the neighbouring outlets. If a franchisee take on a rather undersold franchise, it is likely that s/he will have 'vacant' territories surrounding his/her outlet, which in the short term and until the franchisor sells them, are likely to be serviced from the franchisee's business. As the vacant territories are taken up, so the franchisee may well see their turnover decrease as equilibrium is achieved, and this will be annoying to the dynamic franchisee. The solutions – of which there are two – are simple: the original franchisee either buys up the neighbouring vacant franchises him/herself and accepts that, if turnover is going to decrease, at least it will be going to one of his/her outlets, but let us not forget the difficulties that have been mentioned previously. The alternative is to deepen market penetration in the franchisee's existing territory by trying to attract new customers from market sectors they may have previously ignored, which might well prove to be the better long-term strategy.

Another potentially huge drawback is that franchisees are entering into a long-term 'marriage' with their franchisor, having had a relatively short courtship. While the promotional material sent out by the franchisor might make for interesting reading, and might well promise the opportunity of untold wealth, in reality the franchisor may be unable to provide the level and focus of training that the individual franchisee might require in order to meet these expectations. A specialist lawyer and franchise consultant will guide the franchisee in their task of identifying the pitfalls of a prospective system, and the advice given should be heeded.

The next shortcoming of franchise systems is that they are rather like leviathans: they gather speed and momentum but are pretty difficult to stop or to change direction once in motion. The entire concept of franchising is that it is based on operations manuals and standardized business methods, so it is not the most flexible of systems. Moreover, one of the core principles of franchising is that the individual franchisee will have virtually no power over the most important policy decisions that will influence his/her business, especially as it is often the grass-roots franchisee who will spot the danger signs, but will be unable to make adjustments to the business's trading style because of the fettering nature of the franchise agreement. To counter this phenomenon, there needs to be a free flow of information downwards, upwards and around the franchise operation, and all parties must be prepared to listen with an open mind to the concerns or suggested solutions of others.

There are franchisors who try to dampen the fellowship nature of the franchise system by discouraging too much fraternization between franchisees. Inevitably, it is companies who are insecure or worried about dissent among franchisees that take this course of action, and predictably it is these organizations that are the most rigid and inflexible, and consequently the weakest.

The penultimate drawback of franchising from everybody's point of view, but mainly the franchisees', is one we touched on earlier, in Chapter 2, and that is the subject of the individual franchisee who seeks to cut too many corners and damages the overall quality of the product offering. It might have appeared an amusing and unlikely analogy of the individual rogue franchisee poisoning his/her customers, but such things do happen, and when they do, it is often catastrophic for the entire system. The adverse publicity affects the potential of every single franchise outlet, tarring the good with the brush of the bad. Consequently, the actions of one franchisee affecting the livelihood of other franchisees can be said to be a weakness of franchising in general, which is why franchisors will come down extremely heavily on franchisees who in any way damage the brand or reputation of the system, and the extreme penalties for brand pollution are written in stone in the franchise agreement.

The final inconvenience in franchising comes when a franchisee wishes, for whatever reason, to relinquish his/her franchise. In a traditional non-franchise business, the owner would find a likely buyer and sell the company; with franchising it is not nearly as easy as this. Remember that the franchisor invested a lot of time, effort and money to ensure that the right franchisee was recruited to take on one of its valuable franchises, and it is reasonable to assume that the franchisor will wish to ensure that whoever takes over a retiring franchisee's business will meet the same exacting requirements.

> **Homepreneurs** *are entrepreneurs who operate a business from home; the phrase could be attributed to home-based franchisees who display an enterprising business flair.*

To try and identify positives and negatives of owning a franchise at either end of the franchise spectrum, there now follows an analysis of both home-based franchises and leading brand franchises. There is a higher-level franchise opportunity known as investment franchising, but the franchisee in this case is seldom involved in the day-to-day running of the franchised business, so it is rather outside the scope of this analysis. Investment franchises are covered in Chapter 8.

ADVANTAGES AND DISADVANTAGES OF HOME-BASED FRANCHISES

A flick through any franchise magazine or a wander through a franchise exhibition will show the prospective franchisee that many franchise opportunities do not need the expense of renting office space, or hiring staff. A growing number of franchise opportunities are businesses that can be run successfully from home.

Indeed, at times when the health of the economy is weak and the small business sector is struggling, there is often a resurgent growth in businesses being run from non-commercial premises. A new term for those who run their businesses from home has been coined: 'homepreneurs', and these are starting to have a substantial impact on the recovering economy.

In the USA, some surveys show there to be more than 6 million home-based businesses employing over 13-million workers; and many of these companies generate substantial six-figure earnings.

The growth of the home-based franchise community can be attributed to many more franchisors adapting their offering to attract more people with less capital to invest, usually brought about by the rigidity of the credit markets restricting funds to high-cost franchises.

Coupling this to the huge advances in communication technology, where even the lowliest of businesses can create the appearance of substantiality, means that the cost-to-value equation is driving dynamic franchisors to offer the flexibility of operating from a home base.

The reduction in the cost of starting up a home-based franchise is fulfilling the dream of many more potential franchisees to run their own businesses, and at the same time is also reducing the costs of franchisors by giving them the freedom of introducing new models of operation and growing their businesses.

It is true that running a home-based franchise, whether it is a one-man-and-his-van or home-based franchise requires a different work ethic from being an employee for a company where the franchisee physically 'goes to work' or even a franchisee who has separate premises. For a start, the franchisee has to be considerably more self-motivated and must be prepared to work hard, but most important, they must not be easily distracted. Running a franchise, any franchise, is going to be extremely hard work; especially if the franchisee wants to excel within the franchise network, or gain the accolades that fall to those who are prepared to go the extra mile.

Consequently, the prospective home-based franchisee should seek a franchisor who *understands* the nature of working from home. The prospective franchisee needs to find a franchisor with a proven track record of developing successful franchisees, with an effective marketing plan, a thorough understanding of how successful franchisees make their system work, and bold enough to try fresh approaches to generate business to keep the network one step ahead of the game at all times. But most of all he or she should have existing, successful franchisees who feel good about the franchisor.

If a prospective home-based franchisee were to talk to a successful established franchisee within the network they are considering, they would undoubtedly hear stories similar to these: 'This is a seven-day-a-week job; when I get home after a day in the van I have all my paperwork to catch up on, and as for weekends off? Well, my customers' plumbing does not respect a nine-to-five, Monday-to-Friday schedule; when I am needed, I work. And when I am not fixing a leaking tap, I'm out scouting for new customers'; or 'The only time that my clients can see me is in the evening, so during the day I spend my time scheduling appointments and in the evening I carry them out; the weekends are spent collating all the informa- tion I have gathered during the week and bringing my knowledge database up to date, as well as doing my accounts and catching up with my colleagues regarding any new strategies they have implemented success- fully' – without a doubt, running a home-based franchise is not an 'easy option'.

Life as a home-based franchisee is fraught with distractions, and many come from the least expected source. The first time a home-based fran- chisee gives in to the 'Darling, can you pick the kids up from school?' will be the thin end of the wedge when it comes to distractions. Shopping, dry- cleaning, dog-walking, kids' taxi, will all become distractions that prevent the franchisee from reaching his/her full potential – and that's even before we get on to that tremendously interesting programme on car maintenance or cookery that is on television in the middle of the afternoon! The self- discipline and motivation that the successful home-based franchisee will need means that s/he must be prepared to lay down some strict ground rules, and to learn that the most powerful word in the dictionary is 'No'. There is a strong argument, almost a compelling argument, to have a designated room in the home that can be called 'The Office', where the home-based franchisee will 'go to work'. Having a dedicated business tele- phone line will also help to prevent domestic distractions.

Success in business can be reduced to a simple equation: minimum costs generating maximum return; and the home-based franchisee has one massive advantage over others in that they do not have the overhead of an office facility, but even the home-based franchisee will incur other busi- ness expenses, such as localized marketing, that need to generate maxi- mum value for money.

Some key facts about home-based franchising are given in Figure 3.3, and understanding these may provide a reality check from the delusions that can often create a misinterpretation in the minds of those who see all the positives and none of the negatives of this area of franchising

The greatest pieces of advice that can be offered to a prospective home- based franchisee are:

1   Find a franchise that you love. It is so easy to be distracted from doing a job that one dislikes or hates. Of course, this is important when

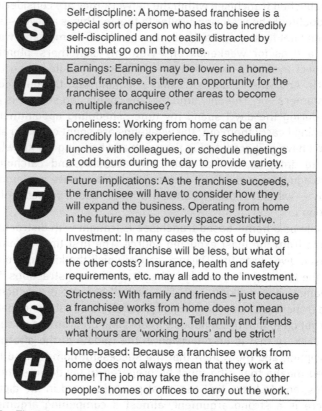

S	Self-discipline: A home-based franchisee is a special sort of person who has to be incredibly self-disciplined and not easily distracted by things that go on in the home.
E	Earnings: Earnings may be lower in a home-based franchise. Is there an opportunity for the franchisee to acquire other areas to become a multiple franchisee?
L	Loneliness: Working from home can be an incredibly lonely experience. Try scheduling lunches with colleagues, or schedule meetings at odd hours during the day to provide variety.
F	Future implications: As the franchise succeeds, the franchisee will have to consider how they will expand the business. Operating from home in the future may be overly space restrictive.
I	Investment: In many cases the cost of buying a home-based franchise will be less, but what of the other costs? Insurance, health and safety requirements, etc. may all add to the investment.
S	Strictness: With family and friends – just because a franchisee works from home does not mean that they are not working. Tell family and friends what hours are 'working hours' and be strict!
H	Home-based: Because a franchisee works from home does not always mean that they work at home! The job may take the franchisee to other people's homes or offices to carry out the work.

Figure 3.3   The home franchise consideration table

choosing any franchise, but when seeking a home-based franchise, with all the distractions that will abound in the home, it is doubly important.

2   Have a getaway. Running a business, any business, is a stressful occupation; franchises do tend to have a lower level of stress than stand-alone businesses, but if the business is being run from the franchisee's home, then the franchisee's family are going to be affected by the business. Getting the right work balance is critical, which means that the franchisee will need an escape from the business (and the home) to recharge his/her batteries.

3   Network, network, network. The flexibility of home franchising gives the franchisee a greater opportunity for networking than a business that needs to have somebody 'minding the shop'. At every opportunity get out of the house and expand your network of contacts; that way you are constantly being proactive and productive.

4   Be selective about which marketing opportunities you take up. As a member of a franchise network, much of the 'national' marketing will

be included in the management fees, but most franchisees will almost certainly have to take additional localized marketing decisions. The world is full of marketers who have the 'ultimate' marketing solution and it is extremely likely that the majority will be a waste of money! Getting value for money means that each marketing opportunity must (a) reach your target audience; and (b) generate an acceptable return of investment.

ADVANTAGES AND DISADVANTAGES OF WELL-KNOWN FRANCHISES

When teaching, lecturers will undoubtedly ask students to identify a brand that they associate with franchising. Not surprisingly, McDonald's, Subway, Domino's Pizza and Burger King typically spring immediately to the minds of students; occasionally, they are followed by other brands, which in the UK may include Bargain Booze, a chain of cut-price alcohol retail franchises. Sometimes seen as a 'licence to print money', it soon becomes clear that the 'Holy Grail' of franchising is to buy into one of the global brands, and some students have even gone on to become franchisees for one of these leading brands, but first they understood the pros and cons of doing so.

Let us consider a few of the advantages and disadvantages of buying into a leading brand.

Without a doubt, if an outlet for a leading burger chain opens in a location, there is immediate brand recognition. The franchisee does not have to spend much time promoting the business or educating the local population about the products that will be offered in his/her business; this is a major advantage because, with smaller, less well known brands, up to 30 per cent of the franchisee's time will be spent promoting the business.

It may also be considerably easier to persuade the bank manager that the franchisee's business will be successful, as the bank's loan underwriters fully understand the franchise concept and accept that the risk element is substantially reduced by supporting a well-tried and thoroughly tested franchise.

Even when looking for a location for the outlet, having a leading brand to offer prospective landlords can be a huge advantage. Not surprisingly, big name brands tend to flock together in shopping centres and retail parks, and approaching the owners of a new mall with a leading brand franchise will generally have the landlord unrolling the red carpet for such a prospective tenant. One big name brand will attract others, and that significantly increases the footfall at the shopping centre.

However, and without a doubt, premium brands attract premium investment. It is highly unlikely that a leading brand franchisor is going to sell a franchise for under a six-figure sum, be that pounds, euros, dollars or even

Swiss francs. Moreover, the ongoing fees will also be at the top end of the scale because of the cost of providing logistical and technical support to the network. The support structures may be huge, but they really do support the individual franchisee with just about any foreseeable difficulty that might arise.

If a prospective franchisee has even the slightest trace of entrepreneurial flair, however, then a leading brand franchise is not going to be the environment where it will flourish. The system has been fully tried and tested, and incorporated in the operations manual. In fact, many leading franchises have several volumes in their operations manual, specifying fine details right down to the most efficient way to sweep the floor; and franchisees are expected to follow the prescribed methods to the letter. This is why, whether a customer visits an outlet in Michigan, Manchester or Moscow, the customer experience will be standardized.

Taking a franchise with a less well-known brand may not have the expectations that a franchisee will eventually become a multi-unit owner, which a leading brand might expect. Many leading brand franchisors seek to recruit area developers rather than single unit franchisees because their costs of recruitment and training are high and they want to maximize brand exposure and achieve the greatest value for money.

Finally, most leading brand franchises are corporate entities where the individual franchisee is an impersonal number who contributes to the overall profit and loss of the business; at the upper echelons of the business it is highly unlikely that management will even know of the individual franchisee's existence. One of the major attractions of franchising to many franchisees is the almost paternalistic family feeling of being part of a business where power distance is relatively short.

What needs to be emphasized to prospective franchisees is that, in seeking the 'Holy Grail' there are certain tough conditions that have to be met; if a franchisee is prepared to meet these conditions, big-name franchising can be extremely lucrative. At the same time, so can small-name franchising; McDonald's, Subway, Domino's and Burger King all had to start somewhere!

The secret to buying a franchise is to buy the whole experience, not just the brand name; the age-old criteria for choosing any franchise are just as applicable whether the franchisee opts for a well-known brand or a lesser-known one. Below are a few questions for a potential franchisee to think about:

1 How much is in the budget to buy and establish the franchise? Do not cut corners to make the brand fit the budget, especially not the corner that is marked 'working capital requirement'.

2 Will the franchise meet the franchisee's financial and other commitments? Nobody goes into a business of any kind not to make a profit,

and it is important that the franchise is able to meet the income expectations and timescale that the franchisee anticipates.

3   How much time can be devoted to the business? If a franchisee is looking for a fill-in job to occupy time while the children are at school, then big name franchising is probably not the route to take, as many leading brand retail franchises work long and anti-social hours.

4   Does the franchisee possess the skills that the franchisor is seeking to grow their business? Franchising is a marriage of skills and talents; if a franchisee persuades a franchisor s/he has skills that s/he does not possess, then divorce will surely follow.

5   Is the franchisee able to follow the system? Franchising is all about replicating a tried and tested system, and each franchisee works the system in a precisely prescribed manner; it is not about trying to 'tweak' the system or cut corners, because that way lies the route to disaster.

Excitement, or even passion, about the business is crucial, because if a franchisee does not enjoy completing the tasks of the franchise, it will not matter how much money the business makes, as the franchisee will not find true job fulfilment – and that is equally true of whether a franchisee has a leading brand franchise or is the first franchisee of a new-start operation.

(WHAT DO YOU THINK?)

In this chapter we have identified the pros and cons of franchising, and have looked at the advantages and disadvantages of either being a home-based franchisee or being associated with a big name brand.

How much value does a recognized brand bring to a franchisee's business? Can it be quantified against increased turnover?

Does the flexibility and relative low cost of operating a business from home outweigh the inconvenience and disruption that will impact on your family life?

Further reading

Duckett, Brian, *How to Franchise Your Business*, 2nd revd edn (How To Books 2011).

Illetschko, Kurt, *Get Started in Franchising (Teach Yourself)* (Hodder Education 2010).

Seid, Michael and Thomas, Dave, *Franchising For Dummies*, 2nd edn (Wiley, 2006).

Sugars, Bradley, *Successful Franchising (Instant Success Series)* (McGraw-Hill 2005).

4 THE FRANCHISE RELATIONSHIP

INTRODUCTION AND LEARNING OUTCOMES

The purpose of this chapter is to examine in some depth the relationship that exists between franchisor and franchisee, which is unique in commercial relationships.
The reader will be able to:

* Understand how the relationship changes over its course, from negotiation to separation.
* Appreciate the responsibilities that each party undertakes to ensure a smooth and happy partnership.
* Gain an insight into what makes for a happy relationship that benefits all parties.

Franchising is a unique and peculiar business arrangement, which differs from a traditional model because of the number of business owners that are integrated into the network.

Moreover, the relationship that exists between an individual franchisee and the franchisor is subject to drastic alteration as the franchisee changes from being a 'prospect', through recruitment and development, up to the point when s/he is the owner of a flourishing business and starts to become less dependent on the franchisor.

Invariably, if one talks with a failed franchisee about the reason why his/her business did not succeed, the answer will fall into one of two categories: either there was a problem with the macro environment (for example, poor economic conditions, such as a recession, at the time they were starting their franchise), or that they had a poor franchisor whose system was flawed or whose support structure was inadequate. Seldom will one hear the franchisee discuss the third option: that their attitude was unsuitable, or that they did not follow the business format in the manner the franchisor had established. In truth, there will probably be an element of all three in the true reasons for failure, and this highlights the special nature of the relationships that exist in a franchise system.

> *Relationships between franchisor and franchisee are like marriages, and like most marriages the relationship has its ups and downs.*

This relationship is almost like a marriage, which starts life as two people who are attracted to each other, and this attraction develops into a courtship and engagement before the marriage takes place, and as the marriage develops, so does the confidence with which the couple face difficulties, but they grow in strength together and fulfil so many of their ambitions, until either death or divorce separates them. The analogy applied to the world of franchising is easy to see, with only three real differences existing. First, in franchising, there is always one dominant party and it does not matter how long the relationship has existed, the established franchisee will have no more rights or any greater freedom than the newest franchisee. Second, one party will be in a 'polygamous' relationship whereas the other will usually be prevented from having several partners. Third, the relationship has a fixed term, whereas marriage is for an indeterminate term – and long may that remain the case!

NEGOTIATION

The most important phase of any relationship, be it civil or business, is the early stages, where the ground rules are set by both parties, and this is where the most important skill of both the franchisor and franchisee becomes evident – the art of negotiation.

Negotiation is not something that is going to be covered in any great detail in this book – there are far better books written by far more competent writers on the subject available at any good bookstore – but readers will appreciate the importance of good negotiation and understand how failing to negotiate well may well commit either party to far-reaching cost burdens that could easily be the difference between the success or failure of the entire venture. If both parties to an agreement have negotiated successfully, both will emerge with a 'good deal'; typically they will spend less, sell more and generate higher profits that will form the foundations of the ongoing successful business.

In any negotiation for the purchase of a business, if the purchaser pays more than necessary s/he will be burdened with a debt, which may well be financed by an expensive loan, for many years to come. Furthermore, if the borrower does not negotiate with the lender the level of interest to be charged on the loan, s/he may well be paying thousands of pounds/dollars/euros more than they need to throughout the life of the loan.

Let us examine this further. If a prospective franchisee borrows, for example, £75,000 to fund the cost of the franchise purchase, over a period of ten years at 8 per cent interest, then the interest charge over the term of the loan will be £86,919. If the prospective franchisee was able to negotiate the interest rate down to 6.5 per cent for the same amount over the same period, the amount of interest payable would be reduced to £65,785. This, of course, shows a lesser amount of interest payable on the loan of £21,134, which may not sound a great deal over the term of the loan, but if the business is working on a 15 per cent gross profit margin, this relates to over £140,000 worth of sales the business must transact, just to service this additional loan interest charge. If the prospective franchisee does not think this is worth negotiating for, then perhaps s/he would be better off in an employed position, because s/he is unlikely to be successful in business!

Most franchisees will need some kind of vehicle for use in the business, and this is an area where you need to negotiate hard. At the time of writing, in post-recessionary times, many car dealers are offering exceptional deals because sales are extremely difficult, but this still remains the starting point of any negotiation. Remember that many dealers make a profit out of any finance deal that is negotiated, so not only does the prospective franchise have to haggle the purchase price down, but also the interest rate charged on any finance arranged; the motor trade is extremely adept at giving with one hand while taking with the other! Negotiate hard, shop around and always buy at month end, when dealerships are struggling to get their monthly quota satisfied. The best piece of advice that can be given is, 'If the salesperson is still smiling at the end of the deal, you didn't negotiate hard enough!'

> Negotiations in franchising tend not to be between the franchisor and franchisee, as each franchisee in the system must be seen to receive the 'same deal'.

Sadly, many people enter franchising believing that whatever the franchisor, or the bank, or the car salesman tells them is set in stone, and whereas this may be true of the terms of the franchising agreement, it almost certainly is not in respect of the conditions, the bank rate or what the franchisee ends up paying for the vehicle.

When negotiating, most people should remember that they are blessed with two ears and one mouth and that is roughly the ratio that they should be used. Listening more, talking less and not being afraid of silence will greatly improve one's negotiating skills. As will slowing down; many people seem to develop an overdrive gear for their mouths when negotiating; the rule of silence determines that he who speaks first, has lost.

The 'negotiation respite' gambit is a great tool to employ. If things are getting out of hand, or you find yourself stuck between 'a rock and a hard place', gather your papers together and politely leave. This often throws the other party into total confusion, but in reality you are only pacing the negotiation to your own timescale. There is nothing unfair or insincere in seeking a respite so that you can reconsider your position; in fact, it is an extremely useful gambit that has often led to some remarkable concessions being made by the other side in an attempt to restart the negotiation.

How many times have you been contacted by a telesales operative with the 'latest and best' deal available, if only you would sign-up on the telephone right now? Personally speaking, I must be the telesales person's Nemesis – I never buy anything over the telephone. If the company is not prepared to put its latest, greatest offer in writing then I will not buy. I am introducing the 'negotiation respite' into high-pressure telesales, and they hate it!

Finally, on the subject of negotiation, do not plan the negotiation with any certainty as to the result. When negotiating, you should know what you hope to achieve, and sometimes, because it is human nature to try to be fair and equitable, this is achieved quickly – and sometimes too quickly! There is a story of an antique dealer who bought an antique clock for £100; the seller was asking £130 and the dealer's first bid was £100, whereupon the seller almost dislocated the buyer's arm by snatching the money from his hand. Perhaps he could have negotiated better and got a much better price, but perhaps he wanted to be 'fair' to the dealer. Too many negotiators try to see both sides of the negotiation, when in reality they should concentrate on their own side.

The franchisee's business plan will show how much the franchisee can afford to pay for the loan; the negotiation does not have to stop when that point is achieved, because any greater negotiation beyond the 'affordability point' can only boost the profit margins of the franchise, over what has been budgeted in the business plan.

There are those who are natural negotiators, and those who are not; the majority, like me, fall into the latter category, and we have to learn how to negotiate; typically, we do so through the experience of having made many bad deals. Learning the basics of negotiation before entering into any hard and fast commitments with a chosen franchisor will greatly improve the negotiation and go a good way towards alleviating the negative emotions (covered later in this chapter) that the franchisee might experience after buying the chosen franchise.

INNOVATION

Of course, it has long been recognized that it is often experienced franchisees that have the best ideas to develop the business, and it is well-known that McDonald's Big Mac was invented by a franchisee from Pittsburgh called Jim Delligatti. Franchisors who encourage their franchisees to 'think outside the box' and be innovative, invariably are the more successful franchised businesses; but woe betide any franchisee who ploughs his or her own furrow and is innovative without the sanction of his/her franchisor, as that is the road to a very messy parting of the ways. The franchise system must be always controlled by the franchisor, but incentivizing the franchisees to put their innovations forward will enable the franchisee to feel respected and recognized within the organization. The whole basis of franchising is that of consistency and uniformity, with the franchisee being licensed to use the system, brands and know-how that the franchisor imparts or includes as part of the agreement; specifically, franchisees are not licensed to operate a business that merely resembles the business of the franchisor, and allows for various 'personalizations' that differentiate the franchisee's business from that of the franchisee in the next town. Of course, in retailing it may be that the stock mix of a franchise may differ slightly to allow for local tastes and preferences, but the full range should still be available to a customer shopping out of area, and there should be uniformity in the marketing, layout and delivery of the product or service in every outlet.

In the early stages of negotiation, it is unlikely that the franchisor will lay all his or her cards on the table and, as in personal relationships, a greater knowledge and awareness of the attributes of the system, together with a greater appreciation of the know-how and intellectual property will be gained as the discussions progress. The skill of tantalizing the prospect sufficiently to keep his/her interest while not revealing the full extent of the franchisor's secrets is almost a tease, and this involves a fair amount of skill, but if the applicant progresses through the torment of temptations and reaches the 'promised land', then usually he or she is not disappointed. This approach may seem cruel, but it is necessary to protect the intellectual property and the rights that can only be revealed once the franchisee has been accepted into the network. What softens this approach is the mutual respect in which both the franchisor and franchisee are held by the other party, and this 'respect' is the key to successful franchise relations; if one party does not respect the other, then the franchise relationship is doomed and it is better that both parties walk away from any commitment – again, rather like marriage!

Those of us who are married are fully aware that any relationship needs to be worked at, and a huge amount of effort is needed to maintain the relationship that exists between the franchisee and franchisor, because, without a doubt, during the course of the agreement the relationship will be tested and relations will become strained by any number of difficulties or disagreements, most of which will be able to be resolved by open communication, but some may require slightly more effort before a resolution can be achieved.

EMOTIONAL TURBULENCE

It is quite true that franchisees experience a whole gamut of emotions during the development of their franchises, and to give the reader some idea of extent of the emotional range, most franchisees will experience optimism, elation, disillusionment, irritation, self-confidence and insecurity at various times during their term as a franchisee. The psychological management of a network of franchisees, each of whom will be going through a different emotional experience at any given time, is enough to give most franchisors a terminal headache, but in order to maximize the potential of the system, the management of these emotions must be handled effectively and efficiently. This is why most franchisors will devolve the everyday management of individual franchisees to their own development manager who has the enviable roles of being friend, mentor, coach, confessor, confidant at different times.

Franchisees will typically pass through several stages before they reach their full potential, presuming, of course, that they are committed to their business and are prepared to work hard at dealing with their difficulties, as well as being adept at overcoming the hurdles that life will undoubtedly throw at them. Some franchisees will glide through all the stages with ease; others will meet each challenge and become frustrated with the options open to them, often becoming resentful; while some others will not have the resilience to overcome the difficulties, will run-up the white flag at the first sign of trouble and quit franchising for a more relaxed and mundane lifestyle.

Understanding the stages through which franchisees will probably pass makes life considerably easier for both franchisee and franchisor, as, if this is the case, the event or series of events that makes the franchisee consider quitting is less likely to arise. Some franchisees will pass through to the 'Teamwork' phase quite quickly, and even perhaps jump some of the earlier phases, especially if they have previous experience as a franchisee. Others will linger longer at each stage and it could take up to two years before they arrive at the final, productive stage. The speed in which the franchisee travels through the phases is generally dependent on how efficiently the franchisor manages the emotional turmoil his/her franchisee is experiencing.

These various emotions can be displayed as a wheel to depict the various stages that franchisees will travel through before becoming fully effective, the different shades representing the 'warmth' of the franchisor/franchisee relationship (see Figure 4.1).

Usually, the first emotion a franchisee will experience is one of elation or excitement, an emotion that typically lasts for about three to nine months after becoming a franchisee, depending on the previous level of business experience. The franchisee still has stars in his or her eyes and is

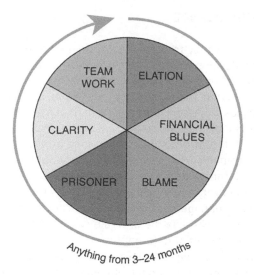

Figure 4.1 The emotional wheel of franchising

satisfied with just about everything the franchisor does. Positive emotions are running high and the franchisee is highly motivated after overcoming all the obstacles and being granted the franchise rights from his chosen franchisor. S/he still anticipates making huge amounts of money, because s/he thinks s/he will have the best franchise the system has ever recruited and is encouraged by the positive commitments of the franchisor at the opening ceremony. S/he is excited about his/her new business and full of hope and optimism for the future.

When the franchisee begins to understand the finances of the business a little more clearly, s/he progresses to what could be called the 'financial blues' stage where s/he will begin to question the size and necessity of fees. The franchisee is beginning to understand the accounts of his/her business and sees a large percentage being creamed off his profit margin in franchise fees. S/he will start to wonder what exactly s/he is getting for his/her money and whether it represents good value. The franchisee begins to sink into a depression as his/her satisfaction level is diminished. Some franchisors recognize that this is going to happen and build into their fee structure a discount they can offer their franchisees when they reach this stage; obviously, because of the standardized structure, the discount cannot be deducted from royalty payments, but might be possible through ancillary costs – for example, through goods purchased or through a rent review of the franchisee's premises. This could be a dangerous game to start, however, as it tends to set a precedent that, when things get tough, the franchisor will realign his prices to make the going easier.

Invariably, however, the next stage the franchisee will experience will be one of 'blame'. It is a well-known psychological trait of humankind that human beings are prepared to accept the credit for good things but seek to apportion blame for things that go wrong. A good example of this would be the student who achieved an 'A' grade recognizing that he did well because he studied hard, whereas the student who received an 'F' grade might well argue that he did poorly because the teacher did not like him. Psychologists call this the 'attribution theory', which goes to the root of personal perception of the rational or irrational acceptance of the causes of an event. This translates well in the franchisor/franchisee relationship because the franchisee will start to think that his or her own success is purely a result of his/her own efforts and hard work; however, if things are not going so well it will undoubtedly be considered as the result of poor support from the franchisor, or adverse trading conditions, or the fact that it was a full moon yesterday ... any reason other than accepting responsibility for poor performance. One area where this does feature significantly, as the franchisee moves around the wheel, is why the franchise is not as financially sound as it might be – because the 'greedy' franchisor is taking most of the hard-earned profit out of the franchise, which is affecting its financial stability!

At this point, the franchisee is starting to feel a bit like a 'prisoner' in the franchise. The franchisee is starting to realize that, despite running his own business, the restrictions of the system confining the way that the business is run are starting to feel like fetters, and the franchisee looks for ways to break free and stamp his/her own personality on their business. Undoubtedly, the franchisee is becoming more experienced and less in need of support from the franchisor, and is beginning to want more and more independence; the operations manual that the franchisee found to be the source of all solutions a few months previously is now starting to feel like a dead weight around his business. Resentment is high and the need to break free of the franchisor's restraint is paramount. The franchisee will start to try to push back the franchise boundaries, or even try and test the enforceability of the contractual agreement. This is a very dangerous area for the relationship, as at this point some franchisors might opt for the line of least resistance and seek a forced sale of the franchise, or a termination of the contract.

The high level of negativity that exists at this point can impact on neighbouring franchises as the disgruntled franchisee tries to enlist support from his colleagues; the dissatisfied franchisee is now the weak link in the chain and extreme care is required by the franchisor as s/he works to alleviate the causes of the frustration.

One of two things will generally occur at this stage of the cycle: either the franchisee will remain a malevolent discontent until the franchisor's patience is exhausted and termination occurs, or the franchisee will experience a 'eureka' moment and move forward to the 'clarity' stage, probably after a great deal of effort by the franchisor, who does not want to lose a potentially good franchisee. This will undoubtedly be the turning point in the relationship between the franchisor and franchisee, and green shoots will start to appear in what was beginning to look like a barren desert. This is when the relationship becomes a lot clearer and more understandable to the franchisee.

The franchisee comprehends the value of the system and why franchisees have to follow the 'golden path to glory' that has been laid down by the franchisor, and s/he starts to appreciate that if every franchisee did his or her own thing, then standards could not be maintained or the product offering be standardized across the network. Getting from the 'prisoner' stage to the 'clarity' stage involves some frank and open discussions between the franchisor and the franchisee, but this is a healthy sign, because conflict will never be resolved if the root causes are not addressed; sadly, however, many franchisors choose to treat the symptom rather that the cause of the problem and this makes for a superficial remedy.

The only way malevolence can be countered is by facing the situation like adults and trying to find a solution that is acceptable to both parties, without abrogating the principles on which the franchise is founded. It will probably not be a pretty sight, with both parties coming away feeling somewhat bruised and battered, and if blame for past misconceptions and misunderstandings is to be apportioned, then it will probably be shared. Both the franchisee and the franchisor need to put past differences behind them and move forward towards a greater understanding of each other's points of view and an appreciation of the other's specific needs.

Some enlightened franchisors might even include franchisees in their board meetings and strategy discussions, either on an elected or appointed basis, so that the franchisee can report back to the network in 'franchisee-speak', getting the message across in a language that other franchisees understand. These elevated franchisees who sit on the board or are included in strategy discussions might be used to help show the malevolent franchisee the error of his/her ways and reaffirm the company policy, as often a word from a peer is better than a directive from the executive. From this, we can see that the 'clarity' stage is where the perception of the franchisee changes and s/he starts to appreciate the value of the strength of the group system.

The final stage is 'team work' where the franchisee acknowledges that s/he does need help with certain areas of his/her business, and the franchisor recognizes that the franchisee has a valuable input to make in the continued development of the business, by being able to channel ideas for the franchisor's consideration; there is thus a true sense of affiliation. The change in perception from 'independent' to 'interdependent' has occurred and the franchisee accepts that life will be a lot easier and considerably more fruitful if s/he stops swimming against the tide and starts working with his/her franchisor rather than against him/her.

One can almost see an analogy of a child growing up as one considers the various stages through which the franchisee travels. The 'prisoner' stage represents puberty and the 'clarity' stage is when the hormones are starting to settle down again before maturity is reached in the 'team work' phase, but it is worth remembering that, if the franchisee is not making adequate profits and/or feels as though the franchisor does not value his/her contribution, then the 'team work' stage will never be reached. Franchisors who treat franchisees differently, or do not deliver on obligations are likely to find they will never shake themselves free of their dissatisfied and disillusioned franchisees.

On the other hand, franchisees who have negotiated the path to the 'team work' stage are an asset to the franchisor; they will have settled down to a quiet 'middle age' where they are reaping the bountiful harvest of their investment, while at the same time developing healthy business relationships with the franchisor, their suppliers, other franchisees in the system, and their customers.

STAKEHOLDERS

This brings us neatly to the stakeholder analysis, where we can see the various stakeholders in a franchise. In the franchise stakeholder model shown in Figure 4.2, the franchisor is represented by the paler circle that encompasses the other stakeholders' circles.

The five main stakeholders in the franchise are the franchisor, the franchisees, the employees (both those employed directly by the franchisor and indirectly by the franchisees), the suppliers and, most important, the customers; how they interact with each other is described in the captions on the model. For example, the franchisee and the customer interact together in the area of brand development through the quality of service given and perceived; if the quality of the service received is good, the brand is enhanced, but if it is bad, the brand deteriorates. Similarly, the customer is the ultimate quality assurance inspector, because if the product is poor and not up to the required standard, complaints will increase and sales will decline, which will ultimately lead to the supplier being replaced.

Equally, head office employees will work with the suppliers to improve the quality and value of the product offering, resulting in a higher-quality product being made available to customers through the franchise network, and the employees of the franchisee (and franchisor) will enjoy the higher employment benefits and standards that are associated with working for a high-profile brand.

Figure 4.2 Franchise stakeholder diagram

There is even a cross-over impact derived from diagonally opposed stakeholders; for example, the franchisee relies on the supplier to ensure the continuity of supply of the base product, and customers rely on good service from the franchisee's employees to enhance the purchasing process – the franchisee's employees are, after all, the public face of the brand and they are the people with whom the customer is obliged to deal!

If all the components come together and work cohesively in concert with each other, the ultimate prize will be the establishment of a winning brand that will become respected and continue to provide a good income for all stakeholders as time progresses.

In the event of one of the stakeholders not performing to the required level expected by the franchisor, then the reputation of the brand will be diminished and this will have a snowball effect across the whole franchised business. Remember that a satisfied customer will tell on average five people, but a dissatisfied customer will tell on average 19 people; it is not hard to imagine that the more satisfied customers that are generated, the more successful the franchise will be, whereas the more dissatisfied customers there are will disproportionately impact on the success of the business.

Franchising is a vibrant business and as the parameters of the franchise changes, so the dynamics of the relationship and the management mechanisms also change. As the market changes, so must the franchise,

| Accounting & finance |
| Health & safety |
| Human resources | Franchisor responsibilities |
| Marketing |
| Information technology |

| Franchise accounts |
| Human resources | Franchisee's local responsibilities |
| Promotion |
| Operations |

Figure 4.3 Franchise responsibilities

whether the change is financial or territorial, or the range offered. Remembering that, when the franchise was created, a balance existed between the franchisor and the franchisee, and it is incumbent on the franchisor to ensure that the balance does not tip too heavily one way or the other, as change occurs.

This need for change is one of the main reasons why franchisors try to retain control over the core business functions. Figure 4.3 shows how these are generally apportioned.

Whereas the franchisee often retains control of the localized functions, as we have seen, many franchisors are now providing their franchisees with integrated business packages that take away the need for franchisees to spend too much time sweating over administration, because much of it is dealt with centrally. However, responsibility and accountability for accuracy of accounting and the timely submission of returns remains the task of the franchisee, who will always be held responsible.

Retaining control over the core business functions is the only way that the franchisor can respond quickly to market shifts, as it is easier and more efficient to implement changes centrally than to try to implement them piecemeal across the entire network, especially if the network is very large.

The elements of the core functions over which it is important for franchisors to retain control can be detailed as follows:

- *Accounting and Finance.* Invoice submission and tracking, debt management, payment for subcontract labour and parts, reconciliations, forecasting and projections, loan repayments, and expansion planning.

- *Health and Safety.* Risk assessment and documentation, updating log, accreditation to trade bodies, and equipment inspection.
- *Human Resources.* Employee relations, contracts of employment, employee handbooks, disciplinary matters, training, managing subcontracts, continuous personal development.
- *Marketing.* Brand development, national advertising, sponsorship management, product development and promotion, campaign planning across multiple media, company appearance and policies, gaining new and retaining existing clients.
- *Information Technology.* Specification and purchase of systems to deal with accounts and customer management, website development, software updates, hardware purchase and disposal, selection of and hiring IT employees or contractors.

The parts of the business at a more localized level are best left with the individual franchisee to manage and control, and can be identified as follows:

- *Franchise Accounts.* Production of physical accounts and book-keeping for the individual franchise unit, payment of local suppliers, salaries/wages of locally employed staff.
- *Human Resources.* Staff planning and rostering, maintenance of local health and safety logs, local staff training and development, hiring and firing of local staff, administering discipline in accordance with central policy.
- *Promotion.* Local promotion of the franchise, maintaining brand image, gaining and retaining a local customer base.
- *Operations.* Premises and maintenance, vehicle leasing and maintenance, day-to-day management of the company.

THE SECRET OF A GOOD RELATIONSHIP

At the beginning of this chapter there was a strong analogy comparing the relationship between franchisor and franchisee to that of husband and wife, and comparisons were drawn. In the same way as there is no set formula for resolving marital disputes, neither are there exact guidelines, or books to read, or formulas to apply, when it comes to relationship counselling between franchisor and franchisee. It boils down to a plain and simple commonsense approach that is strategically motivated and constantly nurtured, developed and enhanced.

There are three elements that, when combined, will ensure a happy relationship (see Figure 4.4), and these are not dissimilar to the elements one applies to any association where both parties seek understanding and

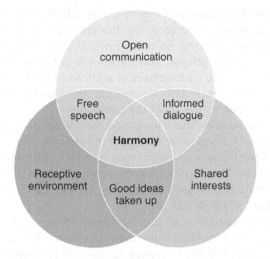

Figure 4.4 The three elements of a good relationship

a willingness to progress, so let us take a look at franchise 'marriage guidance'.

For any relationship to continue once it has been established, it must be maintained, and the first requirement of successful maintenance is effective, two-way communication. Without doubt, the onus of providing the medium for communication lies squarely with the franchisor. Some franchisors, as we have seen, establish formalized channels whereby franchisees are represented on the board of directors, or they establish franchisee committees to encourage free-flowing communication.

Sometimes, these franchisee committees are used to ensure that any modifications to the system that the franchisor wishes to implement are accepted by the network, but this narrow, one-way approach will diminish the value of the committee. The real purpose of the franchisee committee should be to monitor the core requirements of the franchisees, and to create an environment whereby the franchisees feel confident to discuss their concerns, questions, ideas for improvement with the franchisor, or even to recommend changes. The open-ended exchange with the franchise committee should enable the franchisor to improve the implementation of its agenda by locking into the 'combined intellect' of all parties involved.

Another good method of encouraging open dialogue is the generation of an extranet site, which is available to the franchisor, franchisees and staff members to access. It provides an environment for franchisees to access FAQs, or to upload their questions, concerns or ideas to management or to other franchisees, as well as giving all parties immediate access to the latest corporate news, current programmes and business development opportunities. It can also act as a forum for open and uncensored discussion of thorny topics, which should never be used punitively but monitored to ascertain the areas of concern that the network is currently experiencing so that remedial action can be taken before the concern become official. The intranet is a fantastic tool to generate an opportunity where all members of staff, from the CEO to the most recently recruited franchisee staff member, can have their worries heard or find out corporate information about the company.

The infamous in-house magazine, be it in hard copy or online, generates a multiplicity of communication. It formalizes and gives warning of the latest advertising campaign, new product roll-outs and other system occurrences. This communication medium allows the franchisor to inform and educate franchisees on strategy as well as to augment their role as 'custodians of the brand'.

As a consequence of the franchisor offering these communications channels, the individual franchisees feel more integrated into the system and are typically more willing to voice their concerns, or share their thoughts, and bring different perspectives forward for discussion, as well as acting as the courier of the brand's daily challenges.

The success of any franchise structure is the quality of the franchisees: without their willingness and enthusiasm the system would never reach its full potential. Established franchisees are an immense fount of knowledge and perspective about the business. They are one of the core resources of any successful franchisor, because the hands-on experience they have and their vast knowledge of the operational idiosyncrasies of the system are invaluable.

The other big advantage to this commitment to a two-way communication environment is that it generates a feeling of mutual respect and trust between the parties in the working relationship. This trust generates the capacity within the network to influence business opportunities and then to respond much faster to the changes in the vibrant marketplace. The readiness of the parties to be persuaded by one another is a good indicator of how much trust exists between them.

Multi-way communication also helps to break down the 'them-and-us' culture that invariably exists within the network where both parties try to convince themselves that the other side has a different agenda from their (right) thoughts. The 'them-and-us' culture is corrosive in any business, but in a company that relies so heavily on the willingness of the network to be dynamic, it could be catastrophic. It will lead to unnecessary disagreements, and will sap the energy of the business that ought to be channelled to improve health and profitability.

Opening the communication channels to two-way dialogue will allow for amicable and frank discussions, and will help to identify that, rather than being something unique, most of the concerns and frustrations are 'shared interests'. There is most certainly a high degree of similarity between the interests of the franchisee and those of the franchisor, and this overlap is a valuable commodity that, if used wisely, can re-energize a brand. Understanding and appreciating the parallels encourages growth and strengthens the brand, and a strong, growing and robust brand is unquestioningly the most precious asset that can be developed by a franchise.

Consequently, the art of listening and sharing the combined intelligence and expertise of the network's members is the key to building a growing brand. By making a commitment to open collaborative communication, franchisors and franchisees are able to reinforce the strategies and consumer-level implementation that will drive the brand's growth.

CASE STUDY 4.1

Kwalikleen: all that glisters is not gold

When David and June Reynolds bought their Kwalikleen specialist cleaning franchise back in 2006, they were treated like royalty. The American salesman had spent so much time discussing things that were important to them, David's old Jaguar motor-car that he was lovingly restoring, and June's love of skiing were both subjects that the salesman was able to discuss with some confidence. They felt they were building a lasting friendship with somebody who understood life as they did, almost a kindred spirit.

David had been in business before, running a successful property management company in Brighton, in the UK, but had taken early retirement and was becoming bored with his new-found freedoms. 'I used to dream of spending every day on the golf course,' David reminisced, 'but it soon got boring, I missed the excitement of business, the "cut-and-thrust" of making a deal, the satisfaction of a job well done. Of course, it was satisfying getting my handicap down, or getting the brakes to work on Betsy, my old Jaguar Mark 10, but it was a poor substitute for being at the leading edge of business!'

So David decided to come out of retirement and buy a franchise with his wife, who was going to look after the administration of the business. David even discussed taking his wife's brother into the business, who had once been a minor television actor, but had until recently been working as a painter and decorator, until he had been made redundant.

David spent many days researching the various franchise opportunities that were available in the UK, visiting the big franchise exhibitions with June and her brother Mark, or reading the specialist franchising magazines, but nothing really attracted them, until they read a small ad from a specialist industrial cleaning company called Kwalikleen, based in Michigan in the USA, that was seeking to set up a franchise network in the UK.

→

CASE STUDY 4.1 *continued*

Daniel, the American salesman, was enthusiastic about David joining their company right from the very start. He talked about the realistic sums that their American franchisees were earning, and said that David's management skills coupled with Mark's practical skills and June's administrative ability seemed like the perfect combination for a successful franchise operation.

But David was sceptical; it all sounded just that little bit too good to be true and he was worried that the earnings potential in the UK would be less than in the USA, where the company had been established for many years and had a good reputation.

Daniel had the solution. 'Why not fly over to Detroit and see how the system works, and meet with our President, Chuck Kaplinski? Let him tell you how you can make this thing work for you back in England. Heck, we're that confident that we'll even book your flights for you!'

So, in March 2006, David and Mark set off to Detroit to meet the Kwalikleen team and see just how good this proposition really was. Daniel even drove out to the airport to meet them, and apart from his habit of always chewing gum, David thought he was a genuinely nice guy.

The next day, Chuck Kaplinski met David and Mark and showed them the operation; it wasn't a flash operation, but it was efficient and everybody on the support team seemed to know what they were doing. The company chemist, Bernard, was a real character with his shock of white hair and milk-bottle-bottom glasses; he was every schoolboy's perception of a mad scientist, but he really did know his stuff. The products, which were all designed for deep-cleaning engineering factories, worked superbly, and the fact that the work was mainly carried out overnight meant that disruption to the client's business was minimal. Both David and Mark were impressed. Bernard told Mark all about his Kwalikleen cleaning system while Chuck talked to David about running a franchise. They were hooked!

After a brief discussion and a quick call home, David and Mark signed up to become franchisees and were immediately accepted on to the next training course. However, over the next few days David became concerned that Mark was more interested in the social side after training, rather than the training itself. Instead of networking with the other trainees, Mark had found a new drinking buddy in Bernard and the two often went on to a nightclub after the post-training relaxation session finished, rather than studying for the next day's instruction.

Towards the end of the course, Chuck took David to one side and told him that Mark was becoming a bit of a nuisance, talking to the office girls in a rather too familiar manner and David felt he should speak to Mark about his behaviour on the course. Mark was indignant and said that it was none of David's business what he got up to after the training had finished, or for that matter if he fancied one of the girls! It

→

CASE STUDY 4.1 *continued*

soon became clear to David that Mark was not going to be an easy colleague with whom to work.

On the last day, both David and Mark graduated as the new Kwalikleen franchise team for their chosen area in the UK. They were promised that their van kit would arrive within the next six weeks and they both went back to England believing that they were at the start of a very fruitful time of their careers. They ordered their new van, interviewed for a 'trainee' to help Mark carry out the physical cleaning work, and David set about generating contracts.

Then things started to go wrong. Discussions with Kwalikleen in America began to be increasingly difficult, calls were not returned, the franchise support team manager was invariably unavailable, Bernard went into rehab, Chuck started playing too much golf and was never around when David rang, and even their best friend Daniel, the salesman, took early retirement.

David became even more concerned when the promised Kwalikleen van kit did not appear in the six weeks that it was due. In a rare conversation with Chuck Kaplinski, the promise was made to 'sort something out', but nothing materialized. David became more and more frustrated, and Mark became more and more drunk!

Then, early one morning, David took a call from Carlos, another franchisee from the London region whom David had met on the training course. Carlos asked whether David was experiencing any difficulties contacting Kwalikleen in America. Initially, David was a bit guarded, but it turned out that Carlos was in exactly the same situation. He, too, had paid over his $20,000 for his franchise and was now having no luck at all in getting his starter kit or being able to talk with Kwalikleen in the USA. It seemed as though efficient communication was not a major concern to the franchisor.

David started to look around for more established franchisees in the UK and found Ted who had been running a franchise for about two years. Ted also said that he had had difficulty getting his starter kit, because Kwalikleen only shipped the kits when they had five new franchisees, as this reduced the shipping costs. Ted also said that he had given up trying to talk with Kwalikleen and had resorted to dealing with them by fax. He said that he was getting some work, but nothing like what had been promised when he signed up. David asked him whether he was happy with his $20,000 investment, 'Twenty grand?' asked Ted incredulously, 'I only paid $8,000 and that was too much!'

With no communication, no equipment, no support and a backlog of orders he has no hope of being able to fulfil in the immediate future, David became very worried. Ted had offered to take over the contracts David had negotiated, but the amount he was offering was laughably small.

→

CASE STUDY 4.1 *continued*

David contacted Kwalikleen in Michigan and asked for his franchise fee to be returned as the franchisor had not performed on the agreement signed between them; he is still waiting for a reply, and communication is non-existent. Taking legal advice, David has discovered that the Kwalikleen contract was drawn up under the laws of the State of Michigan and that any claims would have to be filed in the American judicial system, which, he has been advised, would be a prohibitive cost. David is resigned to the fact that he has lost $20,000 and has not earned a penny from his new franchise. His Jaguar, 'Betsy', that he was lovingly restoring, has been sold, he and June were not able to go skiing last year and will not be able to afford to go for the foreseeable future, David is looking to come out of retirement and get back into the property management rat-race; June and her brother Mark are not speaking and he is not speaking to David either; and David rues the day he ever thought about buying a franchise.

So what went wrong? First, Kwalikleen was not a member of the IFA in America; second, David did not check out Kwalikleen with existing franchisees before buying into the system; third, they were taken in by a plausible salesman's patter; fourth, the locus of control was too distant with Kwalikleen in America trying to manage franchisees on the other side of the Atlantic; fifth, they did not take advice from a reputable franchise consultant or lawyer; and sixth, there were no established communication channels existing for franchisees to be able to get the support that they needed in the fledgling days of their business.

In fact, just about everything that David and June did was wrong. They were not naïve, but they were conned by some very effective operators who prey upon the good nature of overseas prospective franchisees. The salutary lesson for all is that 'all that glisters is not gold', and when communication breaks down, there are likely to be more problems ahead, not less!

Note: Though this case study is based on a true story, the names of the unlucky franchisee, all other players and the industry in which they operated have been changed for legal reasons. The Kwalikleen franchise used for this illustration is a fictitious business and does not reflect on any existing business, whether franchised or otherwise.

Therefore, the three golden rules of keeping franchisees happy can be summarized as follows:

1 *Openness*. Franchisors who are transparent and share information openly with their franchisees are most highly prized by the prospective franchisee. Much of the confusion that caused the global financial crisis that began around 2007 was generated through the cloak of secrecy

that existed in the world of banking, and consequently formerly respected names from the banking world are now regarded with as much suspicion as dodgy second-hand car dealers. Transparency has a way of permeating the whole of a business and it soon becomes clear to consumers and customers of the good business practices being employed by the company, which reinforces the belief that the franchisor has both a respectable and an honest business.

2   *Adaptability*. It might come as a bit of a surprise to realize that one of the other 'happiness factors' that franchisees appreciate is adaptability. The business world is moving into a more dynamic phase, where only those companies that are prepared to be flexible will survive, so franchisees are looking for franchisors who are prepared to be innovative; and innovation goes considerably further than generating new products or services. The level of adaptability in the manner that the franchisor's business operates will often give it the edge over rivals. Of course, this must still be achieved in the relative inflexibility of the franchise system, but innovation *must* be welcomed, as innovation is the lifeblood of any dynamic twenty-first-century business.

3   *Support*. Support from franchisors has traditionally been a 'top-down' approach; in other words, it is the expected duty of the franchisor to provide the franchisee network with all the support they need; but times, they are a-changing! Many of the more sought-after franchisors are now encouraging their successful franchisees almost to mentor new or below-par franchisees within the network by sharing the secrets of their success. This 'nouveau' approach should come as no surprise to prospective franchisees coming from a team-oriented organization; team work makes systems strong, and the stronger the system, the more recognizable the brand becomes, and the more valuable the assets that the individual franchisee owns. So a lateral support network would score highly with prospective franchisees.

Therefore, transparency, adaptability and support clearly demonstrate that franchising is moving to a more collegiate method of doing business and away from the more franchisor-dominant approaches that have existed in some systems up to now. Readers are reminded of the franchise stakeholder diagram shown in Figure 4.2 above, and note that when the concept was envisaged, care was taken to ensure that the diagram was in the round, because franchising tends to work better when thought of as a complete circle. The task of the future-oriented franchisor is to get the transparency, adaptability and support to shine through the entire circle.

> ### WHAT DO YOU THINK?
>
> In this chapter we have learnt that the success or failure of any franchise system is geared to the relationship that exists between the franchisor and franchisee.
>
> In the Kwalikleen case study it may be seen that the company had little regard for their franchisees; how do you think this will affect their long-term business opportunity?
>
> Assuming that Kwalikleen is a genuine business and not just a scam, what might the company do to ensure that their business has greater success?

Further reading

CPR Institute Franchise Mediation Program, *Managing Franchise Relationships Through Mediation* (BookSurge Publishing 2009).

Hurwitz, Ann, *Building Franchise Relationships: A Guide to Anticipating Problems, Resolving Conflicts, and Representing Clients* (American Bar Association 1996).

Nathan, Greg, *Profitable Partnerships: Improve Your Franchise Relationships and Change Your Life*, 7th edn (Franchise Relationships Institute, Queensland, Australia, 2011) (Amazon Media EU ebook).

Pratt, John, *The Franchisor's Handbook: Your Duties, Responsibilities and Liabilities* (About Face Publishing 2006).

5 ENTREPRENEURS AND FRANCHISING

INTRODUCTION AND LEARNING OBJECTIVES

The purpose of this chapter is to examine whether the concepts of franchising and entrepreneurism are mutually exclusive. Is there a role for an entrepreneurially minded Franchisee within any (or no) franchise system?
The reader will be able to:

- Analyse whether they would fit well within a franchised system.
- Appreciate the need for a franchisor's expectation that franchisees do not become loose cannons.
- Understand the concept of the intrapreneur, within a franchised system.

It has been said that franchisees enjoy all of the benefits of business ownership without the responsibility of establishment, and to some extent this is correct. This is the enigma of franchising: the freedom of being self-employed within the constraints of a fixed and typically inflexible system.

However, one of the main distinguishing features of successful franchisees is the capacity to think and act as an individual and to retain some level of independence. To some extent, all of the really successful franchisees fit this mould, in that they are consistently looking at ways of developing and expanding their business within the system.

As a general rule, franchisors like their franchisees to be compliant and unquestioning disciples of the tried and tested system, and it is true that many franchisees make a good living out of being flock followers; but the really successful franchisee is the person who still retains a certain element of independence and, to some

> *An **intrapreneur** is an employee within an organization who displays entrepreneurial traits in his/her employment.*

extent, obstinacy. Such franchisees will examine decisions and ask questions, and they will retain the right to make decisions about *their* businesses that are right for their development. This independent streak makes the successful franchisee entrepreneurial, or perhaps a better definition would be *intra*preneurial.

An *intra*preneur is an entrepreneurially minded person who works within an organization, and to my mind this pretty much sums up what a franchisee ought to be; indeed, intrapreneurs within franchising have even acquired their own unique label, as they are often described as *'frantrapreneurs'*. While many franchisors would love their entire network of franchisees to be like sheep and to follow their instructions to the letter, very few achieve this desire; there will always be those franchisees who retain the belief that they are masters of their own destiny, and who retain the right to resist being led down a path that they suspect will lead to disaster; these might be described as the franchising 'goats'. Invariably, these are the more successful franchisees.

Without a doubt, the main reason why people buy a franchise is that most of the hard work in setting up a business has already been carried out by the franchisor. A market already exists for the product or service, the brand is recognized, the operating systems have been fine-tuned so that they work – all this means that the franchisee can 'hit the road running' rather than spend a huge amount of time, effort, energy and money – which is what they would be committing to had they decided to start a business from scratch. It goes without saying that the more established a system, the better tried and tested are the marketing systems, and typically the business operations procedures are extremely efficient. Couple with this the established brand and you will see the reason why most franchisees buy into the system rather than setting up an independent outlet.

Nevertheless, it is the absolute duty of any business owner (which is what franchisees are) to protect their businesses. This means that even though the franchisee has a signed contract that says that they must operate within the confines of the system, if the system is not working as efficiently as it might, or your business is being constrained by the system from reaching its maximum potential, you have not renounced the right to free thought and the entitlement to seek to modify what needs modifying.

It is a pretty fair bet that, if things go awry with a franchise system, the first stakeholder the franchisor is going to protect will be themselves. Irrespective of the fact that they have portrayed themselves as the paternal protector of the system, if it goes wrong they will always protect their own interests before those of others; and in accepting this trait of human nature, the franchisee had better seek to protect his/her own interests just as fervently. It should be remembered that franchisees, as individuals, have other responsibilities in addition to those that they have to their franchisor – they have a responsibility to their family, and to their mortgage provider, to name but two!

> *A **frantrapreneur** is a franchisee who displays an enterprising trait in the operation of his/her franchise.*

Retaining objectivity and independence while expecting or anticipating changes in the business environment means that the shrewd franchisee will also seek reassurance that there will be some degree of flexibility in the agreement, should market conditions change during the term of the contract; and how much protection this *flexibility* will afford the franchisee to protect his/her own interests.

There was once a franchisee who ran a specialist food franchise from a High Street location in a busy market town in the Midlands in England. As the recession bit, many of his neighbours ceased trading and their shops were taken over by fast-food outlets, which despite not being direct competitors, were certainly indirect ones. In the early days of the recession, the franchisee saw his turnover drop by more than 30 per cent, while at the same time his local commercial taxation rose by 7.5 per cent and, because he had negotiated a flexible rate on his business loan, the interest rate also increased by 1.25 per cent. Irrespective of the fact that the franchisor was

> *Franchisees are not likely to be 'entrepreneurial' but they are running their own businesses and have a responsibility to ensure that they are being run correctly.*

fully aware of the changed circumstances, he resolutely expected turnover to be maintained at the agreed, pre-recession amount, and that monthly fees were paid promptly and fully at the rate expected prior to the economic downturn.

Some of this franchisee's colleagues gave up their franchises as it was no longer viable for them to continue trading, and even this franchisee came close to walking away from the business he had spent the previous four years building up. Then he had a 'eureka' moment. It happened on a Sunday lunchtime when he was enjoying a pint of ale at a pub and someone commented jocularly about his business woes that, if the customers wouldn't come to his shop, then he must go to where there are customers.

Within three weeks, the franchisee had proposed to his franchisor that he set up a mobile unit, at his own expense and meeting the standards expected by the franchisor, and took his specialist wares on the road. The franchisor agreed to this, and even offered to use his greater purchasing power to acquire and set up the mobile outlet, which took the form of a refrigerated trailer unit that could be towed behind a family car. Not only was it considerably less expensive than the dedicated vehicle that the franchisee had anticipated acquiring, but it proved to be much better value for money as the operating overheads were much reduced.

This intrapreneurial franchisee now stocks the mobile unit from his own retail stock, and travels the length and breadth of his territory working any event, indoor or outdoor, where there are a large number of potential customers. These range from car-boot sales to agricultural shows, and motorsport events to local markets.

The end result of his efforts can be demonstrated by the fact that his outlet is now the third-highest performer in the country, behind two others that also had the foresight to follow the franchisee's lead and to acquire the now 'standard option' of a mobile outlet, but have slightly better areas than him for incremental sales. Even sales from his retail outlet have recovered to be close to those achieved pre-recession, as customers he has met while on his travels around the territory come to buy produce from his retail store.

The franchisor is delighted because overall sales have increased substantially so he is receiving higher fees and the brand is gaining wider exposure; the franchisees are happy because, though they may be working longer hours, their income has increased disproportionately; but most of all the customers are happy and keep coming back for more specialist food.

When the franchisee bought into the franchise, he was the fourth to be recruited post-pilot, so the franchisor was not as well established as other options that were available. However, the franchisee believed that this could auger well for a degree of greater flexibility, and while he was happy to follow the operating procedures as laid down for the first four years of his franchise agreement, his franchisor respected his judgement sufficiently to allow for a degree of entrepreneurial, or *frantrapreneurial*, development within the franchise system.

The fact is that while a franchise head office will offer the franchisees in the system as much support as it is able, but when the curve ball is delivered or the googly bowled by some external occurrence, then it is incumbent on every member in the system, from the senior directors down to the lowest level of employee, to try to resolve the difficulty. Now, without wishing to make this sound like a prelude to George Orwell's *Animal Farm*, there is an old adage that 'the sheep will follow the leader, but a good leader listens to the goats!'

Perhaps, therefore, it can now be accepted that there is a genuine role for the entrepreneur in franchising. Possibly not with the established High Street names, but with the fledgling franchisors who are taking their first steps to world domination. Committing to a fresh franchise offering might represent a fantastic opportunity to get in on the 'ground floor' of a business, but equally it can be a highly risky proposition!

The argument is that, with a business model that is still raw and relatively untested, there is greater scope for the entrepreneurial franchisee to work with the franchisor in the development of the business. Many franchisors would welcome this added input, but there are an equal number who would take the traditionalist view and rebuff any assistance offered. The task is, of course, to determine into which camp the chosen franchisor falls. It may sound an easy task, but it is one that is fraught with pitfalls at every turn.

As we saw earlier, the inventor of the world's most popular fast-food item, the 'Big Mac', was a franchisee, and one of the major global franchisors was astute enough to pay attention to what was being suggested.

Throughout this book it has been stressed, and any self-respecting franchise consultant will similarly advocate, that the prospective franchisee needs to talk to existing franchisees to get an unambiguous viewpoint from somebody in the front-line of the business, but in a start-up franchise these are likely to be somewhat thin on the ground. So how can the prospective franchisee ascertain whether they are investing their life's savings in the next McDonald's or a three-legged donkey? The answer, as always, is that there is no 'golden rule' to follow – if there were, then everybody would be following it and making a fortune; but there are some guidelines that might make the decision easier.

1   *Know the franchisor.* Finding out about people and companies is nowadays, thanks to the Internet, extremely easy. Carrying out in-depth research into a franchisor is the crucial first step in determining whether the business or the management team have sufficient expertise and experience to minimize the risk of failure. If the prospective franchisee is entrepreneurially minded, s/he might consider a fledgling system that is run by successful business people who previously have not had an enormous amount of exposure to the franchising industry. The more experience in franchising that the management team has, the less likely they are to welcome a *frantrapreneur* into their midst.

2   *Accept the uncertainty.* When people invest in established franchisors, they will inevitably talk with existing franchisees, and their consultant will be able to source pretty accurate financial predictions as to how well the business will do throughout the duration of the contract. Investment in a new franchise involves considerably more guesswork, and it is likely that there will be few existing outlets to measure with any degree of accuracy the true worth and value of the financial opportunity. Indeed, there may only be the financial track record of the pilot operation with which to work. Nevertheless, this lack of *gravitas* is likely to give scope for a greater degree of negotiation.

3   *Minimize the uncertainty.* While the prospective franchisee might be limited as to understanding the depth and scope of the financial opportunity, there will be detailed information available about the financial stability of the franchisor. It is true to say that one of the main reasons why franchise systems fail is that the franchisor is undercapitalized,

and before any prospective franchisee invests in the system, they should satisfy themselves that the franchisor has sufficient financial backing to ensure growth.

4   *Value the business model.* It has to be accepted that, with a new franchise, the business model may not be as honed as that of an established franchisor. When negotiating with a new franchisor, the business model may still even be a 'work in progress'; and whereas the old adage that investment in a business that one does not understand is a foolhardy gamble might be relevant in many cases, being part of a developing business opportunity where the business model is still being fine-tuned might be the driver that makes investment by the more entrepreneurial franchisee, exhilarating. There does need at the very least to be a rudimentary business model in place before any investment can be considered, but helping to perfect the imperfect may prove irresistible to the entrepreneurial franchisee.

5   *Be inquisitive.* This section could have been entitled 'Ask Questions', but the word 'inquisitive' suggests a deeper and more intense form of enquiry, much in the manner of the infamous Spanish Inquisition of old, which was notoriously good at ascertaining the truth! When investing in any franchise, the prospective franchisee needs to understand the business, but this is absolutely crucial when investing in a new franchise. It is utterly imperative that the prospective franchisee completely understands the corporate strategy of the franchise, as well as being completely aware of the marketing strategies, technology, training and ongoing support. A true comprehension of the franchisor's approach to these key elements will minimize substantially the risk that is being contemplated.

6   *Understand what is being said.* Franchisees enter into a lengthy and complex legal relationship with the franchisor, which is underpinned by an intricate legal contract. When buying an established franchise, it is extremely likely that the franchisor will be extremely adept at providing all the necessary documentation on which the legal obligations will be founded, and it is unlikely that this will vary greatly from what was promised verbally. When contemplating the purchase of a new franchise, the prospective franchisee should assume inaccuracy; not necessarily the intention to mislead, but it is likely that the business will have developed further in the interim between an interest being expressed and the commitment to paper, and much may have changed. The prospective franchisee needs to ensure that the franchisor has covered all angles, and that franchisees are protected adequately. There is a strong argument that prospective franchisees should always consult a specialist franchise lawyer to assist with the legal elements of the franchise relationship, but this point cannot be emphasized enough when dealing with a new franchise.

7 *Use your bargaining power.* It is a well-accepted fact that franchise contracts are inflexible; all franchisees have to be on identical contractual terms, or the system becomes unmanageable. This is undoubtedly true of well-established franchises, but with new franchise offerings there may be scope for negotiation – after all, the risk is higher, so why should the rewards not be increased commensurately? An easier area of compromise will be the size of the territory; the franchisor is looking for coverage, and having a franchisee who seeks to increase the size of the offered territory might seem to be easy opportunity to boost exposure, offset by the lost opportunity of reducing the number of territories available. The franchisor will need to be convinced that the prospective franchisee can develop an enlarged territory, but will also be mindful of the fact that volume discounts on key supplies may not yet be in place. Negotiation and compromise are trade-offs between desirability and realism, and few fledgling franchisors will stubbornly stick their heads in the sand and be unwilling to negotiate with the right prospect. However, the prospective franchisee must also recognize that the success of the system is geared to a certain return on investment, and that will be calculated into the fee structure, so jeopardizing the success of the system for a short-term reduction in fees, which might have to be replicated throughout the developing network, might be a somewhat Pyrrhic victory.

8 *Be enterprising.* We have seen that entrepreneurial flair may be discouraged by established franchise systems that have been successful for long periods, and this applies equally to feedback. It might be true that whereas feedback is not actively discouraged, it is not always given the priority that the giver expects. This can have a demoralizing effect and may result in franchisees feeling as though their opinions are not valued. Having said that, with fledgling franchisors, only a fool would ignore the opinions and views of those who are at the coalface of the business. Franchisees with an entrepreneurial mind will often spot opportunities and threats long before they are noticed by management, and in providing their insights and proposals for improvement of the whole business, they will be helping to secure a better future for not only themselves, but also for the entire network as it develops. This 'developmental' role, however, must always be sanctioned by the franchisor, as a franchisee who 'ploughs his own furrow' might be seen as a 'loose cannon', if the reader will excuse the mixed metaphor.

9 *Consider longevity.* It used to be said that the only thing one can be sure of is death. Surely then, the only guaranteed franchise opportunity would be that of an undertaker or funeral parlour! Of course, this is not the case, but it is nevertheless worth bearing in mind. Prospective

franchisees are always seeking a modern, contemporary franchise opportunity, but at the same time they are not seeking to invest in a craze, which will be out of fashion in six months' time. Many franchises address niche markets, so a prudent prospective franchisee will examine carefully the opportunities available in their communities and discover what is lacking, and then sound out consumers' needs, wants and opinions. It is worth noting that while the current trend is towards a healthier lifestyle, fast-food burger and designer-coffee franchises are still growing and succeeding, mainly because of the change in their product offering to satisfy the desires of a more nutritionally-minded clientele. They remain modern and contemporary businesses, whereas the more faddy healthy options might not still be around as tastes and fashions change in the future.

10 *Be enthusiastic.* The reason why most people go into business for themselves is because they are enthusiastic about the content of the business, whether it is real estate or selling burgers, and often the reason why their business fails is because they lose this enthusiasm. The same applies to franchising – enthusiasm for the business is the key to its success. Franchisees need to enjoy the idea and get pleasure from doing the jobs that make the franchise grow. All the time that the passion for the business exists, the business will usually flourish, but as soon as the love for the business starts to wither, that marks the start of the decline that leads to failure. Entrepreneurs and intrapreneurs are highly enthusiastic people, and if a franchisor, whether s/he is a fledgling or established, takes on a *frantrapreneurial* franchisee, s/he needs to nurture that entrepreneurial flair for the development and benefit of the entire system.

So, it can be seen that there is possibly a small role for entrepreneurial flair in franchising, though probably not in a rigid and well-established franchise. New franchisors make the industry exciting, despite some being destined to fail; however, should a new, fledgling franchisor and an entrepreneurial and enterprising franchisee meet, then it might just be a match made in heaven ... the difference between success and failure!

WOMEN IN FRANCHISING

In writing this book, I have been advised that I should remove this entire section, but I have strenuously resisted doing this; women have had a huge and positive impact on the work environment since the early twentieth century, and their influence is starting to have a similar impact on franchising; indeed, there is a whole section of the industry that is focused on attracting women into franchising.

There is no doubt that, throughout the twentieth century, the world of business underwent a huge transformation. In the early part of the century, women were little more than second-class citizens; however, following emancipation, and particularly after the Second World War, women quickly established their equality, even if some businessmen still try to suppress the advantages of women with the much denied 'glass-ceiling' that still exists in modern business.

Following the war, in particular, women quickly established themselves as people who could turn their hand to taking on the jobs and responsibilities that their menfolk had previously assumed to be their sole domain. During the war, some women learnt to drive, some turned to engineering or farming, others took over the running of family businesses, and they did it willingly, as it freed the men to fight the foe for their beliefs. Of course, after the war, when the men returned, they expected the women to go back to being subservient home-makers, and some did so ... but others took their new-found freedoms and developed them to become highly successful in areas that had previously been seen as the sole province of men.

Now here I am going to be rather radical in offering the suggestion that the average man can do some things better than the average woman, but perhaps a rider should be added to the effect that the average woman can do many things better that the average man. Of course, there are exceptional men and women who defy the basic rule of thumb, but as a generalization as well as physiologically, men and women are not the same, but they are equal in their skills and attributes – it's just that those skills and attributes are different. Many businesses would be stronger and more durable if the business*men* who run them were to embrace the importance of the attributes that women can bring to business.

Franchising is no different from other businesses in the development of women as both franchisees and franchisors. Interestingly, in a recent survey of franchisees in America, 46 per cent of all respondents were women franchisees, and it was clear that, of those who did respond, the women were more highly educated than their male counterparts. Why might this be the case? It may be a combination of women returning to the workforce after a period of childcare coupled with their traditional attitude towards risk; if it could be shown that women are less likely to be involved in 'risky' businesses, then this might explain the positive attitude towards franchising held by women, as in general franchising offers a much reduced risk to business start-up than traditional go-it-alone businesses. Certainly, franchise businesses that are more attractive to the recruitment of female franchisees ought to consider the benefits of addressing the risk element more thoroughly in their franchise proposal.

The American survey also showed that women franchisees were less optimistic about the potential of their business, and were more likely to think that their franchises did not meet their financial aspirations. This may result from the fact that many women franchisees own 'lifestyle' franchises, which they run to suit their domestic schedule, rather than adapting their familial responsibilities to suit the needs of the business; indeed, many franchised businesses have grown up specifically to be attractive to women who want a lifestyle business.

Recently, I had a conversation with a well-respected senior manager at a large corporation, and when I asked whether his wife complained about the number of days he spent overseas, his response startled me: 'Oh, she's OK about it,' he proudly announced, 'I bought her a cleaning franchise to keep her occupied now that the kids have left home!' Careful later research showed that the senior executive's wife is one of the company's top performing franchisees! Last year she made well over $150K, about triple what the franchisor's average franchisee makes!

I asked what made her so successful in the franchisor's eyes: 'She's focused, she's never been afraid to ask for help, but most of all she's determined to succeed.' When asked if the franchisor knew who the franchisee's husband was, the franchisor confided, 'Yes, and I think that's the reason for her determination. You see, women have a different set of skills and abilities. She doesn't try to be a man! She leverages her unique characteristics and that's what makes her successful; she's smart, able to multi-task, intuitive and gets on with just about everybody she meets. She knows her strengths and acknowledges her weaknesses, and trains hard to make sure the latter don't have a negative effect on her business.'

The growth of franchise opportunities that allow greater flexibility to franchisees with other commitments is probably the main reason why so many women are being attracted to franchising. Unlike many men who have yet to achieve a sensible work/life balance, most women accept that other responsibilities may complicate their ability to work, and franchising may be flexible enough to allow for the impact of these 'complications' to be diminished.

Successful women franchisees have identified five key points that drive their success:

1 Identify your priorities and strike a happy medium between home and work. Initially, it may seem hard to find the right balance between the two, but making room for both in your life will certainly ensure that both aspects can flourish in a mutually inclusive and complementary manner.
2 Never be afraid to ask for assistance if things are getting out of hand. It is often said that a problem shared is a problem halved, and that is equally true in franchising. It is highly unlikely that you will have found a totally unique set of circumstances that is adversely affecting your business; the chances are that there is an easy solution to the dilemma that is ruining your business, but if you don't talk about it, nobody will be able to offer a solution.

3   Join a network. In North America there is a strong network for women franchisees in both the USA and Canada, with the Women's Franchise Committee and the Women's Franchise Network, respectively; elsewhere there appear to be plenty of online resources but little physical networking.

4   Get the family involved. If nothing else, it will give the kids a fantastic opportunity to understand how a business operates, and gives them the chance to develop skills that will help their future development.

5   Remember that you are a franchisee and as such you are part of a network of similar franchisees all experiencing similar problems to those that you face. Use the franchisor's network to make your business life easier.

It might be bold to suggest that these five points could easily provide the backbone of *any* successful franchise, and it would be rather unfair if it were noted that women suggested them.

In other discussions with women franchisees who run 'traditional' franchise outlets, I could find no real difference from their male counterparts when the subject of potential or franchise earnings was discussed; indeed, some believed that their franchise outlets were run considerably better and more profitably than some other outlets run by male colleagues. It was interesting to note, however, that most of these women franchisees acknowledged that it took longer for their businesses to reach maximum potential. Perhaps this phenomenon can be attributed to the previously discussed natural aversion to risk, and the desire to underpin and reinforce decisions taken to minimize the hazards of uncertain strategies.

One thing that is clear, however, is that women are quickly becoming an even greater constituent in the world of franchising and they are bringing a clearer perspective to the industry. Strategies that would have been implemented in the recent past are being calculated further to minimize risk and whereas this cannot be attributed totally to the emergence of a strong body of women franchisees, their presence in the market has certainly been a force for good.

WHAT DO YOU THINK?

Are the concepts of entrepreneurism and franchising mutually exclusive? Can an entrepreneurially minded franchisee have a positive effect on a franchised business, or will they always be seen as trying to 'reinvent the wheel'? Perhaps you can identify distinct areas in which an entrepreneurial viewpoint might benefit a growing franchised business?

Further reading

Duckett, Brian, *How to Turn Your Business into the Next Global Brand: Creating and Managing a Franchised Network* (How To Books 2008).

Kroc, Ray, *Grinding It Out: The Making of McDonald's* (St Martin's Paperbacks 1992).

Mathews, Joe, DeBolt, Don and Percival, Deb, *Street Smart Franchising* (Entrepreneur Press 2006).

6 THE ROLE OF ETHICS IN FRANCHISING

INTRODUCTION AND LEARNING OBJECTIVES

The purpose of this chapter is look at how government intervention, or the involvement of self-regulatory bodies, attempts to guide franchisors to behave in an ethical and socially responsible manner towards the stakeholders in their business, primarily the franchisees and ultimate consumers.

The reader will be able to:

- Understand the importance of being associated with a franchisee who willingly meets and exceeds the strict guidelines of the industry.
- Identify any sharp practice by a potential franchisor when considering the purchase of a franchise.
- Appreciate the necessity for the franchisor to be considered as the 'guardian' of the system.

In the past, franchisors have been heard describing their businesses as being 'ethical' companies, because they source their products only from 'free-trade' sources, or that they have installed very expensive pollution-filtering apparatuses in their manufacturing processes. Whether or not the businesses are acting ethically has not been answered; yes, they may be acting in a 'socially responsible' manner, but the ethical question has not been fully addressed, and this is a common misunderstanding in business.

Social responsibility may be characterized as the code of conduct which ordains that businesses should contribute to the well-being of society and not be driven exclusively by the maximization of profit. Ethics is better defined as the system of corporate moral principles that guides a business's behaviour.

Both are important, but for the sake of this book, we shall define 'ethics' as 'the standards of

> Responsible franchisors work to a strict **code of ethics**, which can be imposed by a trade association, written into law, or be voluntary.

behaviour by which the parties operate in the franchising process'. We shall deal with the importance of social responsibility later in the chapter.

Responsible franchisors work to a code of ethics. More frequently, a code of ethics is imposed on the franchisor's business by the trade association operating in their country, assuming that they elect to become a member. Sometimes the code of ethics is built into the legislation that governs franchising, as is the case in Australia.

Codes of ethics vary from region to region around the world, and to highlight the differences, the various ethical codes for the European Franchise Federation (EFF), the International Franchise Association (IFA) in America and the World Franchise Council (WFC) will be considered. I was going to include the code of conduct as adopted by the Franchise Council of Australia (FCA) but there are 50-odd pages of the 'Trade Practices (Industry Codes – Franchising) Regulations 1998, amended in 2008' and I felt that might eat up too much of the extent of the book! Lovers of Australian legalese can find the full text available on the Franchise Council of Australia's website.

For two reasons, the first being my geographical location, and the second that there is a genuine belief that the EFF code is one of the most comprehensive ethical codes the author has read, this book will explain the role of ethics in franchising as moderated by the EFF's Code of Ethics for Franchising.

The first section of this Code is devoted to definitions, and as the official definition of franchising has already been given in Chapter 2 of this book, we shall start at Section 2 of the code, which covers 'Guiding Principles' (see Appendices on page 240).

GUIDING PRINCIPLES

The first and most important guiding principle answers the 'chicken-and-egg' quandary that was mentioned earlier, and clearly states that 'the Franchisor is the initiator of a franchise network, composed of itself and its individual Franchisees, of which the Franchisor is the long-term guardian'. This clause makes it clear that the franchisor is the originator of the franchise network, which comprises the franchisor and the franchisees within the system, and that the franchisor must be considered to be the guardian of the network and to protect all franchisees against damage, either from a third party or from a rogue franchisee. This goes some way to explaining why the franchise agreement is always skewed in favour of the franchisor; the franchisor in his/her role as guardian of the network has to protect innocent franchisees sufficiently against the malicious intent of somebody who seeks to do harm to the business concept. In all fairness to the franchisor, this is only right and proper, as s/he has considerably more to lose than the individual franchisee should a rogue franchisee decide to act in a manner that might devalue the brand.

The next point that is covered looks at the general responsibilities and obligations undertaken by the franchisor, and these stipulate that the franchisor must:

" ▪ have operated a business concept with success, for a reasonable time and in at least one pilot unit before starting its franchise network,

▪ be the owner, or have legal rights to the use, of its network's trade name, trade mark or other distinguishing identification,

▪ provide the Individual Franchisee with initial training and continuing commercial and/or technical assistance during the entire life of the agreement.

Looking at these points in greater detail we can see that it is only fair to any prospective franchisee that the system into which they are buying has been tried and tested, and has proved to be sufficiently trialled as to be able to give the franchisee a reasonable chance of success, but there is an element of uncertainty built into this clause. Who or what defines success? The minimum level of success that most people would expect from a franchise is that it was capable of giving the franchisee a reasonable return on their investment, and was able to offer the franchisor sufficient profitability to make the venture into franchising viable by the collection of franchise

> *Franchisors owe it to the system to ensure that they have exclusive rights to use the brand of the system, and that no competition exists from others also using the brand.*

fees from the franchise network. Nevertheless, there is no qualification contained in the principle, franchisors could equally claim 'success' as being derived from the fact that people recognize the brand, or the footfall of customers in their trial franchise outlet, irrespective of whether the outlet has generated profits.

What is a 'reasonable' amount of time? Even if one accepts that different industries might have different circumstances, and the nature of differing businesses may impact on what is defined as 'reasonable', extraordinary conditions may affect the 'reasonableness' of the timescale: unusual weather conditions, or exceptional economic conditions, or the strength of one currency against another may all impinge on how long is a 'reasonable' amount of time. Even the originality of an idea may influence what is considered to be reasonable and what is not, as when the novelty wears off and the business settles down to normal trading conditions. Generally speaking, though, 'reasonable' is unlikely to be less than one year.

In specifying that a trial must have been conducted in at least one pilot unit makes an important point. In an ideal world, the franchisor would conduct pilots in several diverse locations to demonstrate that the products and service are universally accepted and viable for prospective franchisees wherever they choose to open their business. However, financial constraints on the franchisor invariably mean that one or two pilots are established, and the prospective new franchisee will need to establish whether s/he feels there is sufficient potential in his/her chosen area, relying on the experience of the pilot unit(s), but not exclusively so, as personal judgement will also play an important part.

The second point is also quite logical, as it requires the brand to be free from competition from a third party who is also trading under the same trade name or trade mark; franchisees have the right to expect that their business is protected against another person opening a business in their vicinity with the same brand or trade name. The clause requiring 'legal rights' to a trade name is related to the existence of a master franchisor who does not own the brand but retains the rights from the brand holder in a given area. In such a case it is equally imperative that the master franchisor is able to assign his/her rights to franchisees under a sub-licensing agreement, which needs to be demonstrable.

Finally, and again logically, as most franchisees join the system with little or no experience of the industry into which they are moving, they will need to be instructed in the way that the system operates, as well as how to use the products or services they will be selling. This final point is absolutely in the interests of both parties because, in order to maximize franchise potential, franchisors need to ensure that their franchisees are fully trained, and to ensure that they continue to be up to date with the product offering. Continuous training and ongoing technical support is vital, and this 'technical support' may even include national advertising and marketing as a chargeable (obligatory) extra. That does not mean, however, that the franchisor should constantly be looking over the shoulder of the franchisees, rather that the franchisor provides direction and the franchisee performs accordingly.

Moving on to the next section of the second paragraph of the Code's guiding principles, we find the general obligations of the franchisee, which at first sight may seem out of place, as generally franchisees are not members of the national trade association that has undertaken to adhere to the Code of Ethics, but as most franchise agreements will require observance of the Code, stating standards that the trade association is unlikely to be able to enforce makes it easier for the individual franchisor to set them as minimum standards. Moreover, if a franchisee seeks to take action against a franchisor and cites unethical conduct, then the courts will tend to look at the franchisee's compliance with these minimum ethical standards on the basis that a franchisee would be unlikely to succeed in his/her claim of ethical misconduct if s/he had not adhered to the ethical standards themselves.

The general obligations stipulate that the individual franchisee shall:

" ■ devote its best endeavours to the growth of the franchise business and to the maintenance of the common identity and reputation of the franchise network,

■ supply the Franchisor with verifiable operating data to facilitate the determination of performance and the financial statements necessary for effective management guidance, and allow the Franchisor, and/or its agents, to have access to the individual Franchisee's premises and records at the Franchisor's request and at reasonable times,

■ not disclose to third parties the know-how provided by the Franchisor, neither during nor after termination of the agreement.

Considering these terms in greater detail, many seem to be rather stating the obvious. Why would a franchisee not seek to promote the system of which it is a member? Promoting the system and gaining greater exposure for the system in which they belong makes brand awareness and exposure greater, which potentially will increase their business, as well as that of other franchisees. Nevertheless, if one delves a little deeper, you can begin to understand what the authors of this clause were trying to convey: the franchisee has an obligation to work hard and to ensure that what s/he is offering the consumer meets the quality standards laid down by the franchisor. Despite a franchisee running his/her own business, s/he is also a member of a network, and a network is only as strong as its weakest member, therefore hard work and a high quality product/service will ensure the strength of the network.

The second point is probably the most valid, as few franchisees relish the thought of completing the numerous requests for information from their franchisor. The argument is that it reduces the amount of time they can spend selling the product or service, but in reality the information sought by the franchisor will probably enable him or her to refine and perfect the offering to enable the franchisees to be both more efficient and more effective. The other aspect of this section is to ensure honesty. Many franchisors rely on the honesty of the franchisee in correctly declaring his/her turnover to be able to assess the level of fees due; it would not only be unethical, but also fraudulent, for a franchisee to withhold information from his/her franchisor in order to avoid paying the correct level of fees. Openness and truthfulness are fundamental in any franchise agreement.

The third point is undoubtedly firmly planted in the franchise agreement, together with other restrictive clauses preventing the franchisee from competing with the franchise, so the inclusion of a non-disclosure clause in a Code of Ethics might seem rather superfluous; however, it does reiterate the importance of the value of the private information, such as know-how, to which the franchisee is privileged during the term of the contract. Confidentiality is absolutely crucial to the franchise network, and any attempt by the franchisee to use the confidential information gained while operating within the network amounts to dishonesty and is certainly unethical. Very few courts would side with the franchisee who has appropriated his franchisor's trade secrets for his own ends.

The final point of the second section is the provision that is likely to arouse a fair amount of discussion. The clause considers the ongoing obligations of both parties, and states that:

> " Parties shall exercise fairness in their dealings with each other. The Franchisor shall give written notice to its Individual Franchisees of any contractual breach and, where appropriate, grant reasonable time to remedy default;
> Parties should resolve complaints, grievances and disputes with good faith and goodwill through fair and reasonable direct communication and negotiation.

This concept of 'fairness' is subjective in nature and in no way objective. Who is to decide what is fair and what is not? What seems fair and equitable to one franchisor or franchisee will not necessarily seem reasonable to another. Moreover, as a franchisor or franchisee becomes more independent, or less dependent, what may have been considered to be 'fair' will by then seem to be unreasonable and inequitable.

However, in accepting that the 'fairness' clause of the Code of Ethics merely sets the scene for the franchise relationship, and creates a benchmark by which the franchise will be judged, it is as well to remember that the concept of fairness applies as much to the franchisee as it does to the franchisor.

Throughout the relationship, there will be circumstances which require fairness to be applied, from the point when the franchisee is negotiating with the franchisor, right through to the renewal of the licence or the sale of the franchise. For example, it would be considered unfair for a franchisor, having decided that a prospective franchisee is unsuited to the role, to drag out the assessment period merely to collect some pre-contract fees to defray his costs of a failed recruitment. Similarly, it would also be unfair for a franchisor to put obstacles in the path of a franchisee wishing to sell his/her licence, thus delaying unnecessarily the sale of the asset; it would be extremely unfair if this was being done with the intention of reducing the value of the asset to enable the franchisor to buy back the licence at a reduced cost so s/he could resell at 'normal' prices and make a profit at the expense of the retiring franchisee.

Inevitably there will be occasions when 'fairness' has to be determined by the courts, and the yardstick by which common law seems to define fairness is 'what appears fair to a reasonable person'; if this measure is applied in one's dealings either as a franchisee or a franchisor, it is unlikely that one will fall short of what is expected.

Undoubtedly, the whole point of paragraph 2.4 (The ongoing obligations of both parties) is to offer guidance as to how dispute resolution should be handled, and it is worth noting that the clause in fact says three separate things, the first of which is 'fairness in their dealings with each other', which sets out clearly the guidelines under which any arbiter will consider disputes. Both parties, if they hope to maximize the potential of the franchise, have to act fairly towards each other.

The second element of the paragraph is guidance covering the situation where, if a franchisee breaches the contract, s/he must be given the opportunity to remedy the breach before the franchisor can legitimately terminate the contract. This will be expanded on in Chapter 9, which deals with franchise contracts, but the paragraph clearly identifies the franchise contract as the cornerstone of the relationship that exists between franchisor and franchisee.

The third element of the paragraph is that of complaint or dispute management, and it imposes a duty on both parties to discuss the situation in an open and frank manner, and to try to reach an amicable solution to the grievance. This may cause some further resentment, as it is highly unlikely that franchisors will be prepared to discuss modifications to the system, and this lies at the root of many franchisees' complaints. Nevertheless, eliminating misunderstandings and communicating clearly will often alleviate many problem situations before they escalate.

RECRUITMENT, ADVERTISING AND DISCLOSURE

The third section of the Code deals with Recruitment, Advertising and Disclosure and is relatively short; however, the analysis will undoubtedly be considerably longer!

The first point of this section states that 'advertising for the recruitment of Individual Franchisees shall be free of ambiguity and misleading statements'. Interestingly, the composers of the Code stopped short of imposing positive disclosure, but rather went down the route of setting two clear standards: first, freedom from ambiguity means that advertisements must be clear, speak the truth, the whole truth and nothing but the truth – advertisements that give an incomplete picture or that contain only half the facts, would be considered unethical. Second, that advertisements must not contain misleading statements is relatively self-explanatory; however, it is worth remembering that not saying something that might have a bearing on the decision-making process is just as misleading as saying something in a way that is intended to mislead.

This concept of 'misleading' is further emphasized in the second point of the third section, which states that 'any recruitment, advertising and publicity material, containing direct or indirect references to future possible results, figures or earnings to be expected by individual Franchisees, shall be objective and shall not be misleading'. At a first glance this may appear to be crystal clear, but the reach of this clause is further than might initially appear. Effectively, franchisors who are making claims as to the future wealth of the franchisee would be expected to justify their claims. Franchises that have been established over a period of years would have established accounts to support their claims, but new Franchisors who do not have the benefit of a wealth of anecdotal and accounting records to support their assertions would need to be able to state clearly the basis and the assumptions upon which the anticipated returns were calculated, together with the criteria underpinning the claim. It might be safer to have the anticipated returns audited independently and presented in such a manner that the reader can see clearly that the claims made have been independently checked by an unbiased third party.

The third bullet point of this section is quite clear and descriptive, in that there can be no real dispute with the wording of the phrase stating that

> " In order to allow prospective individual Franchisees to enter into any binding document with full knowledge, they shall be given a copy of the present Code of Ethics as well as full and accurate written disclosure of all information material to the franchise relationship, within a reasonable time prior to the execution of these binding documents. Franchisors must give the prospective Franchisee full disclosure of all relevant information prior to their signing the legally binding agreements or contracts, plus a copy of the Code of Ethics within a reasonable time prior to the execution of these binding documents.
>
> (Section 3, Item 3.3)

But again, the slight vagueness of 'within a reasonable time' creeps in to muddy the waters. Being open and honest from day one is the best advice that can be given to counteract the vagueness of the condition; if all parties have been open and candid from the outset, there can be no charge that full disclosure has not occurred within that 'reasonable' timeframe.

To expand on what might be considered to be 'relevant information', we need to explore the material a franchisor may have that would benefit the decision-making process of a franchisee, and the best place to start would be the business and financial standing of the franchisor. If a franchisee is being asked to invest a large amount of money to buy into another company's business, it is not unreasonable for the franchisee to request to be told how the business was established and over how long a period the business developed, so that a clear picture of the experience of the franchisor can be assessed. Similarly, it is also reasonable to expect that the franchisee would be able to see that the business had sound financial foundations, by means of the latest certified accounts that would certainly be no more than 12 months old, plus a current financial statement by the franchisor, or at least a declaration to the effect that there has been no deterioration in the financial standing of the franchisor and that s/he has sufficient resources to fund the present financial requirements. Moreover, it should be expected that the franchisor is able to demonstrate that s/he has not been subject to legal action for the recovery of debts, or if s/he has, that s/he defended the action with reasonable grounds. Even if the franchisor is part of an extended company, some financial information should be available, especially where the group corporate accounts do not provide the necessary information for a franchisee to obtain a clear picture of the franchisor's business.

Who runs the business is another area of disclosure that franchisees have a right to access; that is, the directors (whether active or not) and the senior executives, together with details of their responsibilities and commercial background, plus confirmation that they are of 'good character' and have not been declared bankrupt, been convicted of a criminal offence, or are disbarred from holding the position of director in a limited company.

The prospective franchisee needs to know the details of the franchise offer, including a detailed breakdown of the business format, and what is included in the initial fee and the ongoing fees in the form of services or benefits to the franchisee. If the system is in the early stages of development, a clear indication of the level of piloting to which the franchise has been subjected, or in the case of an established franchise system, the opinions of existing franchisees of the franchisor's performance.

Included under the general heading of franchise offer disclosures would be the actual franchise contract, or at least a sample of the current contract with no amendments or significant differences from the contract that the prospective franchisee would be expected to sign. The franchisor should in all circumstances strongly advise the prospective franchisee that they should find a specialist franchise lawyer and take independent legal advice prior to committing to the purchase of the franchise. In that way the franchisee will have the precise nature and conditions of the agreement explained in language that is easy to understand, and will have no doubt as to what s/he is committing him/herself.

The potential franchisee needs to know who supplies the franchisees with products or services, and what happens if that supply fails. If a franchisor enters into a dispute with a supplier, it would be considered unreasonable for a franchisee to suffer unduly from a lack of product to sell, so a clear supply chain with failsafe mechanisms is vital to ensure that the franchisee is protected. Sometimes, franchisors seek the right to approve the site where the business will be located to ensure similarity of offering across all outlets: size, location, access and car-parking may all be features of the minimum standards that franchisors set, and these need to be fully disclosed in the early stages of discussion.

Another element of disclosure is the number of franchisees currently working in the system; where they are located and from what sort of premises they trade; how many have terminated their agreement prior to the conclusion of the contract during the previous year and the reasons why termination occurred; how many agreements has the franchisor terminated in the previous twelve months and why, whether litigation ensued or is currently in process; and, finally, whether the franchisor has traded previously in the territory under consideration, and what the results of that venture were.

In the first point of this section, it was stated that franchisors must be open about claims they make about the future earnings of the franchise, and as we have seen with established franchisors, this information is gathered from accurate data recovered from the franchise network, but in the case of less established franchisors, it must be stated clearly how the projections were generated. Generally, the future financial health of a franchise is given in projected turnover and anticipated costs, giving rise to a profit prediction. However, this is not a guarantee that these levels of earning will be achieved, as the involvement of the individual franchisee is a key element as to how the franchise will prosper; therefore franchisees need to be cautioned that they should take independent financial advice when considering the proposal.

In reality, all a franchisor can do is to demonstrate what an existing franchisee has achieved (with the consent of the illustrative franchisee, of course), or to show the levels of profit that can be anticipated if a certain level of turnover is achieved, and issue a clear caveat that these are illustrations only and do not amount to a warranty of future performance.

Some franchisors offer a 'guaranteed' turnover, but this, of course, does not 'guarantee' profitability. The idea is that the franchisor has such a large volume of work that s/he is able to ensure a certain level of turnover for the franchisee. These may be relevant at the time of selling the franchise, but there can be no guarantee that they will continue over the term of the contract, and leave the door open to all manner of unprincipled and unethical practices by unscrupulous franchisors hoping to lever the prospective franchisee into signing a contract. It could not be said that all these 'guaranteed turnover' schemes are deceitful, but caution would be strongly advised, if one is offered a 'guarantee' of turnover, earnings or profit, to take financial advice prior to any legal commitment.

Nowadays, many franchisors insist on a pre-contract being signed, for which they charge a 'deposit' or an 'advance against fees', and this is not considered to be unethical or bad practice. This is recognized in the next bullet of the Code, which reads:

> **"** prior to the signing of any pre-contract, the candidate Individual Franchisee should be given written information on its purpose and on any consideration he may be required to pay to the Franchisor to cover the latter's actual expenses, incurred during and with respect to the pre-contract phase; if the agreement is executed, the said consideration should be reimbursed by the Franchisor or set off against a possible entry fee to be paid by the Individual Franchisee.
>
> (Section 3, Item 3.4)

Franchisors expend a huge amount of money on recruiting suitable franchisees, and it is not unreasonable for the franchisor to seek compensation if a prospective franchisee withdraws from the process. However, certain conditions have to be met and it is considered good practice to refund deposits after legitimate costs have been disbursed; legitimate costs include any third-party fees the franchisor has expended, but do not include internal staff costs or 'lost opportunity' costs. Should a prospective franchisee proceed to contract, then the deposit should be deducted from the initial franchise fee payable on joining.

In all cases, however, the scale of charges, the level of pre-commitment and the details of any refund of the deposit must be communicated clearly to the prospective franchisee prior to the franchisee being asked to sign any document that commits him/her to any form of legal undertaking with the franchisor. In short, the prospective franchisee must know the level of his/her commitment, and the likely costs of progressing, right from the start.

Similarly, the next bullet point states that 'the Pre-contract shall define its term and include a termination clause', which is only fair, as otherwise the prospective franchisee might unwittingly sign away rights ad infinitum! However, at the same time, the franchisor derives protection of any specialist know-how that might be given to the prospective franchisee in the pre-contract period, under the final bullet, which states that 'the Franchisor can impose non-competition and/or secrecy clauses to protect its know-how and identity'.

Of course, since December 1979, when the Federal Trade Commission's Franchise Rule came into effect, American franchisors have been obliged to provide franchisees with what is known as a Franchise Disclosure Document (FDD). This document must provide necessary information to assist the franchisee in making an accurate decision as to whether to buy into the system.

When a franchisor seeks to expand his/her business into another state, s/he must provide state examiners who will search through the document looking for any discrepancies, which they will expect the franchisor to correct before his/her franchise offering can be registered.

Sadly, it has been noted that franchisors sometimes employ highly competent lawyers to compile the FDD so that it barely meets the minimum necessary information for registration. This would suggest that some franchisors consider the FDD to be a necessary obstacle that must be negotiated prior to registration rather than a sales tool, or even an instrument to assist prospective franchisees in their due diligence.

Consequently, it is often considered that the registration by a state of the franchisor's offering merely shows that the franchisor has supplied an answer to the disclosures required by the state's disclosure and registration laws, and it does not demonstrate that the franchisor's disclosures are either wholly honest or fully inclusive.

Nevertheless, the concept that there should be a document that requires franchisors to give full and complete disclosure to their prospective franchisees is an attractive option for those seeking to further regulate the industry. After all, a franchisor has a duty of care to any franchisee that is recruited, or even considered as a possible recruit to the system, in the same way as they have a responsibility as 'guardians of the network'.

SELECTION OF INDIVIDUAL FRANCHISEES

Section 4 of the Code stipulates that *'Franchisors should select and accept as individual Franchisees only those who, upon reasonable investigation, appear to possess the basic skills, education, personal qualities and financial resources sufficient to carry on the franchised business.'*

On the face of it, this might seem to be stating the obvious; why would a franchisor seek to tie up a territory for an extended period of time with a franchisee that does not meet all of these criteria? Unfortunately, rogues and charlatans exist in all walks of life and the franchise community is no different.

There have been incidents where franchisors have sold territories at an increased initial fee and offer ridiculously low ongoing fees. Using this scenario as an example, it quickly becomes clear that the franchisor does not have any incentive to ensure that the franchisee is successful, whereas in properly balanced franchise agreements, the franchisor retains a definite interest in the continuing success of the franchisee, because the more successful the franchisee, the wealthier the franchisor becomes; in our example this is not the case. So, without proper support and nurturing, the franchisee withers and fails, and the franchisor can resell the franchise for the same inflated fee, while the original franchisee is left with nothing. This situation would be highly unethical, as typically the only criterion that would count for the rogue franchisor is whether the prospective franchisee has sufficient money to be able to buy into the system.

Consequently, it has been found necessary to state the obvious so that it is clearly understood by all parties that unless the prospective franchisee meets the strict criteria given, it is likely that their application will fail; thus it protects the franchisee against opportunistic bad practice.

There are other techniques that are often employed to close the sale to a wavering franchisee, which may breach the various codes of ethics, and which should be apparent to the prospective franchisee that the franchisor is indulging in sharp practice. Here are a few of the more common ploys currently in use, that are not considered to be ethical:

- **Speeding up the process**. After a franchisee has identified a franchise that appeals to him/her, time is needed to consider the investment fully, and this often takes up to eight weeks. The franchisor who pushes the prospect into an early decision is behaving unethically; if, after a few gentle hints that you need to slow things down but the salesman is still pushing, the best advice would be to RUN (don't walk) away from the deal.

- **Discounting**. Franchisees within a network should all (assuming a level playing field) be paying the same amount for the purchase of the franchise and the ongoing fees. Apart from the fact that it makes the franchisor's job ludicrously more complex to have different franchisees on dissimilar contracts, franchisors who offer discounts to attract franchisees are unnaturally desperate; in most cases, the offer will not be a bargain, but will turn out to be an albatross, and the advice given for the previous ploy would be equally applicable.

- **The delay**. Sometimes, franchisors are reticent about providing accurate facts and figures about the franchise. In America, these are included in the Franchise Disclosure Document, but still some franchisors drag their heels in sending the prospective franchisee the information that is needed to make a qualified and accurate decision. Prospective franchisees suspicious about any franchisor who is not open and candid about the facts they need should dig in their heels and not budge until they get what *they* need to make the decision that is right for *them*, and franchisees should not be swayed by any franchisor who delays about providing necessary information.

- **Restrictive reference lists**. Most franchisors will give their prospective franchisees a list of franchisees who will act as referees for the franchise system. Sometimes franchisees are offered a 'comprehensive' list of five existing franchisees they can contact. The potential franchisee should ask: 'Have they really only got five franchisees who would speak highly of the franchise? Would the majority of franchisees who are not included complain and tell the prospective franchisee some unpleasant truths about the franchisor?' If the franchisor refuses to give a prospect a fully comprehensive list of franchisees, it is time for the prospect to dig out a few of their own and ask for candid responses to some searching questions.

- **Lawyers and consultants**. Without a doubt, the best advice that can be given to prospective franchisees is to get themselves a competent franchise lawyer; not the guy who did the conveyancing for the house purchase, or who handled Aunt Mildred's will, but a lawyer who understands franchising. Some dubious franchisors might even tell a prospect that they would be wasting their money if they consulted a lawyer, because the contract is non-negotiable in any case. It is not unusual that contracts are not negotiable, but a franchisor who plays down the importance of the prospect seeking independent legal advice, is acting unethically, and this approach should make a wise prospective franchisee visit a very good lawyer sooner rather than later!

THE FRANCHISE CONTRACT

How to construct an ethical franchise agreement or contract will be dealt with in greater detail in Chapter 7, which will also give guidance to prospective franchisees as to what they should look for in a proposed agreement, but in this section we look specifically at the importance that the EFF places on the agreement. It is clear that the EFF regards the franchise agreement as the cornerstone of any franchise offering, as the section that deals with the contract is the longest in the Code of Ethics.

The first point of Section 5 deals with compliance and reads 'that the *Franchise agreement shall comply with the National law, European community law and this Code of Ethics and any national Extensions thereto'*. One of the difficulties the EFF faced when creating the Code of Ethics, even back in 1992 when this version appeared in its original state (it was modified slightly in 2003), was that it had to apply to 12 sovereign states, each with a different approach to franchising; now, of course, there are 27 member states, and the differences in approach have become much more marked, though the wording of this paragraph is still applicable. It is interesting to note that while much European legislation is supranational – that is, where legislation generated by the European Community automatically supersedes national law – it is National Law that takes the prime position in the wording of the Code of Ethics; this recognizes the existence of local differences, and acknowledges that franchising law should remain in the local domain rather than the almost federal nature of European legislation. Continuing, the expectation is that in generating a franchise agreement, the *spirit* of the Code of Ethics should be applied, and franchisors should not just rely on the wording to substantiate legality.

The second point of Section 5 states that

" The agreement shall reflect the interests of the members of the franchised network in protecting the Franchisor's industrial and intellectual property rights and in maintaining the common identity and reputation of the franchised network. All agreements and all contractual arrangements in connection with the franchise relationship shall be written in or translated by a sworn translator into the official language of the country the Individual Franchisee is established in, and signed agreements shall be given immediately to the Individual Franchisee.

Again we can see that the EFF is emphasizing the importance of the franchisor as the 'guardian' of the network's reputation and as such controls the compliance of the individual franchisees with the system and the uniformity of the product or service offering.

It is not unreasonable that anyone who is signing a contract should be able to understand his/her rights and obligations, together with the spirit of the terminology, and as such it is reasonable that the franchise agreement should be written in a language in which they are competent. At the time of writing, there are 23 official languages in Europe, and about 50 currently in use by indigenous people living within the territory of the Union. If one ventures into the French overseas departments and territories, there are about 50 other local dialects that can be added to the list. This means that potentially there will be well over 100 languages and local dialects that may be applicable to a franchise agreement in any European Union (EU) country, with the free movement of workers and the right to establish businesses in any EU state, and that does not take into consideration any of the Asiatic languages that have become established as a result of the multicultural nature of the EU, so the EFF has taken a pragmatic stand on this issue and stipulated that the franchisee has to be given a franchise agreement 'translated into the official language of the country in which the Franchisee is established'. Even that will pose difficulties in countries where there are two official languages – such as Belgium and Finland – but it is still less of a problem than what might have been the case had the EFF taken a less practical stance.

Handover of contracts would, naturally, take place at the time of signing; it would be highly unusual if they were taken away by either party and then forwarded to the other at some later date.

Paragraph 5.3 considers the clarity of the franchise agreement, and says that 'the franchise agreement shall set forth without ambiguity, the respective obligations and responsibilities of the parties and all other material terms of the relationship'. It is well-known that lawyers love to tie up contracts with phrases written in 'legalese' that require a degree in law to even begin to gain an understanding of them, but the EFF makes it clear that franchise contracts should be written plainly and without ambiguity, in a manner that is easy to understand. The agreement must contain all the terms by which the parties are obligated; nothing should be left to separate agreements or vague statements of intent. Quite apart from the fact that it is almost certain that a court sitting in arbitration will only enforce the terms of the contract, and will not consider what it was *intended* that the terms should mean, it would be most unethical for a contract to say one thing when it meant to say something different.

In recognizing that franchise contracts and agreements will be both company and industry specific, it would clearly be an impossible task for the EFF to be too prescriptive as to the requirements that ought to be included in a franchise agreement. However, in saying this, there must be minimum requirements, and these are covered in Item 5.4 of the Code of Ethics in a series of bullet points, which we shall analyse here.

The first requirement is that the franchisor clearly sets out *the rights granted to the Franchisor* under the agreement. These rights will be company specific, but will generally include the right to enforce his or her rights under the contract and to control the network, to be paid fees by the franchisees, and the right to receive information. If a franchisor is a master franchisor, this section should detail the rights extended to the franchisor by the rights holder, and should any proprietary software be used in the network, the rights extended by the holder of the copyright of that software. These third-party rights must be provable.

Second, the clause stipulates *the rights granted to the individual franchisee*. Franchisees are granted rights by the franchisor in order to carry out their business, a good example being the right to use the brand and trade name of the system. All the rights that have been discussed and form part of the contractual obligation must be listed clearly here, including any third-party rights that are extended through the franchisor for the benefit of the franchisee. This can be summarized as the tangible and intangible elements prospective franchisees will require to enable them to become active and effective members of the franchise system.

Next, the code considers the *obligations of the franchisor*, which to all intents and purposes relates to the levels of support extended by the franchisor to the franchisee during the term of the contract, together with the provision of goods and services that the franchisee needs in the continuance of his/her business.

Then follows the *obligations of the individual franchisees*, and these need to be detailed precisely and without ambiguity. The obligations listed here would be the legal obligations; the 'operational obligations' are typically contained in the operations manual. There is a fine line of distinction here; the operations manual contains the working methods by which the franchisor's system is to be implemented by the franchisee so that the franchisee can fulfil his/her responsibilities as defined in the agreement. It would be most unethical for a franchisor to rely on legal obligations being contained within the non-legal framework of an operations manual, which may be varied or amended as the system develops.

Considering next *the terms of payment by the individual franchisee*, it is important that franchisees are able to calculate exactly what they are contracted to pay, and how that payment will be calculated. As a general rule, franchisees should benefit from the economies of scale that bulk purchasing power affords the franchisor, but at the same time it is recognized that often price lists for goods supplied may be printed in advance and that the franchisor has to weather any negative impact as well as benefit from a positive impact. Passing on cost variations as they happen may well put an additional burden on the administrative capacity of both the franchisor and the franchisee, unless some sort of electronic stock control and pricing is used; nevertheless, if the benefit to the network is good, it would equally be unethical for franchisors to withhold the benefit from the franchisees.

The next point raised looks at *the duration of the agreement, which should be long enough to allow individual franchisees to amortize their initial investments specific to the franchise* and is worded in such a manner as to make for confusion. At first reading it seems to stipulate that sufficient time should be contracted to allow for the franchisee to recover the cost of purchasing the franchise, but does not cover premises that had to be acquired or vehicles purchased. The secret lies in the use of the plural 'investments', which may be taken to include these costs; however, that makes the clause somewhat subjective and unenforceable, as the costs will not be the same depending on where the franchise is located. If premises are sourced in the capital city of a country, the costs are likely to be significantly higher than if they are sourced in the provinces, so how can a term be calculated that allows for regional fluctuations in costs? Moreover, the clause also specifies that only sufficient time to amortize the initial investments need be calculated, which means that any costs incurred after the initial set-up outlay are not included.

Most franchisees will seek a renewal of their contract for at least one additional term, so the next clause deals with *the basis for any renewal of the agreement*. Not every franchise agreement makes allowances for renewal, but if it does then the conditions imposed should be detailed in the agreement and should be fair and equitable. There is an advantage in franchisors seeking to renew contracts, as the incumbent franchisee does not need to be trained, and s/he knows the system and many of the existing customers; however, should a franchisor seek to impose restrictive renewal conditions, including the charging of unreasonable renewal fees, that would be considered unethical. As a general rule, renewals should be for the same term as the original agreement unless there has been a change in legislation that makes this impossible; should be at a discounted fee commensurate with the saving that the franchisor will make in not having to train a new franchisee and work him or her up to full effectiveness; and should not make substantive changes to the terms of the agreement without allowing for some degree of negotiation or flexibility if such changes place the franchisee in a vulnerable position, although normally renewing franchisees will be expected to sign the franchise agreement that exists at the time of renewal. A good example of such a substantive change could be in the size of the territory: a renewing franchisee has a larger territory than is customary in the latest version of the franchise agreement, but most of his/her customers are outside the confines of the proposed new territory, it would be unreasonable to expect the renewing franchisee to have to buy two or more 'new' franchises, just to keep the existing customer base, as that would constitute an excessive and unethical financial burden which would substantially affect the viability of the franchisee's business.

Remembering that the franchisee is running his/her own business, it is reasonable that s/he is free to sell that business, or transfer it with the approval of the franchisor, and this area is covered in the next point, which deals with *the terms upon which the individual franchisee may sell or transfer the franchised business and the franchisor's possible pre-emption rights in this respect.* The terms and conditions where a franchisee might sell or transfer his/her business must be laid out clearly in the agreement, including the scenario where the franchisor retains the right to buy the franchise back from the franchisee. The agreement would be considered highly unethical if it contains provisions for the franchisor to buy back the franchise at below a fair market value, and similarly, highly restrictive clauses preventing the reasonable sale to a competent prospective franchisee would also be frowned upon. There have been horror stories in the past where franchisors have raised semi-legitimate reasons why a franchisee could not sell his/her business to many different purchasers, which has resulted in either the franchise term lapsing and the franchise defaulting to the franchisor, or the franchisee selling the franchise back to the franchisor at a substantially reduced price just to be rid of it. Both of these practices are grossly unfair to the franchisee and would be considered highly unethical.

It would not be unreasonable for a franchisor to charge an outgoing franchisee a fee to compensate them for transferring the business, especially if the franchisor is managing the resale, recruitment and training of the successful purchaser, almost in the manner of a broker.

Whether the franchise returns to the franchisor, or whether a new franchisee is found by the franchisor and approved to purchase the franchise, it is only right that the outgoing franchisee receives the full market value of his/her business as if it were being sold on the open market.

The next bullet point looks at the protection of the system in a clause that reads: *'provisions relevant to the use by the Individual Franchisee of the Franchisor's distinctive signs, trade name, trade mark, service mark, store sign, logo or other distinguishing identification'.* The intellectual property rights that are associated with a brand or trade name belong firmly with the franchisor, and it is incumbent on the franchisor to protect the reputation of this intellectual property for the benefit of the network as a whole. Therefore, omission of these provisions by the franchisor would be commercial suicide, though s/he will need to take precise legal advice as to how to handle the various property rights that s/he holds and is licensing.

Nothing in life ever stays the same, and a franchise system will evolve over time, so some elements of the system will change and how the franchisor deals with this change is covered in the next point, which deals with *the franchisor's right to adapt the franchise system to new or changed methods*. Many of these changes will be at the operational level and will be modified by updates in the operations manual to keep the system competitive in the market place. Essentially, the contract must cover the procedures that the franchisor and the franchisee must follow in the event of such changes being necessary.

An important clause of the contract will be how the franchisor may terminate the agreement, and for what reasons, but provision must be made for such an event and this is covered in the next point. Typically, termination may occur if there is a significant breach of the terms of the agreement or the laws that govern the type of business, and the timescale employed may vary depending on the offence committed. For example, a rat infestation at a fast-food outlet would need a considerably shorter timescale for remedy as the adverse publicity would be likely to damage the brand reputation, than perhaps something like a failure to complete required documentation by a due date. Both circumstances breach the terms of the agreement, but the severity of the first and the relatively minor nature of the second would require that they were dealt with differently. Nevertheless, there is greater scope for ambiguity in the area of forced termination of agreement, and so this needs to be set out clearly with no room for indistinctness or doubt to creep into the termination process.

Finally, when an agreement is terminated for whatever reason, all rights to use the franchisor's property cease, so there must be '*provisions for surrendering promptly upon termination of the franchise agreement any tangible and intangible property belonging to the Franchisor or other owner thereof*'. There is, however, an area of doubt in this final provision, which is incorporated in the final four words. In the event of a master franchisor (sub-franchisor) having his agreement terminated, it may be that the franchisees are licensed to the sub-franchisor, there is no legal contract existing between the franchisees and the franchisor, and that the legal rights of the franchisee network to use the property of the franchisor will terminate when the sub-franchisor's contract is terminated.

It is crucial that franchisees buying into a system controlled by a master franchisor or sub-franchisor ensures that there are provisions in their contract for continuation in the event of the sub-franchisor's contract being terminated, especially as Section 6 of the Code of Ethics specifically states

'This Code of Ethics shall apply to the relationship between the Franchisor and its individual Franchisees and equally between the master Franchisee and its individual Franchisees. It shall not apply to the relationship between the Franchisor and its Master-Franchisees.' It would be wholly unethical if the individual franchisee was not protected in such a circumstance.

ANALYSIS OF THE OTHER TWO CODES OF CONDUCT

Some companies go much further than the mere implementation of the Code of Ethics, as we can see in Figure 6.1, which represents the management structure of a highly ethical franchisor who has chosen not only to implement the Code of Ethics, but also to agree a franchisee committee which holds an elected seat on the Board of Directors and when corporate strategic decisions are being reached, the whole committee is consulted both to gain input and to ensure transparency of communication over decisions which may affect the conditions of the franchisee network. Whereas the franchisee Committee does not have the power of veto, if concerns are

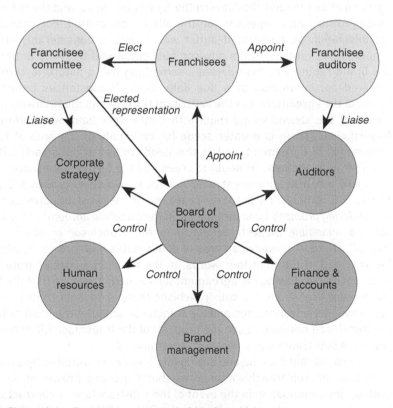

Figure 6.1 Ethical management within franchising

raised the Board of Directors work with the Committee to ensure an amicable resolution. More importantly, the company encourages the franchisees to appoint an independent auditor to examine the company accounts and to produce an independent report for the franchisee network; the franchisee Committee does not appoint the independent auditor, but rather the franchisee network elect an auditor from a shortlist prepared by the Committee and the auditor reports both to the committee and the annual franchisee meeting. The franchisor pays for the independent audit on receiving an invoice from the committee. This is a highly unusual arrangement, but it works well and the franchisor has a high level of franchisee satisfaction and an extremely low franchisee attrition rate.

CASE STUDY 6.1

The rough guide to buying a franchise

Janice Wheldon has run successful home-based franchises in both the USA and in Britain and even though differences exist, in that the US franchise industry is heavily regulated and the UK industry is not, she says that the ground rules for buying a franchise remain the same.

Janice knows that suspicions will become roused when you start researching the various franchises that interest you. You may think that you have achieved your peak when you have found a business that satisfies your needs, aptitudes, way of life, and financial constraints, but that is really only just the start of the journey ... how can you really be sure that your chosen franchisor employs ethical and responsible business methods?

The answer is, that you cannot be 100 per cent sure! But here are her tips, which she calls the 'Rough Guide to Buying the Right Franchise', for avoiding many of the pitfalls:

1. Without a doubt, the biggest indication of ethical credibility is when the franchisor is a member of a recognized trade association like the British Franchise Association in the UK or the International Franchise Association in America. All of these organizations actively promote ethical franchising and, where laws exist to protect franchising, will even review franchisor's legal documentation to ensure compliance with their ethical standards.

2. Legal documentation should be clear and comprehensible and in many cases there are specific requirements as to what this documentation should include. For example, in the USA the Uniform Franchise Offering Circular (UFOC) comprises some 23 sections ranging from full details of the franchisor, any predecessors and affiliates, right through any earnings claims, up to patent copyrights and other intellectual property on which the business relies. Coupled with this comprehensive document will →

CASE STUDY 6.1 *continued*

be a set of the franchisor's audited financial statements and a copy of each form or contract a franchisee is expected to sign if he/she intends to buy the franchise. In the USA the UFOC is obligatory ... they have to be given, by law! These documents are quite complex, so getting legal advice is essential.

3. Claims as to how much the franchisee will earn are purely speculative 'sales puffs' and no reliance should be given to accuracy as to what a franchisee might realistically earn from their franchise, unless the franchisor explicitly commits to specific figures in their UFOC or other legally binding franchise documentation. Promises of unrealistic wealth are to be treated with extreme suspicion and viewed as unethical.

4. Review period. This is the time that a prospective franchisee has between receiving the legal documentation and when they are expected to sign the contract or make a payment to the franchisor. Generally, this is minimally fourteen days, but it can be longer. If the franchisor uses any pressure to persuade the prospective franchisee to sign earlier, either by means of inducement or implied threat, then they are behaving unethically and may even be using illegal tactics.

5. Talking with existing franchisees. Ethical franchisors will provide a full list of existing franchisees, not just those who can be expected to talk up the benefits of the system. Prospective franchisees should seek to contact existing franchisees to get their sales and operational perspectives of the franchisor, although it should be noted that they are not obliged to share this information ... it will be at their discretion. Bear in mind, as well, that each individual franchisee will have differing lifestyles and expectations, but at least the prospective franchisee will gain valuable intelligence about the honesty and integrity of the franchisor.

6. In any business relationship there will be disputes between the parties; that is the third 'fact of life' behind dying and paying taxes! How does the franchisor resolve disputes with their franchisees? Is there a dialogue that seeks to resolve the matter equably? Or is the communication between the franchisor and franchisee closed and one-sided? Getting an insight into how disputes are resolved will give a good indication of the ethical perspective of the franchisor.

These six points are not the blueprint for success, but can go a long way to helping the prospective franchisee to form a good and accurate picture of the ethical and legality of the franchisor and the system being proposed. In many countries, franchise laws change regularly and franchisors are obliged to meet the new regulations and apply them retrospectively.

However, says Janice, the greatest piece of advice that can be given is to trust your own instinct: if it sounds implausible, it probably is.

→

> **CASE STUDY 6.1** *continued*
>
> Take as much advice from respected and knowledgable professions like lawyers to scrutinize the legal agreements and accountants to analyse the accounts and projections to find any discrepancies. Ask the franchisor questions about anything that you do not understand ... and expect prompt and detailed responses.
>
> Remember, though, that this is your business and you must feel relaxed with the product, system, brand, as well as the franchisor's philosophy and goals ... it should fit your expectations like a comfortable shoe. If the franchise is ethical and all other aspects meet your particular needs, you should have few worries.

SOCIAL RESPONSIBILITY AND FRANCHISING

In a capitalist society, it is often argued that the role of business is to generate profit for the owners (shareholders) of that business and, among others, Milton Friedman has argued that only people have social responsibility, the only responsibility of business is to maximize profit to their shareholders, and that business holds no responsibility to society. This approach is rather out of step with the contemporary corporate philosophy of the twenty-first century, where it is becoming more widely accepted that corporate social responsibility (CSR) can appreciably improve long-term corporate prosperity because it reduces threats, risks and inefficiency while offering many potential benefits such as increased brand reputation and employee commitment.

The World Business Council for Sustainable Development, in their publication Making Good Business Sense (2000), written by Richard Holme of Rio Tinto and Phil Watts of Royal Dutch/Shell Group, suggest the following all-encompassing definition:

> ❝ Corporate Social Responsibility is the continuing commitment by business to behave ethically and contribute to economic development while improving the quality of life of the workforce and their families as well as of the local community and society at large.

Of course, there are those who merely suggest that CSR is employed by companies to distract attention from the potentially questionable ethical concerns of the core business operations. The argument goes that businesses engage CSR purely to derive commercial benefits through their elevated reputation in the eyes of the customer base. Franchisors in particular have faced criticism in this regard, with companies such as McDonald's being accused of dubious marketing practices by seeking to promote the Ronald McDonald House charity, and more recently their increased involvement with high-profile 'football ambassadors'; or KFC seeking to improve the educational abilities of Third-World countries such as Ethiopia.

The fact is that businesses exist in the societies where these franchises operate, and they have both a moral and a social responsibility to contribute to the general well-being of the area where they are located as a good and responsible neighbour.

The Quaker sect has long held these beliefs, and many of the early pioneers of social reform in business were members of that religion: industrialists such as Joseph Rowntree and Joseph Storrs Fry of York; Cyrus and James Clark, the shoe manufacturers of Somerset, UK; and Richard and George Cadbury, two brothers from Birmingham, who as early as the third quarter of the nineteenth century had set up social reforms in their businesses to improve the working conditions of their workforce. Ironically, there is no evidence that Henry Parsons Crowell, the founder of the Quaker Oats Company, was in fact a Quaker, but he was a devout Christian who gave away almost 70 per cent of his wealth to help the needy of Chicago, and certainly emulated many of the social reforms of other Quaker industrialists. The working conditions at the Quaker mill were second to none. These philanthropic businessmen also set up charitable foundations that even today do much good for the underprivileged in society.

The secret of success in business is to ensure that the social, economic and environmental elements of a business work together harmoniously, as demonstrated in Figure 6.2.

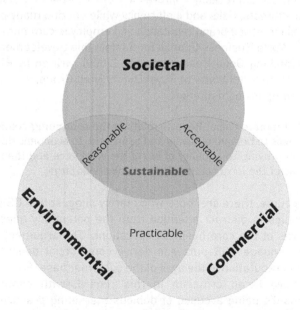

Figure 6.2   Sustainable corporate social responsibility

It is entirely reasonable that responsible franchisors would seek to invest in the society in which they operate, but true social responsibility goes further than the sponsorship of a local youth football team, or giving money to an educational charity. True social responsibility involves obtaining products from sustainable sources and seeking to reduce the carbon footprint of the business operation, and this is an area that the franchising industry is only just starting to recognize.

Brands such as Coffee Republic in the UK, and Tim Horton's in America, are proud that they source their coffee products from sustainable or 'fair trade' sources, and Gourmet Burger Kitchen have a unique 'farm-to-fork' philosophy in their distinctive approach to fast food. Cartridge World recycles inkjet cartridges, which reduces the amount of waste as well as the carbon-footprint of each cartridge refilled. Shared Earth is a franchise dedicated to trading fairly and ethically while benefiting artisans and craftsmen.

At a CSR conference in 2009, José Manuel Barroso, the President of the European Commission, stated that *in the current exceptional circumstances, corporate social responsibility is even more crucial than ever. The crisis resulted, in part at least, from a failure by some businesses to understand their broader ethical responsibilities. Now all businesses must rise to the challenge.* Calling for a *'new culture of ethics and responsibility'*, it was clear that the President was stressing that it was imperative that trust in business had to be re-established. *'This is essential – not just to restore the brand image of particular enterprises but to restore people's faith in the market economy itself. People still want markets – but they want markets with a conscience.'*

CASE STUDY 6.2

A Well Kneaded change to fast food

Well Kneaded's signature savoury is the fresh Firebread – a wood-fired sourdough base of fresh tomato, pesto or roasted garlic (or a mixture of all three), popped in a wood-burning oven in the back of a vintage Citroën 'H' van for a minute or so, and laden with a salad of your choice – or you can just have it traditional style, all melted together *à la* pizza.

Why Firebread? Well, great pizza is almost unbeatable, but thinking that even the best can get a bit samey (not to mention a little unhealthy) they wanted to create something that ticked a few more of the five-a-day boxes and captured something a little more seasonal on the taste buds ... the Firebread!

→

CASE STUDY 6.2 *continued*

'We are working with artisan producers, keeping it as local, organic and seasonal as possible so the menu will vary depending on what's about and what takes our fancy. Think beetroot, goat's cheese and spinach on a fresh garlic base, or chorizo, chili peppers and Portobello mushrooms on fresh tomato.'

The faces behind Well Kneaded are two great friends from university, Bridget Goodwin and Bryony Lewis, who, both having a love for sharing good food and also the growing street-food craze, wanted to give it a go themselves.

Since their launch, they have already achieved phenomenal success by being accepted to be part of London's sought-after Street Food collective, being asked to cater for high-profile events in London, and having been the subject of a review in a national newspaper, as well as scooping the 'Best Pie' award in the 2012 National Street Food Awards in collaboration with celebrity chef Jamie Oliver's acclaimed restaurant 'fifteen'.

The aim of the business is not only to be a commercial success but also to be a successful social enterprise; it aims to nurture those who might have otherwise been overlooked and so seek to apprentice, train up and give young men and women who are struggling to find employment a fantastic business opportunity ... and 'social franchising' is an option under serious consideration to take this innovative business forward.

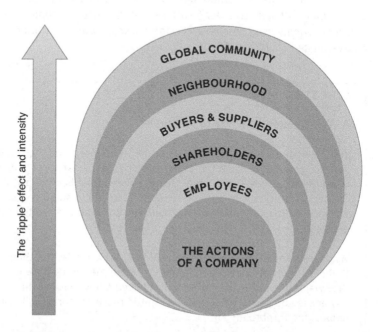

Figure 6.3   Corporate social impact

How a business impacts on society is known as corporate social impact (CSI) and the measurement of CSI is becoming quite a science. It has long been acknowledged that actions have a rippling effect throughout society, and this is truer of the business world than just about any other sphere.

Just as when one throws a stone into a pond the waves spread and widen, even though the ripples are more intense the closer they are to the point of impact, so the waves caused by what a business does can similarly have a far-reaching effect. The rippling effect of business activities is illustrated in Figure 6.3.

> **WHAT DO YOU THINK?**
>
> This chapter has raised the subjects of ethics and social responsibility. Do you think that, in today's tough trading climate, these should play a secondary role to the financial success of the system and its franchisees? Is it possible to quantify any positive elements that ethics and social responsibility bring to the business?

Further reading

Alon, Ilan, *International Franchising in Emerging Markets: China and Other Asian Countries* (CCH Inc. 2005).

Hero, Marco, *International Franchising: A Practitioner's Guide* (Globe Law and Business 2010).

Mendelsohn, Martin, *The Ethics of Franchising: A British Franchise Association Best Practice Guide*, 3rd revd edn (British Franchise Association 2004).

7 CULTIVATING A FRANCHISED BUSINESS

INTRODUCTION AND LEARNING OBJECTIVES

Whereas this chapter is targeted unashamedly at the prospective franchisor, it is also a valuable lesson for prospective franchisees to understand the amount of work and effort that a franchisor has exerted in the system to ensure it is a viable business which the prospective franchisee is being invited to join.

The reader will be able to:

* Appreciate that franchising a business is not a short-term solution to an adverse trading environment.
* Understand that, by franchising a business, the franchisor is devolving much of the responsibility for business growth to others.
* Realize that recruiting the 'right' franchisees is critical for long-term commercial success.

The choice of the word 'cultivating' in this chapter's title is quite deliberate, because the development of a franchise system is a bit like cultivating a rare and delicate orchid; it needs care, it needs nurturing, it needs encouragement, but the final stage is the birth of a fascinating and beautiful, but equally delicate and tantalizing, business. Consequently, as we have seen previously, taking the decision to franchise a business is just the first step on a long and difficult road, but a road that can lead to greater brand awareness, more stability in the marketplace, greater numbers of outlets, and even possibly greater profitability, though the latter might be a bit of a moot point!

The whole concept of franchising a business will require a root-and-branch change in the corporate philosophy, and the approach to business will need to change radically. There are no half-measures; if studies show that franchising will work for your company, you will need to commit yourself, and the entire business needs to be steadfast to the vision. It may even scare the cautious businessperson from taking the leap of faith, while

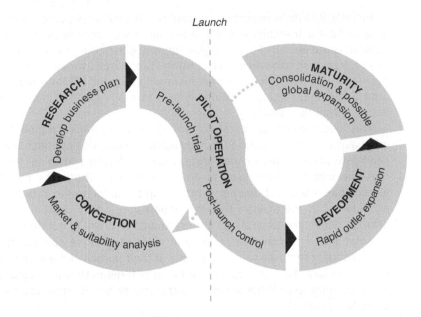

Launch

RESEARCH
Develop business plan

Pre-launch trial

PILOT OPERATION

MATURITY
Consolidation & possible global expansion

CONCEPTION
Market & suitability analysis

Post-launch control

DEVELOPMENT
Rapid outlet expansion

Figure 7.1 The franchisor cycle

others will relish the challenge with alacrity, but whichever camp you are in, there needs to be an understanding that the road ahead may not always be smooth, but the trip will certainly be exciting.

To comprehend the mechanisms that businesses must implement in order to franchise successfully, it is easier to split them into two distinct areas: those that have to be put into action prior to franchising the business; and those that have to be built into the company procedures after launching the franchised business. Consequently, and for the sake of simplicity, this chapter has been split into two parts, considering first the pre-launch undertakings and then taking into account the post-launch procedures.

Before we become too embroiled in the concepts of pre- and post-launch, this would be a good point at which to finally lay a myth to rest. It has long been a belief in franchising that all you have to do is to open for business and customers will beat a path to your door. This may be the case if the franchise is a McDonald's or a Domino's Pizza, but many new franchise opportunities fall into the service sector, rather than retail. Service sector franchises typically do not have a physical presence, such as a shop front, but they are generally much less expensive to set up and begin operating. Having low start-up costs may be a help to businesses in their infancy, but they can create other obstacles that need to be overcome.

Initially, it is most important to identify a franchise opportunity that is a good fit for the franchisee. Sadly, many potential franchisees tend to work on what could be called the 'shotgun' approach to finding a franchise – they go to a franchise exhibition, collect all the brochures available and apply to each, the idea being that any franchisor who responds is followed up. It is a bit like firing a shotgun randomly at a target – some of the shots are bound to find the target!

This less than scientific approach may generate a good match, but the emphasis is on the franchisor to weed out those who do not match the ideal candidate profile. When considering a service-based franchise, the onus must lie with the franchisee to do some of the sifting. The franchisor already has a skill-set that partly makes up the ideal profile of their prime candidate, but the *lifestyle* that the opportunity offers must fit with the desires, hopes and aspirations of the candidate. It would not be a good fit to enter into a franchise arrangement with a franchise opportunity that requires the franchisee to call on people at their homes in the evening if the franchisee has childcare responsibilities which mean they are seldom free in the evening, even if the prospective franchisee fits the franchisor's ideal candidate profile.

Sadly, it is a trait of the industry that numerous franchisees seem to depend far too much on the franchisor to plan, organize and develop their businesses, and consequently they fall into what has become known euphemistically as the 'comfort zone'. They do not believe they need to plan for the business beyond the generation of a formalized business plan, which itself is largely generated from stock phrases available from the franchisor's database of glib expressions. The franchisees hold the ultimate responsibility for their own business development, and it is their responsibility to ensure that their business expands in both a physical and financial direction at a pace with which they are comfortable. To a greater or lesser extent, this correlates directly to the amount of effort exerted – a hard-working franchisee is far more likely to succeed than one who exerts less effort. Talking to existing and former franchisees from the network may give a better picture than the sales pitch of the franchisor's sales team.

Many service franchises are 'management' franchises, where the franchisee manages a team of people who are actually performing the service; some require the franchisee also to perform the task themselves. The prospective franchisee needs to know exactly what his/her role will be in the business, and they need to assess whether they have sufficient skills to fulfil the role: in other words, to understand the entire model. In the franchised service industry,

> **Management franchises** *are where the franchisee manages the business and typically employs others to carry out most of the functions of the franchise.*

management skills are critical; the franchisee needs to understand how to manage his/her business, and this may well involve personnel management skills.

After identifying the ideal franchise opportunity and 'signing on the dotted line', the new franchisee will have to spend a certain amount of time educating his/her target market, who may or may not be aware that they are potential customers, that there is a need for the service, and that the franchisee can fulfil that need. It is a truism that a business might make the best widget springs, but if the people who use widget springs do not know that the business manufactures them, the business will never actually sell a single one. This is all part of the education of potential customers. There is an old sales story of the newly qualified driving instructor whose brand new driving school car merely displayed the legally required 'L' plates. 'I don't want to drive around in a Christmas tree,' he announced when asked when he was getting the car sign-written, 'I will build up my business through personal recommendation from my satisfied pupils and by advertising in Yellow Pages.' The sharp-witted reader might identify the driving instructor as a person who was not really seizing all the business opportunities that were available; he was a man playing at running a business. If a franchisee is in the service sector they need to SHOUT about their business at every opportunity, and whether it be a van or a car that represents your mobile presence, it needs to promote to and educate potential customers that the franchise is there and able to satisfy their needs. Imagine how Dick and Mac McDonald's business would have grown if they had operated a discreet-door eatery when they opened their first hamburger restaurant, and one wonders whether Ray Kroc would ever have founded the business way back in 1954? Education and promotion are the keys to the successful launch of a service franchise.

Part of the promotion process is to identify where your advertising currency would be best spent. Too many franchisees waste a huge amount of time, effort and energy (not to mention money) promoting their business to people who have no need for the service. Successful franchisees target their efforts to find new customers in places where potential new customers exist. Advertising in a local newspaper will possibly reach the 10 per cent of the population that is the targeted customer base of the franchised business, but 90 per cent of the effort is being wasted on people who will never become customers. Spending the same amount on targeted advertising which focuses on the identified customer base will produce much better results, and will appear to the customers to be a more 'specialized' service.

Being part of the community where the franchise's customers live is just as important. A franchisee who offers a high-quality valeting service to the motor trade and specialist owners might, after finishing work, be found at local car auctions talking to the motor trade and expanding his network of contacts, and at weekends s/he might even attend specialist car rallies, talking to potential private customers and promoting the business to proud owners.

In the world of sales there is an adage that 'the customer is king'; perhaps more accurately, 'the customer must be made to *feel* like a king'. In franchising, offering above-average customer service is critical, but with service sector franchising it is even more essential. There are various metrics in the world of marketing which suggest that satisfied customers tell on average five others of their satisfaction, whereas dissatisfied customers will tell 19 people of their dissatisfaction. Keeping customers happy will grow a business, whereas unhappy customers can destroy a business more quickly than can be imagined, so good customer service is even more important in service sector franchising.

Whereas the customer may not be 'king', consistency certainly is. The success of McDonald's is that no matter where you go in the world, the Big Mac does not change. It is consistently good value for money, no matter whether it is bought in Australia, the USA or in the depths of rural Russia. A consistently high level of service based on the franchisor's stated quality levels will ensure that the entire network offers a consistently high standard of service that will ensure customer satisfaction.

Now, having explained the great importance of cultivation when dealing with a service-based franchise, we shall now look at more general tools that will assist with the cultivation of the franchised business.

PRE-LAUNCH

The only real prerequisite for a business to be franchisable is whether that business can be replicated. If a business model cannot be replicated, then the business cannot, in all conscience, be franchised. It is one of the seven golden pillars of franchising that the business can be replicated and that replication sold to the prospective franchisee as an identical business to all the other franchises in that particular system.

The proven method that would-be franchisor companies use to ascertain whether their business is replicable is through a system of pilot testing, where units are set up and run for a period of time as if they were franchises, usually for a minimum of one year. Of course, it is entirely possible to set up a franchise system on the basis of a concept that has not been piloted or tested, but finding suitable prospective franchisees might prove extremely difficult in that case, and it would not comply with the ethical codes of conduct that apply in most countries. Responsible franchisors seek to ensure that their franchisees are properly protected, and the only way that the franchise network can be shielded against damage is by having the armour that can only be acquired by following the protocols that legions of successful franchisors have established over many years. There is no short cut to building a successful franchise system!

However, the first stage in deciding whether to franchise a business would be to generate a feasibility study to see whether it is even worth producing a business plan. Feasibility studies are, to some extent, quite subjective, especially if

> *Franchises must have a replicable business model, and this is generally tested by means of a* **pilot operation.**

they have been generated in-house. It is not unusual for a managing director (MD) to task an underling with the job of drawing up a feasibility study on some project, and the employee feeling as though s/he is almost duty bound to create a study that supports the director's suggestion. Sometimes, 'third-generation' feasibility studies, where the initial study has been generated to satisfy the whim of the MD, who has then commented that a project was too expensive, so the study has been re-jigged to cut costs, to which the director has then observed that the implementation time is too long, so the document has been reworked yet again to cut the timescale. The MD has then taken the study to the board of directors as a feasible project that is both cost- and time-efficient, but in reality is totally unworkable.

To have any value at all, feasibility studies *must* be objective, and with the best will in the world, it is unlikely that this will be achieved by asking somebody within the organization to head-up the team; they are too close to the action, they are too biased one way or another, and they cannot see the wood for the trees! If a business is large enough, it can import a team leader from another division who has the benefit of understanding the corporate culture, but is sufficiently distanced from the department where the study will be implemented; however, not many businesses can afford this luxury or have the resources to apply this pattern.

Usually, the role falls to an external consultant, who has a wealth of experience in franchising but also has the benefit (or otherwise) of not knowing the intimate details of the business. This person can approach the task with total objectivity, and the prospective franchisor can live in hope that the ultimate feasibility study will at least be to some extent unbiased.

The cynicism of the latter statement is drawn from years of experience, both from acting as and employing consultants. There are far too many consultants in business today who either seek to satisfy the whims of their principal by justifying his/her desires (in which case the business might as well carry out an in-house study), or who, through fear of litigation, will sit on the fence and give a somewhat cautious opinion of the feasibility task they were set. Some consultants will even recommend a course of action in which they can play a future role; for example, if a franchise consultant was to say that a business was unsuited to franchising their task would be at an end and they would have limited scope for future income from the business. If, however, the consultant recommends franchising as a way forward, s/he can be pretty well assured that s/he will be retained to draw up and implement the strategies to redefine the client's business in franchising. Do not assume that what is being said is that all consultants are greedy and avaricious sharks, or flaccid jellyfish, because that is not the case. There are good and responsible consultants in the market, and many, if not most, are associated with the national or international franchising bodies; what is being said is that there are so-called consultants who are self-serving and irresponsible out there, and identifying the good from the bad is often a difficult task.

A responsible and focused consultant will give his/her client good and impartial advice, not just polishing the ego of the MD by telling him/her how wonderful is his/her business, but also offering constructive criticism of the things that have been done wrong, or need to be done better. In the main, the consultant should advise his/her client of the difficulties and challenges that the business will face as it moves towards franchising, and not just gloss over the future trials and tribulations.

Surprisingly, banks pay particular attention to who is advising a franchisor, and this will often determine whether they support a franchise offering fully or only half-heartedly. The prospective franchisee will receive plenty of advice from their bank as to the suitability of a particular franchise system, so it is important for the franchisor to ensure that s/he has the best advice available from respected and trusted sources.

Prospective franchisors have to be clear as to the reasoning behind the decision to consider franchising as a business expansion model. Some companies, especially those that have experienced difficult trading times, will consider franchising almost as a 'get-out-of-jail-free' card, and this is probably the weakest platform on which to start developing a franchised business.

Others, particularly retail franchises, are perhaps seeking foreign expansion, and whereas they do not franchise their outlets in their domestic market, they will identify benefits to franchising overseas. Businesses that have excess process or surplus storage capacity may find benefits in considering franchising. Businesses wishing to expand into other markets or to convert low margin outlets into franchises might well find some solace in franchising. Some businesses are even set up with the intention of franchising once they are properly established. Whatever the reason, and whether the business is marketing products or services, the owner needs to take a cold, analytical view of its future and decide whether franchising might benefit the company as a long-term growth strategy.

This is where the business or project plan comes in, which should not be confused with the feasibility study, which looks at franchising from an external viewpoint. The business or project plan will consider whether the project is viable from an internal perspective, and will probably contain more confidential information than has been considered by the consultant or specialist conducting the feasibility study.

A good starting point for any businesses considering franchising would be to look at the current developments in their industry and how they are likely to develop. At the time of writing, the world is in one of the biggest recessions it has ever known; markets are changing, many consumers are spending less and have found lower-cost methods of doing what they used to do. Even if some consumers go back to spending generously, it is likely that many others will continue their new habit of parsimony.

Therefore, considering what consumers in your market are already doing or buying is a good initial analysis, and then asking yourself whether they are expected to continue, or whether their behaviour is likely to change. Can your business, through franchising, offer the consumer a simpler, more efficient, less expensive or better-value option compared to what they are currently purchasing?

It is true to say that just about every thriving franchise has succeeded by giving customers a product or service they need or desire, and doing it differently from (and better than) their competitors. Consequently, a wannabe franchisor needs to ask him/herself how franchising the business can achieve the same aim, and, if the answer is positive, that could be the starting point for developing the blueprint of success.

Banks and other lending sources are keen to know who is advising a franchisee or franchisor, as this often indicates the gravitas and viability of the system.

Having assessed the reasoning behind the decision to consider franchising, the prospective franchisor really needs to understand franchising from the franchisee's point of view; s/he needs to understand why anybody would want to buy a franchise, let alone one of his/her franchises. This insight into the thought patterns of the potential franchisee will give the prospective franchisor a clear understanding of his/her future responsibilities to a franchise network. The reasons why people consider buying franchises is covered in Chapter 8, but it is crucial that both parties understand each other's ways of thinking to be fully conversant and appreciative of the industry.

Assuming that the prospective franchisor has conducted a feasibility study and has determined that there is scope for franchising, and a business plan for the project has concluded that franchising is viable from the business standpoint, the next task is to develop the pilot operation.

To say that it is impossible to launch a franchise operation without carrying out a pilot would be technically incorrect, in the same manner that it is theoretically possible to build a house without laying down foundations – with probably the same result! One of the main reasons that banks like franchising is that it is a replication of a successful business model, and piloting is where one proves the success of the model. If a franchisor does not pilot, s/he cannot prove satisfactorily the ability of the system, and consequently the franchisee's advisers, and certainly their bankers, will treat the opportunity with extreme suspicion.

The pilot confirms three main points: first, that the franchisee can anticipate a reasonable return on his/her investment; second, that the franchisee will be able to afford to pay the ongoing fees to the franchisor; and third, that the franchisor has the scope for a sustainable business funded by the franchisees.

In the initial pilot operation, it is unlikely that the franchisor will achieve profitability, but as the network grows, so the breakeven point will be passed and the system will establish a profit for the franchisor. The pilot merely proves that this is achievable.

So, whereas the final aim of the pilot is a bit vague, the first two are crystal clear. The franchisor must be able to demonstrate that the franchisee will be able to run a profitable franchised business, and that the franchisee will achieve a healthy return on the capital that s/he has invested. Much of this 'proof' will be achieved through financial projections based on the initial year's turnover of the pilot operation, as very few franchises achieve breakeven in year one, but accountants' and financial projection software is perfectly capable of drawing the necessary conclusions as to the viability of the business opportunity in the initial stages. Typically, a clearer picture will start to emerge when two franchise pilots have been operating for two years, but conducting this depth of pilot prior to franchising would place an inordinate financial strain on the franchisor, and very few systems would ever be launched; therefore, most banks and financiers will accept the figures based on a single year's turnover of the pilot as being representative of the prospects of the enterprise.

Another misunderstanding of the pilot is that franchisors do not have to recruit a pilot franchisee; many run their pilot using existing staff, especially in the retail sector. What is critical, though, is that the franchise pilot is run in a similar manner to the way the franchises will be run after launch; it should be in a representative geographical and demographic area and must be run independently of the host business. As many of the conditions as possible that will be faced by the franchisee must be reproduced in the pilot operation, and if operated in conjunction or alongside in-house outlets, the two must be treated as separate entities.

The difficulty of using existing staff to run a pilot operation is that they will be confined by their terms and conditions of employment, so their mindset is that of an employee, not a self-employed independent business owner, and there will always be the 'safety-net' of their contract of employment to save them in the case that the business fails. Apart from the fact that most contracts of employment do not contain restrictive clauses concerning future employment (which a franchise agreement will contain) employees do not have the same attitudes towards efficiency or thrift that business owners have, and this is one of the main reasons why many prospective franchisors choose to run a 'live' pilot using a specifically recruited 'first franchisee', who is genuinely responsible for his/her own business. Obviously, financial incentives would have attracted somebody to take this greater risk, but often getting in at the ground floor is a sound move for prospective franchisees.

However, in saying that, initial franchisees are often over-exposed to the risk of the venture failing, and it could be suggested that it is both irresponsible and unethical to try to prove the system through trial and error. Even if the franchisor offers to reimburse the initial franchisee's investment if the project fails, s/he will not be able to compensate for the lost opportunity. Striking the right balance is difficult, but the success or failure of the entire franchising venture rests firmly on the success of the pilot operation, so that balance *must* be found.

The pilot will also test several other aspects of the business, not least of which is that it will get the product and brand out into the public domain and allow for public reaction to the offering to be gauged; in short it will test the market and the marketing strategy for the product/service. How the outlets are laid out can be tested to maximize potential; the opening hours options tested to ensure maximum footfall; staff shift patterns can be developed, plus designing a staff training package so that franchisees can immediately implement efficient staffing practices; all these can be trialled in the pilot operation. The pilot tries to identify the business 'critical success factors' (see Figure 7.2).

Successful businesses are those that stay one step ahead of the game, and this is truer of franchised businesses than of most others. The fact that many franchisors do not have a direct sales operation means that they are relying on second-hand information filtering upwards from the franchisees,

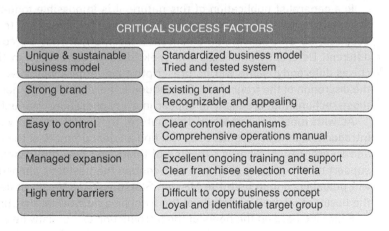

Figure 7.2 Critical success factors

so instilling a culture of free communication will help to ensure that the franchised business is sufficiently equipped to react rapidly to changing market conditions.

The fact is that running a pilot is a learning curve, and during the process aspects of the business will change, but even during this period of experimentation it should still be possible to conclude that running a franchise is a profitable and viable business opportunity to the enterprising prospective franchisee. Moreover, it will also conclude that the transfer of the business system is feasible, and it is possible to teach operating procedures and reassign know-how.

The elements that have been learnt during the pilot operation will all be collated and many will start to form the basis of the operations manual, which is the codified method of running a successful franchise – the point of reference that contains in written format the entire and inclusive systems and methods for operating the franchise. Together with the franchise agreement, it is one of the two most import documents that will exist in any franchised business; it is the fundamental creed of the franchise!

So, why is it that this crucial document, this pillar on which the franchise is founded, has not been honoured with its own chapter? In early drafts of this book, the operations manual was allocated its own section, but then it was concluded that the operations manual is largely developed during the pilot operation, in co-operation with the 'franchisee' who is running the pilot, whereas the franchise agreement is drawn up between the franchisor and his/her legal team and does not involve any input by the franchisee. This distinction is likely to continue as the franchise develops, where the operations manual will have several contributors as it is refined for the benefit of both franchisor and franchisee, whereas the franchise agreement will *only* be amended and adjusted by the franchisor and his/her lawyers to suit the franchisor's requirements.

In a generalist publication of this nature, it is impossible to identify the needs and requirements of the operations manual for all types of franchised business, as even in similar businesses the manual may be completely different. Different franchisors will seek to control practices in the franchises differently; some will be prescriptive and others will leave more to the discretion of the franchisee. Consequently, here we are only going to list those sections that are likely to appear in every operations manual.

As with most documents of this nature, the initial section will be an Introduction, in which franchisees will find a brief summary of the business and an overview of what is expected of them, and how the franchisor will support their business. It should also contain the business philosophy and will probably contain both the Mission Statement and Vision Statement of the business, as well as details of the franchise network at that time.

Following hard on the heels of the Introduction will usually be a detailed explanation of the system and how it is constructed, with an understanding of how each of the essential components of the business fit together. It may well contain a synopsis of the lines of communication, so as to fix its importance in the franchisee's mind from the outset.

The *modus operandi* or operating procedures of the business will be the next contender for inclusion, and will certainly be prefaced by a detailed schedule of the equipment that will be used by the franchisees in their business, what each piece of equipment does, and how to use it. It's likely that a list of service centres will be included should any piece of equipment break down, plus any simple manufacturer recommended repairs or servicing that the operator can carry out. The necessary IT that will be needed to operate the franchise will be included at this point, as will any vehicle requirements and how the vehicle should be stocked. Next will follow the stock control system, which stipulates stock levels and procedures for ordering replacement stock, product standards and pricing levels, together with clear instructions for implementation, ultimately leading to cleaning and refurbishment requirements.

Matters concerning staff will probably come next, and this is likely to be quite an extensive section, dealing with staff training, uniforms, staffing levels, areas of responsibility and lines of authority, job descriptions, disciplinary procedures and so on.

How the business will operate will follow, giving exact details of opening hours and trading patterns, together with how the franchisees will comply with corporate identity and trade mark usage, the standard forms that the business will have to complete, the manner in which the forms must be completed and the reporting protocols, and how to use marketing and point-of-sale material, including where and how to advertise.

Financial operating instructions will probably follow, detailing accountancy procedures, cash control and banking procedures, how to deal with virtual money (cheques, credit/debit cards and so on), the payment schedule for franchise fees, how and what financial records must be kept, and for how long, and VAT/sales tax and employment taxation details.

There should be a separate section dealing with standard forms, both internal and external, which are split into the various responsibilities of the business, including standardized staff employment contracts and all health and safety documentation. In this section it is probable that there will be comprehensive details of any legal forms that might be required for the business.

There should be a franchisor's directory, listing who does what in the organization and how they might be contacted, together with a list of other franchisees and their contact numbers, which should be updated regularly.

Incorporated into the operations manual at some point must be information about the intellectual property of the franchise. The franchisor must retain the legal rights attached to and associated with the trade mark or trading name or brand of the business, which to some extent will have been devolved to the franchisee. This intellectual property is core and central to the success of the franchise system and has to be treated like the Holy Grail and protected with the same vigour. In the presumption that some sort of sub-licensing of the intellectual property exists, so must clear and unequivocal instructions as to how that licensing may be used by the franchisee, and what the penalties are for non-compliance. This will be reiterated in the franchise agreement, but such is the importance of protecting the intellectual property rights of the brand, that it must also be included in the operations manual.

These basic and central sections will vary, depending on the type of franchise one is operating. A service franchise will have different needs and procedures from a fast-food franchise, and they will have a different operations manual from a traditional retail franchise, but the common denominator of all franchises is that at the heart of them is the operations manual. The manual will need a periodic overhaul, not just the distribution of addenda and updates, as franchisees typically are particularly bad at assimilating changes of procedure sent out by the bureaucrats at head office. When overhauled, the manual will replace the previous edition.

As a general rule, franchisors must be involved in the development of the operations manual, even though some consultants will offer to develop the manual as part of their service. Whereas the consultant may be a specialist in the generation of operations manuals, s/he will not in any way be as expert in the franchisor's business as the franchisor himself!

We mentioned above the importance of intellectual property rights and the importance of these to the franchised operation. In many countries it is a requirement that the franchisor owns or has the legal right to use the network's trade mark or trade name, and this being the case, one might think that franchisors would appreciate the importance of such a fundamental aspect of their business. However, this almost appears to be an afterthought with many franchisors. Why is a protected trade mark or trade name so important? In a franchised system, the franchisees are paying for the right to operate with exclusivity in their territory. If a franchisor does not have the ownership or exclusive rights to use the trademark or trade name in an area, then the franchisee runs the risk of competing in his/her 'exclusive' territory with third parties who are also using the brand name, and this breaches a fundamental ethical rule of franchising.

In the UK, there are two types of trade marks, the first being a registered trademark signified by the symbol ®; and second there is the unregistered trademark signified by the symbol ℠; the differences between the two are extremely important.

The registered trademark is protected by statute law, while the unregistered trademark is protected by common law. It is possible to protect an unregistered trademark in a passing-off action, but it is a phenomenally more complex and expensive process, so most franchisors pay the registration fee and ensure that their trade mark is protected under the law.

There are a considerable number of books on the subject of trade mark law, which is a complex field, and consequently it is not the intention here to discuss at great length the details of this specialist area, but any competent franchise lawyer should be able to explain the procedure and cost of getting the franchisor's trade mark registered. As it usually takes some time for the formalities to be processed, getting the application in early is crucial if the business wishes to start trading with a registered trade mark as soon as the pilot has been completed successfully.

European franchisors wishing to expand their business within the EU should seriously consider obtaining a Community Trade Mark (CTM), which is enforceable in all EU member states; however, the downside of applying for a CTM is that if there is an objection to it by one member state, then the application will fail in *all* member states. Franchisors seeking global trade mark protection would make an application for an international trade mark under the Madrid System, all of which will be explained in great detail by a franchise lawyer.

The prospective franchisor has conducted his/her feasibility study and written the project plan, s/he now has his/her system in place, which has been tried and tested by the pilot operation, the trade mark or trade name is registered and the operations manual is written. The franchise agreement has also been written (but more of that in Chapter 8) and now it is time to launch the franchised business into the waiting world.

POST-LAUNCH

What happens to the 'pilot franchise' after the business has been fully launched and is available to the public? The answer to this question depends very much on how it was set up. If the pilot was created as a true franchise, with an initial franchisee recruited to spearhead the operation, it will continue as a stand-alone franchise in the new regime. However, if the franchise was created using existing resources, it may be sold off to the person acting as the 'franchisee' or to a new recruit as a going concern, or perhaps it should continue to operate under the direct (managed) control of the franchisor. Whichever option is chosen, the initial franchise should continue to run as a 'control' mechanism, a benchmark for the development of other franchise units. The big advantage of this initial unit is that it will always be trading at least a year ahead of any other franchise outlet, so valuable information can continue to be gained as the business develops.

However, how the new franchisor handles the continuance or disposal of the pilot unit may have long-term implications for the business. The adage that franchise companies should not mix franchised outlets with company owned outlets may be flawed, but having identified that the philosophy is imperfect, at what mix of franchised and company units does perfection exist?

We have seen that the franchisor has developed a pilot operation which has been used to demonstrate that the system is replicable, and we have considered whether the operation should be sold off to the existing operator, sold to a new recruit as a going concern, or continue to run as a semi-autonomous branch of the corporate entity.

For a new franchisor, choosing the latter option could be, at the very least, challenging. Quite apart from the fact that running a branch is considerably more expensive than running a franchise, and this may be a cumbersome burden on the fledgling franchisor's finances, restricting his/her expansion of the network by soaking up developmental funds in operational costs. It may also lead the prospective franchisees to believe that if push came to shove the franchisor would protect the branch rather than the network, or at best offer the branch more favourable trading terms than those offered to the network.

Let us turn the quandary on its head now, and view it from another perspective. Running branches as 'control mechanisms' can have massive benefits to the franchise network; first, it demonstrates to the prospective franchisees that the franchisor has a stake in the ultimate and continued success of the operation, and that surely must be a vote of confidence for the system.

Second, it should give the franchise network the confidence that any new concept or operational trial can be tested thoroughly in the corporate-owned branch(es) before being rolled out across the network; after all, it demonstrates clearly that the franchisor is taking responsibility for testing any new business concept.

Third, comes market penetration – establishing a presence in a target market can speed up the recruitment of new franchisees as it allows for a brand presence to develop. It is a well-accepted fact that it is considerably easier to sell franchises of a recognized brand, than it is to try to attract attention to the 'Great Unknown' franchise opportunity. Having an established presence makes it easy for prospective franchisees to examine the franchisor's offering closely, rather than to merely rely on conceptual theories.

Fourth, as the branch outlets will typically be established prior to the development of the franchised outlets, they will be at the forefront of any new market research or intelligence, allowing the franchisor a clear understanding of what is current in the marketplace. Relying on feedback from an exclusively franchised network without the ability of testing the intelligence at first-hand seems a rather narrow-minded perspective that has the potential for disaster.

Expansion through the development of corporate branches is not the least expensive option, but if managed correctly could galvanize a wealth of benefits to the brand, not least brand integrity. The franchisor will be presenting an all-inclusive image to his/her customers, consumers and prospective franchisees.

Nevertheless, having spent a large amount of money in the run up to the launch, the franchisor is naturally keen to get a return on his/her investment as quickly as possible, and this is where many franchise systems fall down. The creation of the franchise system has taken place, and next comes the development of the franchise network. Some would argue that this is where the going really does get tough.

It is an easy trap to fall into when a franchisor has worked hard at developing his/her offering, to think that the world-and-his-wife will be beating a path to the door, begging to be allowed to buy a franchise, and it is not at all uncommon for franchisors to think that they will get full coverage in the first year. This, of course, rarely (if ever) happens. The fact is that it takes some time to build up the network.

Most franchisors are over-ambitious in assessing how many franchises will be sold in the early years of the operation, and there is no formula that can be used to predict the success rate with any accuracy. There are too many imponderables. Some businesses will be more attractive than others; some will cost more, and so will attract fewer enquiries; others will be in the wrong geographical area, and so on – the list is endless. Network development is a slow and arduous process, especially if the franchisor is going to minimize risk by being cautious over who are appointed as franchisees.

Desperate franchisors, faced with poor recruitment, often resort to reckless measures to get franchisees on board. Some of these methods are merely foolhardy, others are frankly unethical, and some border on illegality!

As we saw earlier, franchisees who join a new system are taking a greater risk because the franchisor is unable to offer much of a track record apart from the pilot operation. Of course, every franchise network has to start with its first recruitment, but sometimes predatory franchisees see this as a good opportunity to negotiate a 'special' deal. The strength of franchising, as we shall see in Chapter 8, is that all franchisees are on equal contracts and so a 'special' deal is not really in the gift of a responsible and ethical franchisor.

Nevertheless, the desperate franchisor might even instigate the bargaining process by *offering* a 'special' deal. There are areas where some flexibility does exist; for instance, in the initial purchase price, which can be offset against the risk factor, but sometimes franchisors are tempted to offer discounted ongoing fees or royalties, or agreeing to something that is not in the contract, and this will be the start of the breakdown of the strength of the system. In Chapter 6 we saw that this is not only a highly confusing course for the franchisor to embark upon, but is also almost certainly unethical. Each franchise must pay the same ongoing fees as the rest of the network, and each must be on the same contract, otherwise the franchisor will have a network of franchisees all on different contracts, all paying differing amounts, which would not only be a nightmare to administer, but would break just about every rule of the ethical franchisor.

CASE STUDY 7.1

Mutz Nutz Mobile Pet Grooming – advertising and promotion

This case study considers the disillusionment of franchisees and emphasizes some of the pitfalls that responsible franchisors will avoid, but which prospective franchisees will consider before buying into a system.

In an uncertain economy, statistics confirm that more and more people who are interested in running a business are turning to franchising as a realistic option, and many are looking for guidance to help ensure their future success.

Mutz Nutz Mobile Pet Grooming rolled out its franchise offering nationwide in 2008 and immediately started to attract a healthy interest in its van-based, work-from-home pet grooming service. However, aggressive sales pitches and highly polished sales literature coupled with a willingness to recruit any prospect with a pulse, has led what could have been a highly profitable franchise operation almost into bankruptcy.

However, we shall scrutinize the four main areas of concern that were highlighted in the case, and which both franchisors and franchisees need to avoid before commitment:

1 *Is there too much expansion?* Mutz Nutz's fast rate of franchise openings was certainly tempting. The growth of the business was one of the fastest in the industry, and doesn't everybody want part of the action when the business is a sure-fire winner? But what happens when you buy an exclusive area only to discover that, as time goes by, the franchisor opens new franchises almost on your doorstep, or brand saturation sets in among your customers. Mutz Nutz admits to closing more than 150 franchises last year, but a quick glance at their website shows over 225 franchises for sale, which is more than 15 per cent of the company's total number as at the end of 2010.

2 *Were the salespeople acting with due diligence?* With high commissions and the ability to earn a six-figure income, Mutz Nutz salespeople were some of the most aggressive in the industry. Contracts were varied to suit the prospects' own particular preferences, so it was not uncommon for one franchisee to pay

→

CASE STUDY 7.1 *continued*

$20,000 for their territory and their neighbour to pay only $10,000. Nor was it unusual for there to be differing management fee structures applied, or even wide-ranging cost variances when franchisees bought the branded stock from the franchisor. It was almost as if prospects could acquire a franchise territory just by showing signs of life! Amazingly, the conversion times between initial approach and being in operation could be as little as three weeks!

3 *What about national sales campaigns?* While franchisees generally appreciate national promotions and advertising, many do not appreciate the concept of national coupons or nationwide discounting, because even in the USA not every state's market economics is the same. Mutz Nutz franchisees argued that a 'two-for-one' coupon system seriously cut into their profit margins. Franchisees would often visit a pet owner's home in one month for a chargeable sale and then have to travel back the next for the freebie.

4 *What about the economic downturn?* A $40 dog groom is a great business when people are feeling wealthy, but it is not such an easy sale when people are cutting back on luxuries and discretionary spending. Prospective franchisees should always try to imagine how they would sell their services during tough times as well as when times are good; and then try to ascertain whether the products that the franchisor require you to buy are going to be discounted when the going gets tough.

To summarize: numerous Mutz Nutz franchisees are dumping their franchises, often for a huge loss, disillusioned by what they describe as too aggressive a sales pitch by Mutz Nutz sales representatives. Franchisees complain that projected sales figures and turnover estimates were not just deceptive, but in reality pure fantasy, and all have complained that national sales promotions slashed profit margins. Some franchisees are filing a class-action suit looking for compensation from Mutz Nutz and its parent company Doggie Doo's Corp.

Ironically, Mutz Nutz's counter argument is that the charges are false, and they even suggest that many of their franchisees were not suited to operating a franchise, which highlights the lack of due diligence by the company when recruiting their franchisee network!

Note: While this case study is based on a true story, the names of the franchisee and franchisor and the industry in which they operated have been changed for legal reasons. The Mutz Nutz franchise used for this illustration is a fictitious business and does not reflect on any existing business, whether franchised or otherwise.

We saw earlier that it is very important that prospective franchisees are given sufficient time to make up their own minds without pressure being exerted. Often, prospective franchisees are being asked to commit their entire life's savings to buy into a system and they must be satisfied that the acquisition represents a good investment. They need time to talk to their bank, and a franchise lawyer, perhaps a specialist consultant, their accountant, and other franchisees in the system; they need time to consider other franchise opportunities and weigh one against the other to come to their own conclusion that one franchise system represents the best value system available to them. There should be no pressure on franchisees to sign-up without a full consultation, and nor should undue time constraints be placed on the prospect. It is accepted that franchisors only run training sessions periodically, or are occasionally lucky enough to have more than one interested party in a particular territory, and whereas advising the prospective franchisee of the training schedule, or the interest shown by others, are perfectly legitimate negotiating tactics, they should never be used as a lever to force an early decision.

Franchisors need to be open about the number of failures they have had in their system. Franchisees can fail, or need to withdraw from the contract for a multitude of reasons, and switched-on prospective franchisees will understand this; in fact, they are more likely to be suspicious of an established system that declares it has never had a failure, rather than one that is open and above board about the quantity of and reasons behind any failures. If a system has attracted failures much in excess of 10 per cent, this is likely to raise concerns with a prospective franchisee, but in the majority of cases it is unlikely that an established and responsible franchise system will attract anything like this number of failures. Whatever reason a franchisee gives for withdrawing from his/her agreement, whether it is supposed ill-health, or possible emigration, the fact is that the franchise has probably not been trading profitably; the only possible exception for a franchisee to withdraw before time and the reason is not financially motivated, is the franchisee's death!

Franchisors recruit their franchisees in many different ways, but the difficulty in attracting suitable candidates should not be underestimated. It is said that there is a noticeable lack of suitable prospects currently looking for franchises to buy, but this is only an excuse that franchisors use because they have been unsuccessful in locating suitable candidates to apply for their offering.

Faced with a lack of recruitment, many franchisors start to look inwards at their existing franchise network and wonder whether some of their better franchisees could be persuaded to become multi-unit operators. The theory being applied here is that the existing franchisees have already committed to the system, so recruitment costs will be lower; they have already been trained, so training costs will be lower; they already have business systems in place to run their existing franchise, so support costs will be lower; as existing operators of a successful outlet, their bankers will be tripping over themselves to lend money for expansion, so there will be fewer financial hoops to jump through; and all in all, the time necessary to get the new outlet operational will be much reduced. Moreover, having a direct connection with fewer multi-unit operators will reduce the need for heavy administrative support at head office. It is clear that the benefits seem to be beyond measure.

However, this concept is laden with problems, because not every system is suited to multi-unit operation. First, the franchise system is geared to a one-to-one relationship with single-unit operators and any variance from the tried and tested structure is likely to bring problems that will need addressing, not least from those hard-working and contented single-unit operators who might start to feel like the poor relation next to the mega-multi-unit operator.

Second, just because a franchisee is extremely successful at running a single-unit operation does not mean that s/he will be as successful running a multi-unit operation. One often hears of companies that have a policy of promoting their best salesmen into sales managerial positions; inevitably they lose good salesmen and gain bad managers. Not everybody is cut out to be a franchising tycoon. It is worth remembering that while multi-unit franchising is technically defined as 'more than one', two is generally easily achievable with a husband-and-wife team, but introduce a third into the equation and the situation changes massively.

Third, the finances for a multi-unit operation cannot usually be scaled up from a single-unit franchise as territorial overlap may be more likely to occur. The multi-unit operator is most likely to want to run the franchises within a relatively small geographical area, to minimize operational over-heads and enable tighter control. Consequently, running two or more units in adjacent territories will undoubtedly involve some leaching of custom from the original unit. Therefore, while running a multi-unit operation is likely to be more profitable, calculating the benefits is not just simply a case of multiplication.

Without a doubt, multi-unit operation can be beneficial for both franchisor and franchisee, but both parties need to approach the concept warily and with their eyes open; it is not simply a quick fix to a poor recruitment campaign.

Generally, however, increasingly the first port of call of any prospective franchisee will be the franchisor's website, so it is imperative that the franchisor ensures that the website is easy to locate, simple to navigate and franchisee-friendly. Many prospects will have looked at other franchise offerings, so franchisors need to ensure that their offering is as attractive or more so than the competition. Remember, the reason why the prospect is still looking is that the competitors have failed to satisfy the prospect's needs and desires, so the savvy franchisor must ensure that his/her offering is more attractive in terms of initial fee, ongoing fees, turnover and profitability than whatever else is being offered.

Prospective franchisees are becoming better informed; many have been to exhibitions, have read books like this one, read the trade press, talked to the national body, got advice from consultants, and attended seminars, so they are likely to be well informed about what is happening in the industry. Franchisors need to be aware of this and market their offering in such a manner as to attract the maximum number of leads.

However, it goes without saying that, while marketing the opportunity needs to be effective, it must also meet strict ethical standards. Obviously, any claims that are made as to potential earnings must be justifiable, and not puffed up to make them more attractive. In the same way, advertisements, websites and editorials must also be truthful, objective and free of ambiguity. In short, the franchisor should not seek to make any assumptions; it is for the prospective franchisee to draw his/her own conclusions based on clear and objective information provided by the franchisor.

Many countries have legislation, such as the American Franchise Disclosure Document, that aims to ensure full and open disclosure of all relevant information a franchisee needs to make his/her objective decision, but other countries (including the UK at the time of writing) do not. The minimum levels of disclosure are usually enshrined in law, or in the guidelines issued by the governing body in a particular country, but it could be suggested that the absolute base minimum level of disclosure should ensure that prospective franchisees have access to the financial details of the franchisor, including a full set of the latest accounts, audited balance sheet, and profit and loss statement, and a statement that the business has not been subject to litigation for debt, save for any legitimate dispute. Disclosure of who is running the company is essential, with full details of names, qualifications, responsibilities and previous experience, plus an individual statement of their trustworthiness and solvency. Full details of the pilot operation should be supplied wherever appropriate.

Precise details of the offering may seem an obvious disclosure to a future franchisee, but clear and unambiguous description of the business format and precisely what is being offered is the minimum that a prospect can expect. Most franchisors also include supplier details and sources should the main suppliers fail, and a host of other information to help the prospective franchisee make their objective decision.

A complete list of other franchisees and their contact details is a must, together with the date that each opened, the number of terminations and the reasons, details of any litigation, and the territory's trading history going back five years (if available).

The financial projections must clearly state the basis of the forecast and that the franchisor cannot warrant the financial performance of any individual franchise unit, but that they advocate that the prospective franchisee takes independent accountancy advice. That being the case, the franchisor should nevertheless show figures of what has been achieved, and what levels of profit might realistically be achieved if certain levels of turnover are reached.

A generic franchise agreement should be included, but before the contract is signed, the franchisor should suggest strongly that the prospective franchisee takes independent legal advice, and this should be done in writing so that a record is kept.

Details of the franchisor's bankers should be given, with the clear invitation that the prospective franchisee takes up references from both the company's bank and its suppliers. Any trade or industry affiliations should also be declared.

Occasionally, franchisors will have separate distribution networks in place which may encroach on the territory of the prospective franchisee, particularly if the franchisor is currently transferring his/her business from a managed to a franchised operation. The franchisor must be open and clear about any other distribution sources that might affect the franchisee's business, and indicate whether the situation will change and over what timescale.

So, the upkeep and development of the network post-launch is a continuing and thoroughly absorbing task for the franchisor. It cannot be rushed and it must be all-embracing. As the network develops, so the responsible and ethical franchisor will start to really appreciate the adage that 'successful franchisees make for successful franchisors', but they will also understand that the opposite is equally true.

Many businesses are built around a marketing mix, or 'the four Ps' as they used to be called: price; product, promotion and place; many franchised businesses can also attribute much of their success to the adherence to a sound marketing policy, so perhaps we ought to generate a similar model for franchising (see Figure 7.3).

Along with 'the nine Ps' of franchising go the 'seven deadly sins' and in all honesty these are not unique to franchising, but apply just as much, if not more, because it is a foolish franchisor or franchisee that does not take heed! Let us start at the beginning:

1 *Avoiding accountability.* 'It's not my fault', or 'My suppliers let me down': do not avoid responsibility by blaming others for something that should have been anticipated. Customers and clients respect somebody who admits to having made a mistake a lot more than they do somebody who avoids responsibility. Remember the proverb that a man who has never made a mistake, has never made anything.

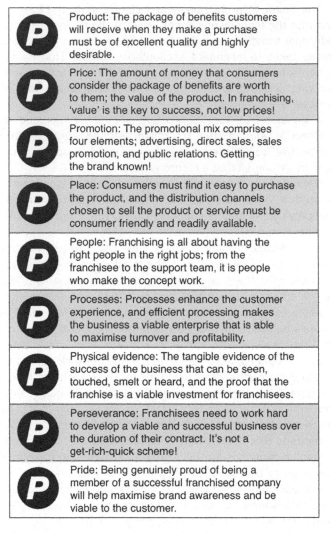

P Product: The package of benefits customers will receive when they make a purchase must be of excellent quality and highly desirable.

P Price: The amount of money that consumers consider the package of benefits are worth to them; the value of the product. In franchising, 'value' is the key to success, not low prices!

P Promotion: The promotional mix comprises four elements; advertising, direct sales, sales promotion, and public relations. Getting the brand known!

P Place: Consumers must find it easy to purchase the product, and the distribution channels chosen to sell the product or service must be consumer friendly and readily available.

P People: Franchising is all about having the right people in the right jobs; from the franchisee to the support team, it is people who make the concept work.

P Processes: Processes enhance the customer experience, and efficient processing makes the business a viable enterprise that is able to maximise turnover and profitability.

P Physical evidence: The tangible evidence of the success of the business that can be seen, touched, smelt or heard, and the proof that the franchise is a viable investment for franchisees.

P Perseverance: Franchisees need to work hard to develop a viable and successful business over the duration of their contract. It's not a get-rich-quick scheme!

P Pride: Being genuinely proud of being a member of a successful franchised company will help maximise brand awareness and be viable to the customer.

Figure 7.3   The nine Ps of franchising

2 *Not understanding your customers' business.* Only a fool thinks that all customers and clients are the same, so the franchisor or franchisee is foolish who expects his/her trading partners to answer the questions that they themselves failed to identify through adequate research.

3 *Building a fence – the 'us and them' scenario.* A business's customers and clients are paying a huge compliment by agreeing to do business with

them; they have a right to expect that their trading partners will help to look after their interests in any and all transactions.

4 *Sell solutions, not products.* Try to imagine a situation where a man walks into *his* local hardware store and buys a 1″ drill. Then ask what the man went into the store to buy. The unwise will assume that the man had obviously wanted to buy a 1″ drill. Wrong! The man really wanted to buy a 1″ hole – the drill was merely the facilitator of what he really wanted.

5 *Never being available.* A business's clients and customers are the lifeblood of its success, and this is more applicable to franchising than to many other businesses. If a customer or a client contacts the franchised business and it takes hours (or even days) for the franchisor/franchisee to return the call, the biggest impression that will be left with the client/customer is that they are so far down the priority list that they do not really matter. If customers or clients really start to believe this, they will go elsewhere and they will be lost for ever. Retention of customers in franchising is one of the first lessons to be learnt, and ignoring them when they want to talk indicates a lesson that has not been learnt.

6 *Help, rather than sell.* Customers and clients are really just looking for help; they are not looking to give the franchisor/franchisee an opportunity of puffing up their company.

7 *Never waste a customer's time.* Sometimes, probably quite often, a company's solution is not the 'right' solution for the client or customer. One of the worst sins a business can commit is to waste the time of a customer or client by trying to sell him or her something they do not need. At best, the business will appear foolish; while at worst they will appear to be con merchants! It is far better to say 'No' than to waste people's time by trying to fit the problem to the product.

WHAT DO YOU THINK?

It is clear from this chapter that franchising a business has to be structured and is not a 'quick fix' to deal with adverse trading conditions; it takes a good deal of time to cultivate a business so that it can be franchised.

Apart from commercial failure, what other potential pitfalls will a business face if it does not follow a structured pathway towards building a franchisable business?

How can business plans ensure that they follow the nine Ps of franchising and avoid the 'seven deadly sins'?

Further reading

Duckett, Brian, *How to Franchise Your Business*, 2nd revd edn (How To Books 2011).

Mendelsohn, Martin, *How to Franchise Your Business*, 6th revd edn (Franchise World 2006).

Sawyer, Clive, *How to Franchise Your Business: The Plain Speaking Guide for Business Owners* (Live It Publishing 2011).

Sun, Shelly, *Grow Smart, Risk Less: A Low-Capital Path to Multiplying Your Business Through Franchising* (Greenleaf Book Group Press 2011).

8 THE STEPS TO BUYING A FRANCHISE

INTRODUCTION AND LEARNING OBJECTIVES

The purpose of this chapter is to give the reader a clear understanding of the processes they would need to go through to identify, negotiate and acquire the ideal franchise for their needs and budget. It also gives the prospective franchisor a clear understanding of the due diligence that prospective franchisees will carry out before committing to a system.
The reader will be able to:

- Identify accurately the process of choosing a franchise opportunity.
- Appreciate that buying a franchise is investing in a whole concept, not just an attractive product range.
- Accept that potential franchisees will need expert advice on the process from a range of professional sources.

Before we become too embroiled in how individual unit operators buy a franchise, there is an area that crosses over the divide between being a franchisor and being a franchisee, and that is the topic of becoming a master franchisee. This will probably not apply to the individual person seeking a 'man-and-van' or single-unit franchise, but will possibly apply to corporations seeking investment in franchising at a corporate level.

Acquiring a master franchise appears to be an attractive opportunity to some businesses seeking to get into franchising – after all, they will be buying into a system that has been trialled and tested in another country. It often appears that they get the advantages of being a 'franchisee' with the safety net of a larger corporation behind them, while retaining the flexibility and independence of being a franchisor. To them, the only disadvantage is that they have to pay the franchisor a percentage of the fees paid by the individual unit franchises, sometimes as much as 20 per cent.

However, before I am accused of digression, the reader who is interested in buying a master franchise should read Chapter 11 of this book, which will give them an understanding of the benefits of taking on a master franchise.

So, let us get back to buying a franchise. One of the vexing questions that is constantly asked by prospective franchisees is 'Am I too young?' or sometimes people say 'Surely I am too old?' The answer is typically that there is no 'right' age for buying a franchise; when the individual is ready to take on a franchise commitment, that is the 'right' age, and for some this may occur on graduation from university, and for others in the twilight of their careers.

However, it may be presumed that, like most business opportunities, having the maximum time to devote to the business and without the worry of the business being a 'success-or-bust' operation, would probably be the best time to consider a franchise. Often this is during the younger years, when one's drive and energy means that 100 per cent of effort can be devoted to the success of the business, and the franchisee is not burdened with the costs of a mortgage, a ton of hire-purchase, children's school fees, and all the other financial encumbrances of successful employment in the corporate world; because with these burdens come responsibilities that will often divert the focus away from the successful running of the business.

With more and more franchises focusing on the younger generation, either through fashion or lifestyle, if the franchisee is also of a younger age, s/he is able to connect better with the customer base. Of course, if the franchise is selling financial products such as insurance or mortgages, or preparing the last wills and testaments of clients, then being older may be an advantage because, for some reason, age does rather project sincere and mature responsibility.

Of course, the younger the prospective franchisee, the less likely they are to attract substantial financial investment, especially as the previously mentioned financial burdens often provide the security that financiers seek when approving business lending. However, this can be less of a problem and more of a challenge as there are, in most areas, specific funds available for young entrepreneurs setting up in business for the first time.

This discussion is not intended to dissuade older franchisees from beginning a second career in franchising, but more to reassure younger prospects that their age is not a barrier. Indeed, there are many retirees who, when tired of playing golf on a daily basis and missing the cut-and-thrust of their previous business life, take on a franchise to re-establish a purpose in their life.

So, to reaffirm the earlier statement, when the individual is ready to take on a franchise commitment, then that is the 'right' age to become a franchisee. In any case, and irrespective of age, before a potential franchisee even gets to the stage of being a *prospective* franchisee, some basic steps have to be taken, and for this very first step in the process, and before

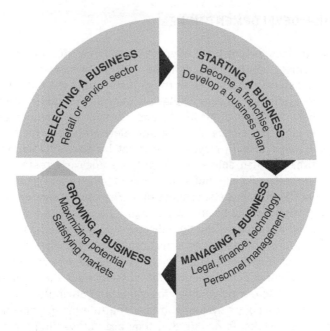

Figure 8.1 The franchise development model

elevation to the dizzy heights of becoming a full-blown prospect, we shall call candidates pre-prospective franchisees.

In Figure 8.1, an attempt has been made to identify the four stages that most franchisees go through. These will be expanded upon in the following pages. The arrow from 'Growing a Business' to 'Selecting a Business' completes the circle and is specifically not as dark as the arrows between the other quarters. The dark arrows denote stages that franchisees must pass through on their road to success; when they reach the 'growth' stage, some franchisees start to want more – they have a successful business that they have enjoyed developing and now want expand it. Some franchisees will take on another franchise from the same brand, widening their exposure in the brand, while other franchisees will take on another franchise in a totally unrelated field (they are likely to be prevented from taking on another franchise in the same industry as their original franchise by their franchise agreement), thereby deepening their involvement in franchising. Many will be happy with their existing business and will not have the ambition to widen or deepen their business; this is why one lighter arrow, as this stage is an optional one, but if the franchisee does decide to expand his/her business in this manner, the process will start all over again.

Of course, franchisors like franchisees to buy more areas as their recruitment costs are reduced; often they pass on some of these savings to the franchisee in the form of a discounted second area purchase.

FRANCHISE DEVELOPMENT MODEL

Nevertheless, before the reader gets too committed to the idea of owning a franchise, one thing needs to be emphasized most clearly: *franchising does not suit everybody*! There, the genie is out of the bottle!

Successful franchisees display peculiar and unique characteristics, and the character traits of the ideal franchisee are summed up as follows.

The ideal franchisee must be intensely ambitious for him/herself, but equally a good team player; s/he must be able to work on his/her own initiative, but also able to work within some very restrictive rules; they must be self-sufficient, but also prepared to be reliant on others. For a pre-prospective franchisee to assume that s/he can mould him/herself to meet these criteria would be an unwise idea.

Buying a franchise and then discovering that one has made the wrong decision is a waste of time, effort, energy and money for both the franchisee and franchisor, which is why franchisors take so much time and trouble to ensure that potential franchisees have the right skills for their business. Discovering whether the skills and attributes exist to be able to operate in anybody's system is a task that the pre-prospective franchisee should undertake, to ensure that they are not wasting their resources by chasing an unrealistic pipe dream.

However, self-objectivity is not a talent with which many are blessed. Asking most people to answer a questionnaire about themselves truthfully is typically as unrealistic as expecting an alcoholic not to crave a drink! A dispassionate and totally impartial approach is needed, and in all honesty this is why the most successful franchisees have begun their careers by taking as much advice from as many people as possible. Obviously, one could immediately recommend a visit to one of the numerous franchise consultants, but at the initial stages of the fact-finding mission, the pre-prospective franchisee would probably be left wondering whether the consultant was working for them or their stable of franchisors, and they would probably be justified in their confusion.

> *Self-objectivity is a skill that few possess, but before embarking on buying a franchise, the prospective franchisee needs to be honestly self-objective!*

The first step in the journey to discover whether franchising is right for the pre-prospective franchisee is to carry out a personal skills or traits audit: write down in the form of a list those skills that have been developed over the years. Do not just spotlight the experience that has been gained, but rather concentrate on the skills that have emerged from the experiences that have been encountered.

Some might argue that it would be unfair to offer a list of skills that are considered desirable by successful franchisors, as the temptation for the

F Flexibility

R Responsible & positive attitude

A Ability to manage multiple priorities

N Need to succeed

C Creative problem solving

H High energy levels

I In no doubt about personal abilities

S Strong people skills

E Eager to learn

Figure 8.2 The franchisee skills acronym

reader would be to look at the list and then identify areas of their own experience that come close to those desirable talents and in some way try to shoehorn their own personalities into becoming the 'ideal' candidate. Such an exercise would be wholly unproductive, as manipulation of the truth seldom leads to a satisfactory conclusion; at best it could lead to an unsatisfactory career change, and at worst to financial ruin.

Nevertheless, there are certain traits that successful franchisors seek in their prospective franchisees, and these can be summarized in the simple acronym shown in Figure 8.2.

Sadly, there are many who believe that running a successful franchise requires some kind of supernatural ability, but in reality all that most franchisors seek is a degree of level-headedness and the desire to succeed. Responsible franchisors will teach their franchisees all about their industry and mentor their franchisees on how to run successful franchised businesses, both before they open the doors to their outlets and continually throughout the term of their agreement.

Next would be an appointment with the local bank manager, assuming that in these days of computerized points-based assessment such people still exist, and ask whether, if one were to consider buying into a franchise network, would the bank be prepared to lend a percentage of the buy-in fee.

Of course, the franchise division of the bank would need to know more details, not least of which being the system that one is contemplating, but what the pre-prospective franchisee is trying to ascertain is whether the bank considers they are a sufficiently good enough risk to consider funding a franchise purchase.

Remember that bank managers are unemotional; they look at opportunities dispassionately; after all, their sole purpose in life is to lend money against minimal risk. If a banker suggests that the bank would consider lending the franchisee enough money to buy into a franchise system, then it could be seen as a pretty fair indicator that others will come to the conclusion that the prospect has what it takes to run a successful franchise. Of course, if the bank manager uses phrases such as 'Hell will freeze over before I give you a loan!', or falls off his chair clutching his sides in merriment, that also might give you a pretty clear indication as to the way he is thinking!

Having received a positive response from the bank, the pre-prospective franchisee should consider three things about themselves, and answer these questions truthfully:

1   Am I the sort of person who spends my time trying to find alternative ways of doing things?
2   Do I like doing things by myself and am frustrated by having to work in a team?
3   Am I the sort of person who enjoys keeping myself to myself and am not much interested in the business of others?

These are the three fundamental questions that pre-prospective franchisees should ask themselves, and should they find that they give a positive response to any of these questions, perhaps franchising would be an unsuitable career choice. This constant self-questioning may seem excessive, but unless the prospective franchisee is committed 100 per cent to franchising and the prospect of running this type of business, then what might have been the start of something beautiful will wither and perish like diseased fruit!

Whatever way that pre-prospective franchisees approach franchising, the fundamental philosophy that should always underpin their considerations is that they will have to adapt to a franchise system – the franchise system is *not* going to adapt to them. The rigidity of franchising is one of the aspects that makes the model unique, and franchisors are petrified of recruiting a franchisee who is always looking to re-invent the wheel; this is why most franchisors, if they are truthful, would admit to not seeking 'entrepreneurs', but are more interested in recruiting able candidates who are willing to follow the system to the letter, but are still keen to run their own business. Former military personnel have some of the right characteristics for franchising; they are used to following orders unquestioningly!

CASE STUDY 8.1

Transition: from military service to civilian life

" *Franchising is a bright spot for veterans: although the financial crisis continues to darken the horizon of the US economy, there is one bright spot: the franchising industry, poised to lead the way out of the downturn.*

Headlines following President Barack Obama's inauguration noted his plans to seek civilian and military officials' opinions about drawing combat forces out of Iraq. How could such plans factor into the US economy and franchising? Franchising has typically withstood past economic downturns. Those whose jobs were terminated, downsized or sought other avenues to build wealth turned to well-recognized franchised brands to fuel their entrepreneurial dreams.

Today, although the recession is often referred to as the most serious the United States has experienced in decades, franchising remains a viable option for those wishing to control their destinies. As thousands of military veterans return from Iraq and other countries to an environment of fewer job opportunities, franchising, with its training, brand recognition and efficient business structure, provides an attractive way to build a career as a small-business owner.

Franchising World, March 2009 © International Franchise Association

Assuming that the pre-prospective franchisees have undertaken a period of self-reflection and analysed truthfully the reasons why they want to buy a franchise, they can now consider themselves to be fully-fledged 'prospective franchisees'; they have survived the rite of initiation and are on the first step of finding a franchise system to buy into.

TYPES OF FRANCHISES

Franchising falls into five main sectors, and it is wise to consider within which of the sectors one feels most comfortable operating. The sectors are:

- *Retail franchise*
  Typically, this type of franchise will be situated in a retail premises; it will sell products or services at times when retailers usually open for business to 'walk-in' retail customers. Because this business is wholly dependent on the premises where the business is located, the choice of

location is critical, as (generally speaking) the majority of customers will be passers-by. To succeed, the franchisee may well need to source High Street premises or a good position in a shopping centre, and because the business is selling products or services to an end user, it is critical to ensure that there is a market for these goods or services in the chosen location. The franchise will be operated during retail hours, which may include weekends and involve long working days. The franchisee will need to employ and manage staff, and deal with the general public, so good interpersonal skills are highly desirable.

• *Management franchise*
 In this sector of the industry, the franchise operator will be using skills s/he has acquired to develop the business and to manage the staff whose task it is to carry out the work of the business. While this type of franchise will also require premises, it is far more likely that the franchisee will be office based rather than operating from a retail outlet. It is also more probable that the business will be focused towards business-to-business (B2B) operations, rather than retail sales. These premises need not be located in high-cost, centralized areas. As the franchise will be marketing a product or a service, the franchisee will usually be required to work at and manage the franchise during regular office hours; this also means that they will need to employ and manage skilled staff and carry out a fair amount of administrative work in the provision of the product or service. Though usually dealing with business clients, there is still a likelihood that, for a small percentage of the time, the franchisee will be working with the general public, so good interpersonal skills are definitely required, especially as it is very likely that the franchisee will need to operate and manage the business in person.

• *Manual single operator franchise, sometimes called a 'Job franchise'*
 The franchisee will usually be directly employed in working at the job or service that the franchise provides. This will often take the form of a trade or skill that involves supplying, selling and/or delivering a product or service. The franchise could potentially be home-based, mobile from a van, or perhaps even requiring small commercial premises. To make this type of franchise a success, the franchisee will need to learn the franchise's skill or trade, as this type of franchise may involve selling a product or a service to the franchise's clients. Generally speaking franchisees will initially operate the franchise by themselves, but as the business grows and develops, may employ staff. It is typically the responsibility of the franchisee to promote the franchise in the local area in order to generate business and, depending on the product or service, the franchisee may find that s/he has to do business with the general public as well as commercial clients. As most of the appointments or schedules are organized via the telephone, it is useful for the

franchisee to have a pleasant but firm telephone manner. In most cases, this type of franchise will be mobile-based, quite often in a van that has been fitted out by the franchisor with all the necessary tools or products to be successful. Franchisees will need to have good administrative skills, as typically they will be responsible for handling much of the administration of the franchise themselves, in their van, at home or in their small office. Increasingly, especially in the case of a franchise involving physical work, and considering health and safety issues, a uniform is likely to be supplied, and the franchisee will be expected to wear this and adhere to the franchisor's dress code. One of the big advantages to this type of franchise is that it invariably has flexible working hours.

- *Executive single operator franchise, sometimes called a 'white-collar job franchise'*
  Again, the franchisee typically will be working directly in doing the actual job of the franchise, which will usually take the form of a trade or profession supplying, selling and delivering products or services to commercial clients or the general public. This type of franchise could be home-based, mobile or perhaps requiring small commercial office premises, but the difference from the previous sector is that this type of work can be classed as 'executive'. There are similarities with the Manual single operator franchise inasmuch as the franchisee will still need to learn fully and understand the business, which may be a trade but is usually a service. Initially, the franchisee will generally be an independent operator, but may subsequently employ staff as the business grows and develops. It will typically be the franchisee's responsibility to market the franchise locally in order to generate business, but in this case it is more likely that the franchisee will be dealing mainly with businesses, although occasionally they may have to deal with the general public, so a good telephone manner is very important. Usually, this type of franchise will be mobile-based and the franchisee might operate from either his/her own home or from small business premises. Typically, the franchise will operate during office hours only.

- *Investment franchise*
  For those prospective franchisees who have access to large amounts of capital, the solution could be an Investment franchise. In this type of franchise, the franchisee invests a substantial amount of money in the business, which may be (for example) a hotel, but generally the franchisee will not personally work directly in the business, but will either employ a management team to operate the franchise, or lease the business to the franchise operator. Perhaps this type of franchise would best suit a person who has had experience in managing professional teams and has a large amount of available capital, but who has

interests apart from the day-to-day running of a business. Executive retirees often find this type of franchise attractive.

THE SIX SEGMENTS OF FRANCHISING

Having ascertained the level of involvement and in what area the prospective franchisee would feel most comfortable working, the next stage is to decide the industry that would appeal the most. Generally, the main industry categories centre on the 'Big Six', which are the following:

- Retailing, which may cover such businesses as Supermarkets, Convenience stores, General stores, Department stores, Clothing outlets, Kitchen and Bathroom suppliers, Electrical goods stores, Shoe and Accessory shops, and Furniture shops.
- Property Services, which might include Estate agency, Commercial and Domestic cleaning, Property refurbishment and maintenance, Interior design and decoration, Garden and landscaping, and Emergency and repair services.
- Personal Services, incorporating Fitness and Weight, Hair and Beauty, Education and Care, Mobile and Home, Holiday and Travel, Distribution, and Computer and Telephone supplies and service.
- Business and Communication Services, featuring Goods and Consumables, Professional and Financial, Employment and Training, Print, Equipment Repair and Maintenance, IT and Communication, and Design and Signs.
- Hotel and Catering, where one might find Hotels, Bars and Pubs, Restaurants, Mobile catering, Fast food, and Commercial and Industrial catering.
- Transport and Vehicle Services, taking in Car and Driver hire, Parcel and Courier services, and Vehicle Repair and Maintenance.

These six main segments of the industry, with the examples that have been given, show clearly that the franchise industry is both wide and diverse. Prospective franchisees could buy businesses as wide-ranging as mowing lawns to arranging business finance, or from running a hotel to washing cars – the list is potentially endless, so it seems quite logical that new franchisees would seek to reduce their options to those businesses that best suit their interests, their capabilities and their skills. Logical it may seem, but that is not the way that many franchisees come to choose the business that they buy; a huge number buy their businesses because of the potential return on their investment. Naturally, everybody who buys a franchise is seeking to make money, and getting a good return on one's investment is a justifiable and perfectly acceptable objective, but to buy a business just because it offers the best possible financial return is a recipe for disaster.

First, ask why this franchise is offering the opportunity of making a better return on your investment than others that have been under consideration. Is it because the franchise is less well established than others, and the franchisor is trying to tempt with the promise of greater potential wealth? Or perhaps the franchisor has cut his/her margins as s/he is finding it difficult to recruit new franchisees; why might that be?

When a franchise is sold, both the franchisor and franchisee are entering a contractual obligation that may last for five, ten or more years, so while making a healthy return on one's investment is important, so is job satisfaction. Whatever a prospective franchisee commits to is going to occupy up to 25 per cent of his/her entire working life, so you need to be pretty certain that you are going to enjoy the business that you join. In franchising, job satisfaction ranks as highly, if not higher, than getting a good return on the capital invested, using the concept that somebody who enjoys what they are doing does it better. While making money may balance the fact that you are doing a job that you hate, this will only be the case in the short term, and eventually the dislike of the task will overcome any amount of money you might be making and the business starts to become unproductive.

> *Franchising is a long-term commitment, and prospective franchisees need to assess whether they have the stamina to sustain such a long-term relationship.*

Though franchising is renowned as a business that takes people from a wealth of different backgrounds and trains them into the way of the system, a quick glance at the 'big six' categories above will show the prospective franchisee that the majority fall within the service sector. This is because franchising is really a tool of the service industry. It may be *used* by the manufacturing industry to aid the marketing of products, but it is very difficult to build a franchise around the skill of manufacturing. Consequently, most of the businesses that the prospective franchisee will consider will have a greater or lesser element of dealing with customers; therefore a skill that franchisee's will find invaluable is the ability to get on with others and to have a likeable personality. Franchising is about service, and good, friendly service brings greater rewards as the franchise develops; marketers often say it costs more to make the first sale and that each repeat sale is free of marketing cost absorption – giving good service and getting repeat business is the key to successful franchising.

We saw above that, on the one hand, franchisors prefer to take people with no experience in the industry, but we also saw that, if one has acquired certain business skills, one will have an advantage over a completely raw recruit. This is one of the paradoxes of franchising, just how much 'skill' gives a prospective franchisee an advantage, and how much is a disadvantage? Even more worrying is that there is no correct answer and no formula to work out the paradox. The main reason why franchisors like to take on people with no previous experience is that these people come without preconceptions and bring a totally fresh mind to the franchise; on the other hand, 'experienced' people may tend to try to tell the franchisor how best to run his/her business.

Nevertheless there are exceptions, and a good example of this in the UK is a substantial franchise that specializes in the rental property market by offering landlords and letting agents regular safety inspections and repair of gas boilers, central heating systems and domestic electrical wiring checks on their rental properties, because UK law states that rented properties must have these checks on an annual basis. The law also states that the only people legally able to offer these services have to be trained by an official body and have certain certificates of competence, so a prerequisite of anybody buying a franchise from this franchisor is that they *must* have the required level of knowledge and competence, and be suitably certificated.

These specialist franchises are, however, the exception rather than the rule, and it is true that generally franchisors prefer prospective franchisees to come to their industry without any prior knowledge.

However, that does not mean that the franchisor is willing to take just anybody, and the real differentiating factor to the franchisor is whether the prospective franchisee has 'transferable skills', such as good administrative ability, proficiency with computers, or a clean driver's licence. Therefore, the paradox may be resolved by the notion that, whereas franchisors want people with no industry experience, they also want people with good basic business skills and acumen.

This can be refined further by saying that, if a prospective franchisee has previous sales and marketing skills, s/he should consider a franchise where these skills can best be utilized; if the prospective franchisee enjoys do-it-yourself (DIY), s/he might enjoy a more practical franchise such as kitchen fitting; if the prospect likes working out of doors, s/he may enjoy a franchise that takes on the mowing of people's lawns; or, if the prospective franchisee is a dog lover, s/he might like to take one of the numerous canine-oriented franchises. These transferable skills are invaluable to a franchisor and really do give a prospective franchisee a competitive advantage over the numerous other applicants.

There is, however, one note of caution that needs to be mentioned. There is a suggestion that entrepreneurs could make a very successful business out of what they enjoy doing in their spare time, and that there is the case of an Estonian connoisseur who has a passion for old British sports cars. Finding it difficult to find spares for his collection of MGs, Triumphs and Jaguars, he took to importing scrap cars and breaking them for spares. This grew into a very healthy business, importing old cars, breaking them, testing the spares and then selling them over the Internet throughout Europe to other aficionados of classic British sports cars. Now he drives a new Mercedes-Benz saloon, not a classic British sports car, because his sideline which developed into a job drove away his affection for his hobby.

The cautionary note, therefore, is, if you enjoy a bit of DIY, how would you really feel if it were to become your job? Is it worth risking losing something you really enjoy to do as a relaxing pastime to it becoming your main source of income. To pursue this theme a little further, remember as well that whatever franchise the prospective franchisee is considering, it has to generate enough income to provide for the franchisee's family – job satisfaction is great, but make a living first!

Perhaps, if the prospective franchisee is considering a career move away from corporate employment to self-employment, then a business-to-business (B2B) franchise may provide the ideal compromise. The B2B franchise can fit into any of the 'big six' franchise groupings, and as such might even extend the groupings to seven.

Business-to-business franchises provide much needed services to other small businesses, saving them time and money and improving their efficiency; the franchised business succeeds as a result of its customers' businesses succeeding.

The principal benefit of joining a B2B business is that there are many franchise opportunities to consider. There are franchises supplying goods, such as ink-jet supplies and refills, photocopiers and office machinery and their associated consumables, office supplies, corporate workwear, business signs and much more. From the service angle, one can find B2B franchises providing many and varied services to small businesses, ranging from postage and courier services, specialist business consulting, staffing and personnel recruitment, IT support, cleaning, tax accountancy and marketing.

Business in the twenty-first century lives in an adhocracy. In the none-too-distant past, it was not unusual for even relatively small businesses to employ a corporate solicitor, or an accountant on the board of directors, to handle any legal or accountancy difficulties, but in the lean, mean and challenging times in which we live, it is now far more likely that firms will outsource specialist expertise. Not only is outsourcing considerably less expensive than employing the specialist internally, but it enables businesses to focus on their core competencies while letting outside service providers handle the more mundane aspects of the business. Consequently, B2B franchising is a rapidly developing sector of the market.

Let us consider the many advantages of running a B2B franchise. The greatest advantage is that, typically, the business operates at the same times as the clients' businesses – generally normal business hours, Mondays to Fridays. Having conventional set working hours is a great advantage, especially to the franchisee who is balancing his/her working time with family commitments; seldom does a client ring the franchisee in the wee small hours of the morning because he has noticed a discrepancy in his tax return. When comparing the advantages of running a business that conforms to a 'normal' business week with one where there is a 24-hour call-out, or a retail or fast-food franchise that could be open for up to twenty-four hours a day, seven days a week, fifty-two weeks of the year, there are undoubtedly massive advantages in considering B2B franchising as an option – not an *easy* option, but a more convenient one.

Let us next consider the skills-set involved in B2B franchising. Many people coming into franchising are moving into it from the corporate world, and a major advantage of B2B franchising is that many of the skills that have been learnt throughout the prospective franchisee's career are transferable to a B2B franchise. As previously mentioned, the franchisee will be visiting other businesses and offering them the goods, services or skills they need to run their companies, so, irrespective of the industry, any experience gained in sales or marketing will be a valuable asset in B2B franchising.

Many B2B franchises, especially in the service sector, can be run from a home office, which reduces the operating cost of the franchise substan-tially, as there will be no massive property overheads. Of course, some B2B franchises will need a commercial base, but generally speaking this does not have to be in premium-cost premises; even businesses such as office machinery supplies or ink-jet refilling seldom need to be on the 'High Street', as customers tend to be willing to travel to your premises. By reducing or eliminating the premises overhead, a greater amount of the franchise's resources can be allocated to marketing and offering better value for money.

Without a doubt, B2B franchising is one of the most rapidly expanding sectors of the industry, and it offers franchisees a relatively high-demand but low-cost business opportunity within the supportive framework of a franchise system.

As noted previously, there are hundreds, if not thousands, of franchise opportunities available on the market, so it should not be too difficult to find one that is perfect for your particular talents, and that will meet the job satisfaction aspect as well as providing a healthy living. The task that faces the prospective franchisee is taking this wealth of opportunity and filtering it down to a few likely possibilities.

The wise prospective franchisee might do well by first contacting his/her national franchise organization (a list of all the national franchising coun-cils that are members of the World Franchise Council, and their website details, can be found in Appendix 4 at the back of this book) and ask for a list of members. At least the prospective franchisee will know that these companies have agreed to a voluntary or compulsory ethical code, and it is pretty certain that these companies represent the more responsible members of the profession in each country. There are no cast iron guarantees of success, of course, but at least the prospective franchisee will understand that the risk is likely to be reduced by approaching an affiliated member.

Very often the prospective franchisee will discover that these professional bodies run training courses to help franchisees adapt to the concept of franchising, or perhaps run exhibitions where the prospective franchisee can meet responsible franchisors in a structured setting.

Beginning the filtration process, the prospective franchisee may well already have discounted certain types of business, and adding to these those franchisors who choose not to be members of a trade association will probably reduce the number of options quite considerably. However, there are likely to be more on the list of filtered prospect franchises than the prospective franchisee is able to handle, so more sifting is needed.

The next level of filtering will probably be financial: the recognition of value for money, and the potential return on the investment. Accepting the fact that the franchisor has invested considerable amounts of capital in developing the system, s/he will be seeking to recover this in two main ways: first, by demanding an initial fee; and second by charging ongoing fees throughout the term of the franchise agreement. Some franchisors load the initial fee to try to filter out the prospective franchisees who have limited funds available, and then reduce the ongoing fees to compensate, while others seek to attract the less flush prospect by offering a low buy-in, but the monthly ongoing charges are quite high. Large and well-known brands are in a position to charge a premium rate for the initial investment and still charge substantial ongoing fees. The prospective franchisee has to cut through the marketing hype and determine which businesses offer the best value for money, that they are also able to afford.

Chapter 9 considers franchise finances, but as a foretaste, the affordability of a franchise is based on the net worth of the franchisee. Net worth is the difference between what is owned and what is owed, and it is hoped that when the prospective franchisee adds up his/her assets and deducts the liabilities, s/he will still be in positive territory! When considering the prospective franchisee for a loan to cover a large percentage of the initial fee, banks will often use this 'net worth' figure when calculating risk. Therefore, it is extremely important in the financial deliberations, as the amount of money a prospective franchisee can borrow added to the amount of liquid cash s/he can afford to invest will determine the level of initial fee that can be considered. Even though a well-known global fast-food brand might be considered as a licence to print money, banks will not provide the wherewithal for the high cost of buy-in if the figures do not add up.

The prospective franchisee will now be at the stage where s/he has looked at what is available, identified the business area in which s/he wishes to work, and has found a selection of franchisors who have franchises available. S/he will have calculated which of the offerings are within his/her price range and which represent good value for money. Probably, by this stage, the prospective franchisee will have reduced his/her potential targets from the many hundreds of available franchises to a shortlist of something in the region of ten to twenty.

The next stage of the whittling-down process will probably involve the prospective franchisee in a bit of detailed research, perhaps applying for and reading the prospectuses of the shortlisted companies. From examining the information sent by the franchisor, the prospective franchisee can easily start to ask some pertinent questions. A good place to start would be with the question, 'Do I think the product/service is a winner?', or at least 'Would I buy the product or use the service?' Look at the offering carefully; identify the precise features and benefits that are unique to that particular product; and try to see the potential market over the five or ten years that one will be committed to spend selling the product or service. It has already been said that many people consider the fast-food industry to be a good money-spinner and a reasonable investment, but will that range of high-saturated-fat hamburgers still be a viable proposition in the more health conscious upcoming years? And is the macrobiotic, vegan, healthy tofu burger franchise just a passing fad that will go out of fashion in the next couple of years as customers eschew healthy food and go back to food that tastes of something? What it boils down to is whether the prospective franchisee feels sufficiently confident about the products to be associated with them over the duration of the agreement. Any the franchisee feels doubtful about should be struck from the shortlist.

The next set of criteria might be more company focused. How long has the business been established? How many active franchises are in operation? Is their Franchise Development Manager perhaps being just a bit too pushy? What is the preliminary training like, and how long does it last? How comprehensive is the continuing support package? Many potential franchises will fall by the wayside at this stage; something will just not seem right with some franchisors, something will seem just that little bit too unbelievably good!

It is true to say that, as with most businesses, the skill of the franchisor significantly reduces the risk to the prospective franchisee. Figure 8.3 identifies the risk factors at various phases of the business's development.

Most prospective franchisees will find themselves competing for opportunities to find franchisors in the 'growth phase' or the 'maturing phase', but very few will be brave enough to enter at the 'immature phase', or have the resources or necessary experience attractive to franchisors in the 'seniority' phase. Therefore. accepting that there is likely to be a

RISK	NUMBER OF FRANCHISES	COMMENTS
High	**1–10**	*Immature phase* The franchisor has expended large amounts of capital and is seeking ways of starting a revenue stream. Inexperienced at recruiting franchisees and is really in the post-pilot phase, where ideas may still change. Not for the faint-hearted!
	11–50	*The growth phase* Like a teenager, the franchisor is developing growing pains; half of the first ten franchises are not performing satisfactorily and he is having to spend a disproportionate amount of time getting them to viability. Stresses and strains are starting to be seen, but the organizational structure should be secure. Just be wary that rapid growth does not overstretch the franchisor's resources.
	51–99	*The maturing phase* In this stage the franchisor should be maturing like fine wine. Plans are being laid for substantial growth, but it is also a time for reflection; is everything going to plan? Some of the existing franchisees will have been with the business for a few years and will be able to give a fair appraisal of the franchisor's strengths and weaknesses.
Low	**100+**	*The seniority phase* Just because seniority has set in does not mean the franchisor is feeble; indeed they are more nimble and able to respond to change in the marketplace quickly and efficiently. The franchisor will have substantial resources to support the franchise network but will also be at the stage where they can be even more choosy about who they recruit.

Figure 8.3 The 'risk factor' table

moderate risk in the investment, the wise prospective franchisee would do well to quiz their target franchisors about their businesses. I am not going to give the reader a list of prescriptive questions they should ask, as different markets will have differing factors that are important, and the local trade association will have a plethora of questionnaires that prospective franchisees can access that are region specific. However, we shall consider the basic questions that just about any franchisee will want to ask anywhere in the world, focusing on the following suggested topics:

* The business background and experience of the directors and officers of the franchisor. This should give the prospective franchisee a clear understanding of the depth of knowledge of both franchising and the particular industry that the company has at its disposal. Other, more personal questions should seek to confirm that the directors are of sound character and have not been subject to embarrassing events in either their business or personal lives.
* How the business has developed. The prospective franchisee will then be able to judge for him/herself whether the franchisor has developed the business with due care and attention to detail, and whether the business has progressed responsibly into franchising. Other questions about the pilot operation and the level of personal investment by the directors will underpin the judgement as to how well the business has been run.
* The plans for the future. How rapidly a company plans to expand will reinforce the opinion of the prospective franchisee as to whether the franchise is moving too quickly, too slowly, or at the right speed. Ask how franchisees are recruited, and the procedures involved in approving or rejecting their applications. Ask about training and how that prepares franchisees to be successful within the franchise. How many franchisees are outperforming the 'average' income figure that the prospective franchisee has probably been given?
* The solvency of the business. The prospective franchisee will expect to see audited accounts, but should also seek to gain assurances that the financial condition of the franchisor has not weakened since the accounts were drawn up; if the franchisor is cagey about answering financial questions, ferret further or walk away with ever-increasing speed!
* Credibility. Seek details of membership of trade associations, and check to make sure that membership is not obtained simply by paying a fee. Membership of organizations that are affiliated into the World Franchise Council do not issue membership without careful checks having been made, and membership of these bodies should reassure the prospective franchisee that the business opportunity is at least credible and viable.
* References. Ask for two trade and two financial (not bank) references, plus details of the franchisor's bankers so that references can be obtained. Assuming that the franchisor does not provide details of his golfing partners as referees, these references should give the prospective franchisee an overview of the way that the franchisor does business, and the esteem within which s/he is held by his/her peers.

- Existing franchisees. No responsible franchisor will ever give a prospective franchisee an 'edited' list of approachable franchisees. Most trade associations would consider a franchisor who gives out a list of 'tame' franchisees to prospective franchisees would be acting unethically, so demand, and expect to receive, a full list of those people who already run one of the franchisor's franchises, and select those who operate their businesses in similar circumstances to the prospective franchisee to be approached for a satisfaction reference. Listen to what the existing franchisee says about the franchisor, but also listen to what is *not* being said; more can often be learnt by what is *not* said than by what is!

The prospective franchisee should now have a pretty good idea about the standing of the franchisor, so the next step is to scrutinize the various business proposals the shortlisted franchisors are recommending. Offers that come from different companies, even in the same industry, are likely to be vastly different, but even though it may be a game of 'swings-and-roundabouts', with nothing much to choose between some of the franchisors, *how* the proposal is structured may make a whole world of difference!

Prospective franchisees can expect their target franchisors to have created a package that in the eyes of the franchisor represents the best opportunity for a new franchisee to begin operations successfully, and this is typically the case. But could the franchisor have done it better? Some of the best people to ask whether the overall package lived up to expectations are the franchisees, and they will usually also be only too willing to suggest ways that the franchisor might modify his/her offering to make it better. Of course, these opinions are subjective, and the franchisor has to be objective: what will work for one franchisee in Cornwall might not work as well for a franchisee in Scotland, and the franchisor has to develop a system that works well for all the franchisees.

> Good training programmes do not focus only on the functionality of the business, but will go into much greater depth, thus providing a true understanding.

Possibly one of the critical essentials of the franchisor's offering often overlooked by potential franchisees is that of training; perhaps 'overlooked' is too strong a word, but there does seem to be a presumption that franchisors will provide sufficient training to run a franchise profitably, and that could be a dangerous supposition.

Quality training programmes will not just cover the service or product, but be much more detailed and will guide prospective franchisees in all aspects of running their business, from the initial set-up, through staff management, marketing, company procedures and reporting, and much more. Without doubt, the easiest way of determining the depth and extent of the franchisor's training programme is to talk with existing franchisees. Did they feel that the training programme prepared them for running the franchise, and what did they think were the strong and weak points? Do not be afraid to ask whether the existing franchisees felt totally prepared for the first day of trading, and how much support was offered in the embryonic stage of the business.

Remember, though, that the franchisor's business has developed since many of the existing franchisees attended their basic training courses, so what they report as weak points may already have been rectified. Equally, the training course that was good when the franchisor started trading may now be obsolete and unfit for purpose. Consequently, it is wise to discuss the training programme with franchisees who have been around for a while, but also with new franchisees that have been trained more recently. By carrying out this in-depth research, prospective franchisees will gain a more complete picture of the training practices of the franchisor.

It is also worth remembering that training does not stop with the initial training; it needs to be ongoing, so the research carried out by a prospective franchisee with existing operators should also ask questions about the level of continuing training offered. Is there a training manual, and if so, when was it last updated? How often do the franchisees receive emailed training updates, or attend supplementary training sessions? How is training provided for new procedures?

Buying into a franchise system costs a substantial amount of money, and the commitment to the ongoing fees adds to this investment. Potential franchisees need to be assured that they will be trained adequately enough to be a success in the business and that, as their business develops over the term of the agreement, the training will allow them to cope with expansion. Therefore, devoting time and thought to the appraisal of a franchisor's training procedures will reap greater rewards in the future as it helps the potential franchisee to decide whether the franchise opportunity is viable or not.

Looking at the offering further, prospective franchisees will quickly identify that some franchisors will work with them to acquire premises and prepare them for opening; while others will provide a 'turnkey' service. This turnkey operation is especially relevant for van-based franchises: the franchisee arrives for training and after successful completion s/he is handed the key to his/her fully kitted-out vehicle. With retail franchises, the franchisee usually attends training and on completion his/her fully-equipped shop is awaiting his/her arrival. Whichever way the franchisor chooses to operate, the franchisee will be responsible for the cost of the shop fitting and stocking, or vehicle stock, either as part of the 'buy-in' cost or as a separate stock item. Equally, whichever way the franchisor chooses to operate, the franchisee should be able to count on the franchisor offering a considerable amount of support as s/he develops the business. The level of support offered and the method of acquiring premises should be key questions for a prospective franchisee.

It is hoped that the prospective franchisee's accountant, lawyer and franchise adviser will be made aware of the target franchise's offering, and will be able to suggest precise and pointed questions that the prospective franchisee can ask of the target franchisor. The sort of information a wise franchisee will be seeking in relation to the franchise offering will generally relate to the following subject areas:

- *Financial matters*. Precisely how much is it going to cost to set up a franchise with a particular company? (Many franchisors are keen to promote a headline 'buy-in' price, but are a little more reticent about giving a total figure until they find out how serious a prospective franchisee might be.) What do the fees that the franchise pays to the franchisor include? What other costs are likely to be involved? What level of working capital should be budgeted? How much gross profit can be expected? What is the average profitability of your franchisees?
- *Operational matters*. What are the timescales involved? Assuming a prospective franchisee signs up, how long is it likely to be before s/he can expect to receive an income? Who will pay for, and provide, training for staff? How seasonal is the business and which months are likely to see peaks and troughs? Is there a launch party, and if so, is it promoted by the franchisor? What national and/or regional advertising and marketing does the franchisor provide? Does the franchise contribute anything to the business, financially or in any other way? Is point-of-sale material provided, and if so, at what cost? What help can the franchisee expect in recruiting suitable staff? What continuing services are provided by the franchisor, and if there is a dedicated support manager, when will the franchisee meet that person? Who owns the equipment the franchisee needs to conduct his/her business? How often does the outlet need refurbishment and who pays for the cost of renovation? Are there systems in place for franchisees to keep in touch with each other? Are there regular franchisee meetings? Of the franchisees who left the network last year, how many actually failed in their franchise?
- *The franchisor*. How does the franchisor make his/her money? Apart from the percentage of the franchise's turnover, does the franchisor have other revenue streams, such as mark-up on product lines, or commissions from suppliers? If so, how much additional income accrues from these? What is head office staff turnover like? How can the franchisee be sure that the franchisor will live up to the promises made? In America, a good question to ask would be: has the franchisor ever been rejected by a state registration board, or have any found that the franchise offering would be risky for investors?

All of the above are legitimate questions that a franchisor should not have a problem answering or discussing with any prospective franchisee. Certain technical and operational secrets may be withheld until there is a commitment by the prospective franchisee – after all, some less scrupulous competitors may try to find out what the franchisor is doing by posing as prospective franchisees! Generally, however, a prospective franchisee should expect their target franchisor to be considerably more open with them than they might expect in an employee/employer relationship; remember, the franchisor is seeking somebody to invest in his/her business, and the ongoing relationship is going to be, to some extent, that of (unequal) partners.

Having taken all aspects of the franchise offering, the franchisor, the market and other salient points into consideration, the prospective franchisee will come to a decision as to whether the franchise represents a good business venture for him/herself and his/her family. The prospective franchisee will have reduced the number of options to the final choice, which he truly believes represents the best value, and that is the franchisor he will seek to pursue.

Typically, by this stage the franchisor would have conducted basic checks on the prospective franchisee and both parties should be in a position to move forward; nothing would be more disheartening than if the franchisee has found his/her ideal match of a franchisor, only to be told by the franchisor that s/he is not interested in taking the deal further. It does happen, and many good prospective franchisees have become disillusioned by a last-minute withdrawal by their franchisor and have gone off to get a job somewhere, mistakenly believing that franchising is a scam!

The secret to a good negotiation is that both parties move forward through the process together, that way the franchisee's time, effort, energy and money will not be wasted if a franchisor decides early in the process that they are not interested in a particular prospective franchisee.

Below is a checklist of tasks that franchisees should follow in their quest to find the right franchise. This particular checklist is the one that is suggested by the World Franchise Council, but is much the same as is proposed by most other national bodies:

- Assess the reason for wanting to own a business.
- Assess the lifestyle and income implications of owning and operating a business.
- Assess the franchise opportunities consistent with the items above.
- Build an understanding of the franchise relationship by reading around the topic.
- Narrow the franchise search to a few systems, then request further information.
- If appropriate, and you are comfortable with the decision, select a system and begin the application process.

- Ensure you have adequate borrowing capacity, including working capital, to establish this type of business successfully.
- Be sure you receive and evaluate all disclosure material during the application process.
- Be sure that all legal and accounting advice from lawyers and accountants with franchise experience is received before making any final commitment.
- Use a cooling-off period to check the facts and figures and determine if you still want to proceed.

Of course, having just given a pretty comprehensive guide as to how a prospective franchisee should go about selecting the right franchise, there is a potentially simpler route and that is by calling on the services of a franchise broker.

Generally, brokers are specialists in the field who will help the prospective franchisee narrow down the plethora of options to a handful that meet the prospect's criteria; typically, they would not be active in the purchase of the franchise, though they would be on hand to advise the prospect in the purchasing process.

Responsible brokers will take much time and trouble to identify the areas of interest of the prospective franchisee and then, bearing in mind any budgetary constraints, produce an initial selection of franchisors for the prospective franchisee to consider.

On the positive side, a broker can save the prospective franchisee a huge amount of time, effort and energy, and help them to avoid the worst of the hard-selling sales personnel by having a comprehensive overview of which franchisors are ethical and responsible. Brokers are concerned with matching the prospective franchisee with the right system, not in selling the franchisee a dream franchise.

While in some cases franchise brokers charge for their services (some receive a commission from the franchisor that the prospect subsequently chooses), they can actually represent huge value for money by focusing the prospect's mind on the whole package, rather than allowing the prospective franchisee to be drawn purely by the product or service that is being offered.

On the negative side, those brokers who receive a commission from the franchisor may seek to guide the prospective franchisee towards those franchises that will earn them the most commission; the criteria will still fit the prospect's profile, but some 'bargains' may be overlooked or dismissed by a broker seeking a higher pay-off.

Another slight negative is that brokers tend not to work with the whole directory of franchise opportunities. As professionals, they specialize and this means that they may only work with a certain sector or with a narrow selection of reputable franchisors; this could mean that the prospective franchisee does not meet the 'ideal' franchisor, merely one who is 'almost ideal'!

There are a huge number of brokers or consultants who allegedly offer similar services, so the secret is to identify the ones that offer the prospective franchisee a problem-free experience in locating and purchasing the franchise that meets his/her expectations. A good place to start would be your local franchise trade body.

The good broker will offer the prospective franchisee guidance and consultation, with a thorough process enabling the prospective franchisee to evaluate the proposals methodically, coupled with an extensive network of independent lawyers, accountants and financing options, to smooth the decision process.

Another point worth considering is to use a broker in the area where the prospective franchisee wants to open a franchise, as a highly competent broker who operates outside this area might not understand the market where the franchise will be opened, and this could lead to inaccurate advice being given.

It does not really matter how brilliant a franchise broker may be, the prospective franchisee must carry out his/her own due diligence, even if only to confirm what the broker is recommending. The prospective franchisee ought to go over the disclosure document with a fine-tooth comb, talking to current and former franchisees, examining the franchisor's track record and verifying his/her earnings and profit claims independently.

WHAT DO YOU THINK?

Is the successful franchisee a particular breed of person? Or can anybody, with the right basic skills and good training, become a successful franchise operator?

How much credence can be placed on what the franchisor says in his/her sales campaign? How important to the potential franchisee is the franchise disclosure document, and how can it be improved?

Write a checklist of all the relevant information that a franchisee has to obtain prior to making the commitment to join a system.

Further reading

Biggins, Michael, *The Journey to Being a Successful Franchisee* (CreateSpace 2011).

Bisio, Rick, *The Educated Franchisee: The How-To Book for Choosing a Winning Franchise*, 2nd edn (Bascom Hill Publishing Group 2011).

Mendelsohn, Martin, *How to Evaluate a Franchise*, 8th revd edn (Franchise World 2003).

Murray, Iain. *Franchising Handbook* (Kogan Page 2006).

Record, Matthew, *Taking Up a Franchise: How to Buy a Franchise and Make a Success of It* (How To Books 1999).

9 LEGAL AND FINANCIAL MATTERS

INTRODUCTION AND LEARNING OBJECTIVES

The purpose of this chapter is to highlight to the reader the immense importance of obtaining sound financial and legal advice before committing to any franchise opportunity.

The reader will be able to:

- Understand the importance of the franchise agreement as a protection measure for both parties.
- Accept that the franchisor has potentially more to lose and appreciate why the agreement is more biased towards the franchisor.
- Comprehend the nature of projected turnover and profitability data that is given in the disclosure documentation.

The two elements of any franchise offering that have the most impact on the success or failure of the venture are the franchise agreement and financial details of the fee structure.

Both of these components are going to be specific to the individual business, but there are factors that will be generally applicable across all franchises, and these are the points we shall consider in this chapter.

The purpose, therefore, of this chapter is not to turn readers into instant lawyers or accountants, and obtaining professional advice in these areas is still going to be a necessity; the most that this book can hope to achieve is to look at the legal and financial matters surrounding franchises, so that when readers speak to their accountants or lawyers, they will at least have some idea what is being discussed. Readers might be able to use their pre-existing knowledge to help them to read a franchise agreement or a set of accounts, and be knowledgeable enough to notice areas of concern, which they can raise with their lawyers or accountants.

There really is no substitute for obtaining appropriate professional advice, and because of the different nature of franchising, *specialist* professional advice. The professional body in the reader's country should be able to offer a list of dedicated franchise lawyers and accountants who are able to advise correctly on the validity and viability of any scheme, whereas a family lawyer or a firm of general accountants might not understand the nuances of the differences that are unique to the franchise industry. Therefore readers should first contact the professional body and obtain a list of industry professionals.

Once this list is in their possession, readers should identify the best professionals they can afford and engage them to begin the development of a team of experts who will help prepare readers for their foray into franchising. The first specialists that should be recruited are the expert lawyer and the industry-specific accountant.

THE FRANCHISE AGREEMENT

Many countries have explicit legislation that regulate the franchise relationship, but others (such as the UK) do not, and in these countries the importance of the agreement is heightened because, when a dispute arises, what is written in the agreement is what the lawyers and courts will consider and rely upon when seeking to resolve the problem.

Without a doubt, the franchise agreement is the cornerstone of any successful franchise operation: good ones will be the key to maximizing wealth creation for franchisor and franchisee alike, while bad ones will serve little purpose apart from the wealth creation of lawyers battling over poorly written clauses and ambiguously worded provisions. Franchisors have only one chance to get it right, so it is worth spending that little bit of extra time to ensure that the agreement offered is something of which the franchise can be justly proud, and it is also worth remembering that what is *not* written might be just as important as what is included!

It is quite often the case that franchise agreements are made up of two separate legal documents, the first being the *acquisition agreement*. The initial phase of the agreement is merely a declaration by all parties that they are keen to proceed to a full agreement subject to certain conditions. At this stage, the gun has been fired and both parties will start to formalize their preparations towards full contractual commitment. The franchisee will talk to his/her bank and ensure that the funds are available for the acquisition, and the franchisor will set about planning for the opening of a new outlet in the franchisee's chosen territory and arranging for training and support packages

> Many countries have specific legislation, while others do not, but whichever system applies, the franchise agreement is the cornerstone of the system.

to be put in place, generating a cash-flow prediction and even to start to check the franchisee's suitability for licensing. It is usual at this time for the franchisee to pay a deposit, which will later be offset against the full franchisee fee.

The concept of a deposit is to show a degree of commitment by the franchisee and to cover the franchisor against losses incurred should the franchisee decide to withdraw from the contract. Deposits are relatively recent phenomena that have been brought in because some potential franchisees were exploiting the good nature of franchisors by allowing the franchisor to run around getting the franchise ready for the franchisee, and then withdrawing at the last minute, leaving the franchisor with non-recoverable costs. Nowadays, there are conditions applicable to the handling of deposits that form part of the acquisition agreement, but essentially if the franchisor concludes that the territory is not a viable proposition, or that there are no suitable premises available, then the franchisee can expect to receive his/her deposit back in full. If the franchisor decides not proceed because s/he has discovered something untoward about the franchisee that has not been declared (for example, bankruptcy or a criminal record), or if the franchisee withdraws, then the franchisor can reasonably deduct his costs from the deposit and return the balance, if any, to the failed franchisee.

If things are not progressing smoothly, then it is often better to cut and run from the deal rather than be tied to contractual obligations for an extended period of time, which satisfies neither party and will eventually lead to resentment and disagreements.

It is worth reiterating to the reader that the concept of 'purchasing' a franchise is slightly inaccurate. The franchisee is not actually 'purchasing' anything, but is paying a fee to the franchisor in exchange for the franchisor issuing a licence to the franchisee to operate under his/her brand and system for a given period of time; it is more of a 'hire' agreement than an outright purchase.

Assuming that negotiations progress smoothly and all parties are willing and able to progress to the next stage, then the next agreement signed will be the actual *franchise agreement*.

It has been said that the whole purpose of a franchise agreement is that it enables the franchisor to keep franchisees in check and while there is an element of truth in this statement, it is not the 'whole truth'.

We identified earlier in this book that the relationship existing between the franchisor and the franchisee is skewed and this is evident in the franchise agreement, with typically considerably more onus placed on the franchisee than the franchisor to perform in a certain way. However, in saying this, the benefits a franchisee can reasonably expect as part of the network are also clearly detailed in the franchise agreement.

The franchise agreement will never be a 'balanced' document because

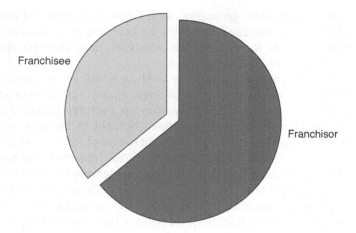

Figure 9.1 The imbalanced relationship

the purpose is mainly to protect the franchisor's brand and the reputation of existing franchisees. Consequently, agreements need to be robust and exacting documents, but they also need to be fair. Accepting that agreements will be somewhat one-sided (see Figure 9.1), there are still limits as to the bias that can be applied. A good example of the level of bias will be those clauses related to fees: franchisees need to be protected against too much upward movement of fees by a greedy franchisor; budgets are drawn up at the beginning of a term, based on information given by the franchisor, and too much of a rise would affect the viability of the franchise. So, movement of the goalposts must be kept within predefined bounds; scope should exist, but not excessive scope.

> *Franchise contracts are never 'balanced' agreements; the franchisor has to protect the whole system while franchisees have merely to worry about their own business!*

Equally, the agreement will often refer to the operations manual, which is an important item in the franchise documentation, but this manual should be reserved strictly for matters concerning the operation of the franchise. Too often have franchisors sought to modify the franchise agreement by changing the details contained in the operations manual, or including items that should really be included in the agreement.

Essentially, all franchise agreements serve four distinct purposes:

1 The agreement puts into writing what has been agreed verbally between the parties, the purpose being to set the boundaries of the relationship and to avoid future disputes, as well as to provide guidelines on dispute resolution, if arguments do arise.

2   The agreement seeks to protect both parties against the abuse of the franchisor's intellectual property rights; his/her brand and trade mark, know-how, secret formulae, and so on.
3   The agreement lays down certain minimum standards of franchise operation that both parties are able to rely upon.
4   The agreement confirms equality and uniformity between the franchisees that make up the network, which is arguably the most important strength of the franchise system.

Agreements are seldom written with the intention of making the transaction attractive to the parties, but at the same time they should not be so complicated as to scare off potential signatories. While franchise agreements are complex and complicated commercial contracts, designed to last for a considerable amount of time, they should be written in plain language. Though lawyers love to use Latin terminology to show their superiority in language, there is no place for confusion in an agreement that binds together two willing parties in a commercial arrangement, so clarity and ease of understanding are paramount.

At one time it was not unusual for franchise agreements to be photocopied and the name and address of the prospective franchisee added as required, sometimes even with a ballpoint pen. Whereas these documents would have the same legal standing as a beautifully prepared parchment scroll that has been lovingly penned in superb calligraphy, it does not create the correct professional image for the franchisor in the eyes of the prospective franchisee. If a franchisor cannot be bothered to type in the franchisee's details on the legal agreement between them, it shows the slapdash manner with which the franchisor regards his franchisees, and might indicate to a prospective franchisee the low regard in which the franchisor regards him/her, *and* the importance placed on the agreement!

> *Franchise industry specialist lawyers have a much deeper understanding of franchising than 'regular' commercial lawyers, and as such should be preferred.*

In the preamble to this chapter, it was stated that franchisees should obtain professional advice from industry specialists, and an example of why this is good practice can be drawn from the unique nature of franchise agreements. Part of the strength of any franchise system is that the contract the franchisee signs is identical to the contracts that the entire network have signed; if individual and different contracts were in existence across the network, there would be no continuity and the system would be fatally flawed. It would be most inequitable if one franchisee were to be tied to a set of terms that were materially different from another franchisee's.

Consequently, industry specialist lawyers understand this phenomenon and will advise prospective franchisees about the positives and negatives of the agreement, so that they have a clear understanding of all aspects as they make their decision to sign the agreement, or not. Time and again, prospective franchisees talk to the lawyer who has drafted their will or handled the conveyancing of their house, who may well understand the principles of contract law, but do not understand franchising. These lawyers will spend a huge amount of time and an even greater amount of the clients' money trying to get the franchise agreement changed so that it is more balanced. Needless to say, they are not successful, as the franchisors refuse to budge and say they will not change a single full stop or comma. Inevitably, the lawyers returns to their clients and advise that the franchisor is 'impossible to deal with', the prospective franchisee should proceed with extreme caution, and the lawyers' advice is that the client should never sign this agreement unless changes are made!

As a result, the client takes the lawyer's poor advice, the franchisors have lost much time with a good prospect who fails to complete, plus they have lost an excellent prospective franchisee; the individual franchisees have lost a good business opportunity and probably a great deal of money in legal costs and lost deposits; in fact, the only people who have 'won' are the inept lawyers, who realistically should be the last people to benefit from their flawed advice!

So, we have seen that franchise agreements will be identical across the network, and that franchisors will not modify their terms and conditions in any circumstances ... well, that is not strictly true, because there is one situation where a franchisee may be on a different contract from the rest of the network, and this is the case with the 'third-party pilot' franchisee.

Often, when franchisors begin the process of franchising their business, they will recruit somebody internally to act as the franchisee – perhaps an existing store manager, if it is a retail operation. Many franchisors, however, set up a totally independent pilot using a real live franchisee to run their pilot outlet(s). These third-party independent franchisees take on a higher risk than if they were to buy into an established system, as they are also fulfilling a developmental role, so it is quite common that the initial agreement for these pilot franchisees will be on more advantageous terms than the 'standard' contract; when, however, the franchisee renews his/her contract at the end of the initial term, s/he will be expected to sign the current agreement and the additional benefits that have been received until that date will cease on renewal.

As the business develops, there will always be a need to amend the contract to reflect current market conditions and trading policies; incorporating amendments to agreements is permissible in this situation and may be implemented from that time forward. It would be inequitable to attempt to impose an amendment retrospectively, or to force a franchisee to sign a new contract mid-term, unless something in the macro environment makes this imperative. Generally, amendments should be incorporated at time of renewal, when all franchisees will be expected to sign the agreement current at that time.

In saying that franchise agreements should be identical does not allow for the *variables* that will always exist in franchise contracts. The most obvious variable will be the name of the franchisee and the address from which s/he will operate. Other variables might include the level of the initial stock, if the floor area of the retail space is larger or smaller than others, and whether the premises are leased from the franchisor or the franchisee him/herself holds the lease. These details are acceptable variations within the standard contract; however, it still remains the case that the substantive parts of the agreement must remain identical.

There will always be at least two, or sometimes three, parties to the franchise agreement. The first party will be the franchisor, who will unavoidably be a limited liability company. Second will be the franchisee, who is also likely to run a limited liability company, but could also quite feasibly be a sole trader, a partnership or, increasingly, a limited liability partnership. Often, franchisee limited liability companies will have only recently been formed and will hold no assets. Consequently, if a franchisee company breaches its terms and conditions of the contract, there will be little or nothing for the franchisor to recover in the form of damages; often the only asset is the licence, which, if the franchisee has breached the terms, is pretty much worthless. This brings us on to the possible third parties to the agreement – the individuals who have formed the company that is nominated as franchisee. Wise franchisors should seek directors' guarantees from those who have set up the company and will operate the franchise; if such guarantees are received, if the franchisee breaches the terms of his/her contract, the franchisor can seek redress from the directors' personal assets. Of course, if the directors refuse to underwrite their own business, that might lead the franchisor to speculate as to the ultimate aims and intentions of the franchisee, and the level of commitment the directors have to the success of their own company.

Having understood the nature of the franchise agreement, we should now try to get to grips with the content of the franchise contracts and at this point it is worth recalling that franchise agreements typically fall into two distinct phases: the 'pre-launch' and 'post-launch' stages.

In the pre-launch phase, the onus is on the franchisor to make sure the franchisee has everything needed for the launch of the business. In the post-launch phase, the onus is on the franchisee to ensure that s/he maximizes the predicted opportunities in the territory, to

> *Some element of exclusivity is central to most franchise agreements; it would be grossly unfair if franchisees had 'carte-blanche' over where they could operate!*

ensure that the franchisor is receiving sufficient income to justify continu-ing support, and that the franchisee is developing the income levels that have been forecast.

Accepting that franchise agreements are all different and unique to indi-vidual franchisors, it is generally the case that the following areas will be covered in some way by the agreement.

DESCRIPTION OF THE FRANCHISE AND RIGHTS GRANTED

What the franchise does and how it goes about doing it is clearly stated so that it forms part of the contractual relationship between the parties. Details of the franchisor's intellectual property is likely to be included in this section, which includes trade marks, methods, know-how, goodwill, copyrights, and how the franchisor intends to protect these against misuse. Inevitably, the franchisor will detail the rights that are being extended to the franchisee to use this intellectual property in the course of his/her business. Remember, one of the main reasons why the prospective fran-chisee is buying into the system is because of the value of the brand, so if the franchisor has not put in place sufficient restrictions as to the use and/or abuse of these assets, the reputation of the brand will suffer and the value of the franchise will be diminished.

Often franchise agreements detail some level of exclusivity, and how this is specified will often depend on the type of franchise that is being licensed. If the franchise is retail or commercial and physically based in a fixed location, it is likely that the undertaking would be not to franchise another unit within a certain radius of the franchisee's business. If the franchise is mobile-based, the territory would probably be determined by some geographical boundaries outside of which the franchisee is not permitted to carry out or tout for business. Getting the level of territorial coverage correct is one of the many challenges that franchisors face: spreading franchises too thinly means that they will be losing business opportunities, because the franchisees cannot in reality cover the amount of business that could be generated by a huge territory. Alternatively, if the territories are too small and the greedy franchisor seeks to cover the country with too many franchises, then the amount of business that each franchisee is able to conduct is insufficient to meet his/her minimal expectations and s/he will become demotivated and lose the drive to be successful. This balancing act is a mix of demography and geography so it is wise to define boundaries clearly, such as by postcode or by county boundaries.

A few years ago, there was a British domestic services franchisor who stuck firmly to a system of county boundaries – which benefited hugely the lucky franchisee in Middlesex, where there were 1.1 million people with a density of 661 per square kilometre; but the franchisee who bought Northumberland was less pleased, with his/her potential customer base of 310,000 spread over a huge county with a density of 62 per square kilometre, and with a considerably greater population of sheep than humans – especially as this franchisee had paid the same fee for the licence!

Neither franchise benefited the franchisor, who has subsequently modified his approach to licensing, as the franchisee in Middlesex found himself working all hours to try to keep up with the massive amount of leads that were being generated, and eventually had a nervous breakdown and lost his business, while the franchisee in Northumberland was unable to make sufficient money on which to live and he quit his franchise before the term ended and in the process lost his entire investment.

THE TERM OF THE AGREEMENT

This section will state the length of the contract, and in reality there is nothing to stop a franchisor from granting a licence in perpetuity, but few would be so bold! It is generally accepted that the 'ideal' term of a franchise is in the region of ten years, as a contract of less than ten years means that the franchisor does not fully exploit the full potential of the franchisee, and more than ten years is likely to encourage a situation where the franchisee becomes contented and loses the hunger to achieve.

In Europe, the waters are muddied by the block exemption of EU competition laws in respect of what are called 'vertical agreements', which include franchise agreements. Without getting too bogged down with the principles of European law, the regulation describes a 'non-compete obligation' as:

> " any direct or indirect obligation causing the buyer not to manufacture, purchase, sell or resell goods or services which compete with the contract goods or services, or any direct or indirect obligation on the buyer to purchase from the supplier or from another undertaking designated by the supplier more than 80% of the buyer's total purchases of the contract goods or services and their substitutes on the relevant market, calculated on the basis of the value or, where such is standard industry practice, the volume of its purchases in the preceding calendar year.
> (Commission Regulaton (EU) No 330/2010 Article 1: Definitions 1(d) of 20.4.2010 on the application of Article 101(3) of the Treaty on the Functioning of the European Union to Categories of Vertical Agreements and Concerted Practices)

Effectively, this means that most franchise agreements in Europe are negotiated for a period of five years, with an option to renew at the end of the term by means of the franchisee signing a new contract at that time.

The new contract is not likely to be on the same terms as the original contract, as the renewal will be on the same terms as a new franchisee joining the system would have imposed on them. Typically, however, the initial fee will be discounted by the set-up and training fees that the franchisor would not have to expend on an experienced franchisee, so the second term actually represents very good value for money to the renewing franchisee.

Whether the term is for five, ten or however many years, the golden rule is that the franchisee must be expected to recover the cost of his/her initial outlay during that period, and show a reasonable return on his/her investment.

It is most important that the franchisee's lawyer closely examines the rights that are being extended to the franchise in respect of the term and the right of renewal, as this might be one of the main causes of a franchisee withdrawing from the agreement if the term clauses do not fit with the franchisee's long-term plans and aspirations.

THE FRANCHISOR'S OBLIGATIONS

Generally speaking, contracts should generate a benefit to the parties that form the agreement, therefore, irrespective of the imbalanced nature of a franchise agreement, it would be most unusual if the franchisor did not commit to a benefit being given to the franchisee; indeed, such a one-way contract might well prove to be unenforceable!

Without doubt, the biggest asset that the franchisor is obligated to share with his/her franchisees is the unfettered use of the company's brand and trade mark; this is the demonstrable and recognizable face of the business, and without this obligation being set in stone, the franchise opportunity is pretty much worthless. Franchisors extend this obligation to keep the brand 'clean' and free from any adverse publicity that could impact negatively on the franchisee's business.

It is usual that franchisors undertake to train the franchisees, and even their staff, so one would expect to find details of the training package included in the franchise agreement as well as details about who pays for the cost of training; inevitably, this will be the franchisee, though it is not unusual for the initial training costs to be absorbed into the original franchise fee. Wise prospective franchisees will want to know how much the staff training costs will be, and whether training costs related to system modifications or upgrades, such as training in new and obligatory equipment, will be met by the franchisor.

Franchisors will undertake to supply equipment and stock, together with all other materials that are needed to run a successful franchise, though the franchisee will be liable for the cost of stock and materials.

Normally, the franchisor will undertake national advertising and it is often the case that the franchisor will levy an additional charge across the entire network to cover the costs of network-wide marketing; all responsibility and costs related to local advertising will remain the liability of the franchisee, unless there is a provision for a 'starter' package of local promotion included in the initial franchise fee.

If the franchise requires premises, it is not unusual for franchisors to assist franchisees in finding the best property available and fitting the premises out in the style of their other outlets. Sometimes, the franchisor is also the franchisee's landlord, in cases where the franchisor holds the head lease, though the property contract will probably be separate from the franchise agreement, as the franchisor may wish to protect their property rental income separately from the franchise income. In the event of a franchise failing they would not wish to be held liable for ongoing rent for the property until a new tenant is found.

Franchisors will also be expected to provide a detailed operations manual giving clear and explicit instructions as to how the franchise will operate. The operations manual remains the property of the franchisor, must be surrendered on termination of the franchise, and the franchisor will expect the franchisee to keep the manual up to date by including additions and revisions as they are published. The operations manual is the 'bible' of the franchise, and adherence to the conditions and instructions contained therein is an expectation of the franchisor; failure to comply to the letter with the operations manual will typically result in disciplinary action against the franchisee, or even a termination of the franchise, and this is usually clearly spelt out in the franchise agreement.

Part and parcel of the franchise agreement is the undertaking to provide continuing support and advice throughout the term of the agreement. Remembering that it is in the best interests of the franchisor to help a struggling franchisee to maximize his/her opportunity, on the basis that a successful franchisee generates more income for a franchisor, the level of support must also be cost-effective. If a franchisor has to dedicate a team to support the efforts of a weak franchisee, the cost liability may exceed the potential benefit, so this level of support is unlikely to continue for too long before the franchisor pulls the plug on the franchisee. In such circumstances, the franchisor is seldom blameless, because if s/he had researched his/her prospective franchisee better before signing a contract, s/he might well have identified that the franchisee would struggle with the business, and have withdrawn before commitment. Therefore, whereas the level of support offered is controlled by the franchisor, there has to be a degree of common sense and understanding by both parties.

Some franchisors undertake the financial management and accountancy functions for the franchisee, in the belief that a franchisee should be out developing the business rather than be stuck in the office chasing overdue accounts or poring over a set of accounts. Other franchisors will undertake to keep accurate stock and accounts information to assist the franchisee's record keeping, which s/he will undertake by him/herself. A third group do little more than provide the necessary record forms for the franchisee to undertake both the administrative and financial functions of the business him/herself. Whichever system the franchisor favours will be detailed carefully in the agreement, and the franchisor will be obligated to offer this level of service during the term of the contract.

Franchisors will always commit themselves to improving and developing the system, and this is one of the major benefits to franchisees throughout the duration of the term. All businesses have to evolve over a period of time, or they will stagnate. Usually, a small-business owner will have to undertake the evolution process on their own, and devote a substantial amount of time and effort to make sure that the business is contemporary and current. Franchisees have the advantage of having a corporate level that undertakes much of this development work, as it benefits the franchisor more to have an up-to-date business, as returns are substantially improved at all levels.

Some franchise agreements will also include rights and obligations extended to and from a third party, and this is particularly the case where the franchise agreement exists between a master franchisee and a franchisee. Undoubtedly, in the background there will be a superior being in the shape of an original franchisor, who may hold some degree of rights over and obligations towards the individual franchisee. For example, if a master franchisee were to go into liquidation, the franchisor's rights and obligations might well default to the original franchisor until a new master dealer was appointed. The obligations of both the franchisor and franchisee are embedded in the franchise agreement, as shown in Figure 9.2, but rather than making the obligations of both parties mutually exclusive, a good agreement will make them mutually inclusive.

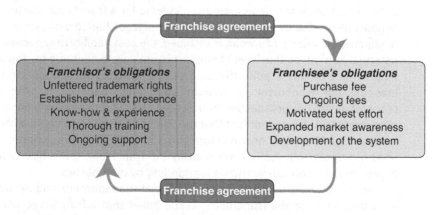

Figure 9.2 Franchise obligations

THE FRANCHISEE'S OBLIGATIONS

The obligation of the individual franchisees are many and varied, but they all relate to the development of the system and to the promotion of the brand; for example, every franchise agreement will include a clause whereby the franchisee undertakes to conduct his/her business in such a manner as not to harm the reputation of the franchised business, or the brand.

The strength of the franchise concept is centred on the uniformity of supply in every franchised outlet of the network, so franchisees will be expected to undertake to follow the operations manual to the letter, including any updates or modifications to procedure that may be notified by the franchisor from time to time during the course of the agreement.

Similarly, franchisees will be expected to purchase their products from either the franchisor directly or through designated suppliers, in the bid to keep franchise outlets selling an identical offering across the whole of the network.

Franchisees will also allow their franchisor unrestricted access to all parts of their business for any purpose, including their accounts, to ensure that standards are being maintained and that the franchisee is operating to the requirements of the operations manual.

Another obligation the franchisee takes on board is the payment of fees. The fee structure is clearly identified in the franchise agreement, and the franchisee is expected to comply with these requirements. Similarly, the franchisee will also commit to keeping minimum standards of accountancy recording and reporting; this enables the franchisor to gather important management information about product sales, and whether profit margins are being achieved, and to calculate the fees due to him/her under the agreement.

It seems quite logical that franchisees will be expected to keep staffing at such a level that customers do not have to wait for their purchases, and to ensure that the staff are properly trained in the operation of the franchise. One fast-food chain has a target that customers should not be kept waiting for more than 30 seconds before being served, and no more than an additional 30 seconds before they receive their order. This often means that, at busy periods, the area around the tills where customers order is frantic, with staff almost tripping over themselves to ensure that customers are not kept waiting any longer than the target time; the fact that staff seem to avoid crashing into each other and causing further mayhem, and that this ambitious target is often surpassed, let alone merely reached, is a testament to the efficiency of training!

Another typical clause will insist that franchisees protect and promote the goodwill of the business. Goodwill is a rather subjective asset of the business that may have taken many years to develop, but which can be destroyed in a moment of madness.

Often franchisees will be restricted in what else they can do at the premises of the franchise. It may well be that they are prevented by the agreement from running another business of any description from the same business premises. It has been known for franchisees to get on the wrong side of their franchisor because their partners are running a non-competing business from a spare office above the franchise shop. Provided the franchisee is able to show that, while the office premises is above the franchise, it has a separate entrance, separate address, separate services and so on, then most franchisors would take a lenient approach.

Franchisors will undoubtedly have carried out a study as to when their outlets are at their busiest, and will often stipulate that their stores will be open to comply with these times. This can be particularly tricky if a franchisee follows a particular religion, perhaps as a practising orthodox Jew who is required to keep the Sabbath holy and not to do any work on that day. In Judaism, the Sabbath is Saturday, which is an exceptionally busy trading day for most retail outlets and it would be unthinkable that a franchisor would allow an outlet to close on Saturdays, irrespective of the religious beliefs the franchisee might hold. The solution might be for the franchisee to appoint a manager to work on Saturdays and thereby avoid an unnecessary confrontation with the franchisor.

Local advertising will usually have a corporate requirement attached, where only approved ads are permitted to be placed to promote the brand. Often, the franchisor will have a series of advertisements and promotional material over which the franchisee can print his/her company's name and address, because keeping the corporate identity in all advertising and promotional activity strengthens the brand image. In the same vein, franchisees will be obliged to use the point-of-sale material that the franchisor provides, and to use whatever packaging or boxes the franchisor stipulates when wrapping customer purchases.

Often, a franchise agreement will stipulate that the premises have to be renovated mid-term of the agreement to keep the outlet looking fresh and clean, and this is something the franchisee will have to budget for in his/her long-term costings and projected accounts for the franchise.

> *Franchisees cannot assign their rights or obligations under the agreement without express permission of the franchisor.*

It would be quite usual to have further restrictions imposed on the franchisee to prevent them trying to solicit business from outside their territory. This may be difficult to enforce in respect of retail franchises, on the principle that the franchise is static, but the customers are mobile and might have seen the franchisee's advertisement in a newspaper with a cross-over circulation. However, in a mobile franchise, where the customer is static and the franchisee travels to the customer's home or workplace, this can be policed by a requirement that the franchisee hands over any leads that have been obtained in another franchisee's area. What may be more difficult to control is the requirement that franchisees do not 'poach' staff from other franchises in the network. In accepting that it might be discriminatory not to employ a suitable candidate merely because they have worked for another franchisee in the network, it is often difficult to ascertain whether an employee walked out or was coerced from their previous employment. Franchisees need to be aware of the general requirement not to seek to entice staff away from other franchises, and be prepared and able to defend their actions should a claim of staff enticement be levied against them.

Franchisees are not permitted to assign or sub-assign the franchise without the express permission of the franchisor. Remember that franchisors take extreme care when recruiting franchisees, and they hold the rights to the franchise licence. Whereas all franchise agreements should be assignable with the permission of the franchisor, there must be restrictions on franchisees deciding unilaterally to re-assign contracts or agreements to third parties of whom the franchisor has no knowledge. Of course, the exception to this rule is where the franchisee is a limited company and the principal shareholder dies mid-term; in this case, the business must be allowed to continue trading until another person is able to assume the responsibilities of the deceased shareholder and be trained as the succeeding franchisee principal. It might even be argued that, even if the franchisee is an individual, the business must be allowed to continue, as the value of the operating business may represent a substantial part of the deceased franchisee's estate. If there is nobody competent to take over the reins in such a circumstance, it would not be unusual for a 'caretaker' or 'interim' franchisee to be appointed by the franchisor until the business can be sold as a going concern, or somebody can be trained to take over, though a 'management fee' would probably be levied to defray the costs of the franchisor assisting in this way. It would almost be an ethical requirement that responsible franchisors are sympathetic in these types of unfortunate circumstances, whereas they may be less understanding if the franchisee declares bankruptcy or becomes debarred from holding a franchise through some other incident.

> *Disputes that are not resolved amicably, typically have a demotivating and negative affect on the whole system.*

Another restriction placed on franchisees is regarding what they are able to commit to in the name of the franchisor, which is typically nothing, or very little. Franchisees will usually be required to advise customers that they are operating under a licence from the franchisor, and that no agency liability exists between the franchisor and customer.

However, in saying that there is no contractual link between the customer and the franchisor, the franchisor will regard the customers of the franchise as his/her customers! This apparent double standard would typi-cally only come into force should a franchisee cease his/her relationship with the franchisor, in which case the franchisor will expect the customer details of the franchisee to be handed over, so that whoever takes over the franchise will have an existing customer base with which to start trading.

It can be seen that the locus of control in franchising is centred on the franchisor, and that the franchisee has very little scope for 'personalizing' their own business, but that is what franchising is all about; the acceptance by the franchisee of stringent operating conditions that have been tried and tested by the franchisor and, if followed, will generate a good income for all parties.

DISPUTE RESOLUTION

Increasingly, franchise agreements are beginning to incorporate dispute resolution clauses, and the reason is that disputes are on the increase. Previously, the usual route for arbitration in a franchise dispute was through the courts, and inevitably this involved both parties briefing highly expensive lawyers, who would get their heads together and thrash out a settlement long before the matter came before a judge. Consequently, franchisors seek a contracted alternative that will resolve the disagree-ment more quickly and more cost-effectively.

Typically, both parties agree on and appoint a recognized expert in the field of franchising who acts as an arbiter and who, to all intents and purposes, sits as judge in the dispute; mediators are slightly different, as they act as a facilitator to a settlement. The parties, in agreeing the appointment of an arbiter, also agree to be bound by the decision.

These methods of dispute resolution have major advantages, not least being the time it takes to resolve the argument – with litigation it may take months before the matter can be brought to court, during which time animosity and resentment fester between the two parties. Typically, arbi-tration, mediation or other informal intercession can be scheduled and take place within a much shorter timeframe.

It is also much less expensive, as legal representation is not necessary, unless the matter involves some legal point; typically, both parties sit down with the arbiter, and both sides of the dispute are analysed before a deci-sion as to the rights and wrongs of the matter is reached. A huge benefit is that the arbiter usually understands the complexities of franchising, because both parties typically appoint a knowledgeable person of standing from within the industry; it is highly unlikely that a judge sitting in court will have as much experience or understanding of franchising.

Mediation typically involves both parties trying to resolve the situation by and between themselves so that an amicable solution is reached.

The two other main benefits of arbitration and mediation are that litigation invariably receives publicity, and not many franchisors (or franchisees, for that matter) are keen to wash their dirty linen in public; arbitration and mediation can be kept private. The final point is that litigation typically ends the relationship; both parties will be bitter and feel animosity towards each other after being ripped to pieces in court by the opposition's legal team, and it will be almost impossible to rebuild the trust that is necessary for the parties to work together harmoniously. However, with mediation and arbitration, the parties can often dust themselves down and get back to a sensible working relationship, as they often feel as though they have resolved the dispute themselves.

Of course, if the 'losing' side still feel as though they have been hard done by, they usually have the option of appealing through the courts. It should be noted, though, that in many cases the courts will concur with what has been agreed at arbitration or mediation.

There are circumstances and failings that cannot be resolved by arbitration and/or mediation and these typically involve a serious breach of contract, some examples of which are:

- Consistently not paying the franchise fees that are owed.
- Not maintaining the quality standards laid down in the operations manual and agreement.
- Failing to operate the system in accordance with the operations manual and contract.
- Consistently not submitting reports in the correct manner, or on time, or submitting falsified reports.
- Not renovating the business or redecorating at the appropriate time as laid down in the contract.
- Sub-assigning parts of the business, or taking in partners/directors without approval of the franchisor.
- Setting up a competitive business and directing customers away from the franchise.
- Being lazy and not committing sufficient time to the business to maximize opportunities.
- Acting in a manner that would bring disrepute to the brand.

These examples go to the very root of the franchise relationship and are fundamental to good franchising. Franchisors facing franchisees who behave in such a manner would probably wish to terminate the agreement and seek a court order to enforce the post-contractual restrictions.

Arbitration and mediation will only work where both parties are willing to reach a settlement,

If disputes between franchisee and franchisor become common knowledge, it can have a negative effect on the public opinion of the brand.

and the arbiter or mediator does not have the power to impose injunctions against future actions. In the above circumstances, neither arbitration nor mediation would be appropriate, because one party is seeking termination and the enforceable imposition of contractual constraints.

TERMINATION OF THE AGREEMENT

Termination of the agreement is going to occur at some point, so it is important that all parties understand their rights and obligations when this occurs; these rights and obligations are likely to be different if the termination is premature than they would be if the termination results from the contract expiring, but not greatly so.

Franchise agreements that do not have a renewal clause tend not to terminate but rather expire; even so there will still be restrictions on what occurs after the expiry.

Generally speaking, franchisors retain the absolute right to terminate franchise agreements where the franchisee has committed a breach of the terms of agreement, though usually a period of time should be allowed between being notified of the breach and any termination, to enable the franchisee to rectify the breach. The word 'usually' crept into that last sentence because there will be occurrences when a franchisor will terminate instantly and these centre on circumstances where it can be shown that the franchisee has behaved in an untrustworthy manner, perhaps falsifying returns, or lying on his/her application form, or the franchisee breaching his/her fiduciary duty to the franchisor by disclosing confidential information to a third party.

Sometimes, franchise agreements have a clause stating that a given period must have passed before a franchisee is free to terminate his/her agreement, and setting down a set of procedures that must be followed when this situation occurs. If the given period of time has not elapsed, then inevitably the franchise would return to the franchisor and effectively be surrendered.

Forced termination by either party is regarded as the 'doomsday scenario' in respect of the agreement as there is no reversal. Both parties will undoubtedly lose out and this is why franchisors will do everything in their power to rescue an errant franchisee and welcome them back into the family rather than invoking termination. A typical recovery of a bad situation will often include the franchisor:

- Sitting down and talking over the problem with the franchisee and trying to identify the root cause of the problem. Often, what the franchisee declares to be the problem will only be the tip of a very large iceberg, and the franchisor should try to seek out the hidden reasons why there is dissatisfaction, or why the franchisee has defaulted. If a rescue package is to be implemented it must be directed at the cause, not the symptoms, of the problem.

- Recognizing that franchisees go through peaks and troughs, franchisors should have a team of trained personnel who are able to offer additional support to a troubled franchisee. It may be that additional training, or a concentrated marketing effort, or assistance in recovering bad debts, will solve the problem sufficiently for the franchise to be salvaged, and then close monitoring can identify whether the franchisee is back on track.

- Accepting that there may be an incurable problem and the franchisee's long-term future is bleak, perhaps there has been an irreconcilable difference of opinion, or mutual trust has completely broken down. In such circumstances, it is far preferable for the conclusion to be reached sooner rather than later. The franchisor should seek to assist the franchisee to build up the business so that it becomes saleable and enable the franchisee to recover as much of his/her investment as possible.

- Assisting, when the situation has reached such a point that the franchisee is unwilling or unable to be salvaged, to sell the business, either back to the franchisor or to a third party, at a realistic value.

- Being aware that, if the help and assistance packages totally fail and the franchisee persists in defaulting, then the franchisor has a responsibility to the other franchisees to ensure that the brand reputation does not suffer, so a termination notice should be served on the defaulting franchisee. If no attempt at reconciliation is made at that point, then the franchise would be terminated.

The usual manner in which franchises are terminated by the franchisee is when s/he has built up sufficient return on his/her investment and is looking to sell the business so s/he can go off and do something different. Usually, in such scenarios, the business has been built up and there is a fair amount of goodwill that has to be quantified prior to the sale of the business. In such circumstances, the rule will still apply that the franchisor has the ultimate right of sanction or veto over any prospective purchaser, and the 'right to sell' conditions will be laid down clearly in the agreement to prevent what should be a happy parting turning sour. Most franchisors will readily assist franchisees wishing to sell their businesses, either by offering leads to qualified purchasers, or even buying back the franchise at its true market value – remember that a successful franchise outlet can be just as valuable to a franchisor as it is to the franchisee!

Sometimes, franchisees have to sell their franchises back to the franchisor, who will then market them as a franchise resale. This practice may be unfair to the franchisee because if s/he were to offer the business on the open market, the market would decide the value based on the number of potential purchasers; this is the law of supply and demand. If the franchisee only has one potential purchaser, then who is to determine that the price offered is a fair representation of the true value of the business? Consequently, if a franchisee is obliged to sell his/her business back to the franchisor on termination, there must be clear guidelines in the agreement as to how the valuation of the business will be reached, and in all consciousness the valuation should be assessed independently, with the franchisor agreeing to the independent valuation. This puts the rights of the franchisee appropriately at the forefront of the purchase, but it also puts the franchisor in a difficult situation. If a commercial purchaser does not like the price at which something is offered for sale, s/he has the option to decline the purchase, but if a franchisor does not like the value placed on a franchised business and the franchisee is determined to sell, the franchisor really has to grin and bear the independent valuation. Perhaps that is the implied penalty for restricting the sale of the franchise!

POST-TERMINATION

Whatever the reason for the termination, whether it is voluntary or forced, the post-termination clauses will generally be similar. These will always require that the franchisee:

- Ceases using the brand name, and any goodwill generated by the business will cease.
- All signs and logos that were used by the business must be removed, and the appearance of the premises of the franchise, be it fixed in the form of a retail outlet, or mobile in the form of vehicles, must be altered so that there is no indication to customers that any replacement business has or had any connection with the franchise.
- Does not contact any of his/her former customers as these form part of the 'goodwill' of the business, which will have reverted to the franchisor or been sold to the new franchisee.
- Stops using the system or any specialist knowledge that has been acquired as a result of the franchisee's tenure. This would be difficult to enforce where the franchise is a 'specialist' franchise which required the franchisee to have certain qualifications prior to beginning to trade; it would be considered a severe restriction of an individual's right to earn a living if, say, a franchisor prevented a time-served tradesperson from practising his or her trade, or a qualified pharmacist from working as a pharmacist elsewhere.

- Does not work in a business that competes with the franchisor, either from the same premises or within a defined geographical exclusion zone for a specified time period. It was quite common at one time for the restrictive zone to cover the whole of the country in which the franchisee had previously operated, and this exclusion would exist in perpetuity, but such a restriction, if challenged, would be considered unreasonable nowadays, in the same way that the restriction detailed in the previous point would be unfair. It would be fair to restrict somebody from plying his/her trade or conducting his/her profession within a reasonable geographical area, and that would generally be the area that was defined as the franchise's territory and/or a wide enough boundary that previous customers could not easily be enticed away from the new franchisee's business, and it would be reasonable to impose a time limit on this exile period.

In an ideal world, the terminating franchisee would give up his/her franchise, take his/her money and retire to Spain or Florida to take up golf or fishing for the rest of his/her days, but that doesn't often happen. The good news for franchisors is that other franchisors are loath to take on experienced franchisees from similar franchises as they come with the baggage and preconceptions of having worked for a competitor franchise; typically, they are more trouble than they are worth as they always claim to know better than the franchisor and are constantly trying to 'reinvent the wheel'.

If a departing franchisee wants to set up with another franchisor, it is highly likely that they will end up working in an entirely unrelated industry, and therefore the restrictive clauses will not be applicable. The difficulty exists when a retiring franchisee tries to set up a cloned business in a similar market, even at a distance from where s/he was previously trading, and then set about franchising this him/herself. The poacher has become the gamekeeper! This would require careful policing and would mean careful wording of the restrictive clauses in the agreement, because the departing franchisee might be operating a competing business as a franchisor without using any of the specialist know-how gained while being a franchisee for their original franchisor. A good example of this would be a fast-food franchisee whose original business was as a franchised pizza retailer, setting up as an independent business or even franchisor in the burger industry, the competition would be indirect and almost certainly none of the directly relevant know-how would be applicable and it might prove extremely difficult for the original franchisor to gain a preventative court order restricting the new business venture.

CASE STUDY 9.1

Café au Lait – protecting the franchisee's investment

So, you have done all the due diligence that you need and have committed to being a franchisee for a reputable franchise brand. You think you have all bases covered, but suddenly and out of the blue comes a bombshell you just did not ever consider a possibility.

Franchisee Charles Lafontaine of Vancouver, Canada, learnt a hard lesson that soured his relationship with his franchisor and nearly drove his business into the ground. Lafontaine already owned two thriving outlets of the Café au Lait franchise in Vancouver; indeed, his outlets were doing so well he thought he'd metaphorically struck gold! Then, without warning, Café au Lait decided to embark on a massive expansion drive and launched three new outlets in Vancouver in just over a year. As might be predicted, some of Lafontaine's customers now had more convenient outlets to visit and his sales went down considerably, but unfortunately Lafontaine's franchise agreement allowed for expansion by the franchisor.

Typically, it is usual that existing franchisees are given the right to buy new outlets that are adjacent to their existing outlets under a clause that covers first-refusal rights; Lafontaine's agreement did not contain such a clause and it was a point missed by all of his advisers when negotiating his agreement. The downside of a first-refusal clause is that often franchisees feel pressured into taking on new outlets to protect their existing trade, sometimes stretching themselves financially almost to the point of non-viability.

Whereas it is usual that franchise agreements give some level of territorial protection, in the case of multi-unit retail outlets in a given metropolitan area, such as a city, where franchisors may want to expand at a faster pace than an original franchisee can handle, it is not unusual that the only geographical protection offered will be a radial boundary to the original store, often as little as one mile. Nevertheless, there are methods that can be put in place to protect an existing franchisee from the risk of disproportionate expansion by a franchisor; for example a simple profit-sharing agreement between the new franchisee and the original franchisee might be a better alternative for the original franchisee rather than trying to expand his/her own business too quickly. Another method would be to put in place protocols or formulas to identify whether an existing outlet has been affected negatively by the opening of a new outlet. Using this methodology, there is a clear understanding between the original franchisee and the franchisor as to the level of competitive impact that the original franchisee's outlet can endure; if the new outlet causes a greater commercial impact than the agreed level, the franchisor compensates the original franchisee.

→

CASE STUDY 9.1 *continued*

Fortunately, franchisees are not on their own when facing such a blatant disregard of the ongoing viability of their business; there are resources at their disposal to help them avoid the pitfalls. First, to make sure that the franchisee's investment is protected, s/he should ask a franchise lawyer to review the agreement *before* signature. At the same time, it is also important to research the franchise opportunity and the franchisor most carefully; the best way to delve into the innermost secrets of a franchise is to speak with as many existing and past franchisees as one is able. This way the potential franchisee learns the positives *and* negatives of being a franchisee with a particular brand. Franchise associations, such as the Canadian Franchise Association (CFA), encourage ethical and responsible franchising and self-regulation through standardized disclosure documents; they impose a strict code of ethics on their members, and a strict vetting procedure for all their members. Franchisees can have a high level of confidence, knowing that their franchisor holds CFA (or other franchise association) membership.

Significantly, at the time of this case, only two provinces of Canada had legislation regulating the franchise industry. The franchising laws in the provinces of Alberta and Ontario imposed a *'duty of fair dealing'* on both franchisor and franchisee. Additionally, the regulations contained widespread disclosure obligations that franchisors had to follow. It is a point worth noting, though, that some would argue that Alberta's *Franchises Act* (2000) was the reason for the slow expansion of franchising in the province. On the other hand, the province of Ontario is where over 50 per cent of the nation's franchises are located. Ontario's provincial legislation is still relatively new and only time will tell if the new legislation will put the brakes on the intensification of franchised businesses in that province. It is expected that additional provinces will follow Ontario's lead in seeking to legislate the industry.

> *It is crucial that trust exists between the* **franchisor** *and* **franchisee**, *so in financial matters there has to be openness and mutual understanding.*

Note: While this case study is based on a true story, the names of the unlucky franchisee and his franchisor, and the industry in which they operated, have been changed for legal reasons. The Café au Lait franchise used for this illustration is a fictitious business and does not reflect on any existing business, whether franchised or otherwise.

FINANCIAL MATTERS

Whether one is a franchisee or a franchisor, all business transactions will involve three elements: revenue, cost and investment. The acid test of whether one is running a successful business might be if there is sufficient profit being generated when one deducts the cost and investment elements from the revenue. For the franchisor, it becomes a little more complicated, because the speed of expansion is going to have a negative impact on profitability while not necessarily generating revenue for a period of time; the good news, however, is that because franchising is a replicated business model, the time lag between investment in a new franchise outlet and the outlet starting to generate profit, is typically less. Nevertheless, the history of franchising is littered with the corpses of franchisors who tried to expand too quickly and without the financial depth to survive the lean period between recruitment and the generation of revenue.

This brings us on to another thorny issue, in that those engaged in franchising enjoy talking about revenue streams, but in all honesty revenue is merely a feature on financial statements; what drives business forward is profit.

As the financial requirements of the franchisor and franchisee differ, we need to (as in other parts of this book) separate them and deal with them independently.

The franchisor

The financial aspect of the franchisor's business is twofold; initially, the franchisor bears the financial expense of establishing the franchised business, and then has to make sufficient profit from the franchisees to sustain lasting viability. And, on top of his/her own financial considerations s/he has to take into account that his/her franchise offering has to be sufficiently attractive to enable him/her to sell all of the territories, and financially worthwhile so that they are profitable.

This fine balancing act is slightly upset by the realization that it is not unusual for franchise networks not to be profitable for up to five years, so the franchisor needs to ensure that s/he has sufficient working capital available to fund his/her business until profitability is achieved.

Sometimes, it may be possible for the franchisor to subsidize his/her negative cash flow with the income generated by the 'in-house' pilot operation, but in any case, before most banks will even look at funding a franchisor's business they will want to see a realistic business plan that incorporates cash flow, profit and loss, and probably even balance sheet projections for the period until the company reaches positive profitability, plus what the overall capital requirements will be for the business.

One element that financiers are very adept at spotting is that, as the system grows, so must the infrastructure. There are very many struggling franchisors who still believe they can run a network of 100 franchisees with the same infrastructure they had when they ran a network of ten. It doesn't work, and the franchisees become increasingly dissatisfied with the diminishing level of service that their discontent will have an adverse effect on the recruitment of new franchisees. Once a franchise system gets a reputation for having a weak support structure, it is extremely difficult to rid itself of that mantle!

The fees that each franchisee pays should represent a growing income to the franchisor, and as the individual franchisee starts to taste success, it might be hoped that they will expand their businesses by investing in new territories, thereby expanding the system and multiplying the income achievable by the franchisor. Consequently, the fees charged to the franchisees need to be finely tuned so that equilibrium is achieved between what is necessary for the franchisor to be profitable and what is needed for the franchisees to recover their investment and realize a good living income; neither party can afford to be greedy.

So let us now consider the fees that the franchisees will be paying to the franchisor. As noted earlier, franchise fees come in two parts; the initial fee and the ongoing management fees or 'royalties'. Having invested a large amount of money in the development of the system, it could be extremely tempting for the franchisor to load the initial payment so as to recover a large chunk of the set-up costs. This would be financial folly, though, as the higher the entry fee, the fewer prospective franchisees will be available with the necessary resources, and if a franchisee's financial backer suspects that the franchisor is loading the front end too much, the likelihood is that it will not fund the purchase. So, by being too greedy, the franchisor is risking strangling the development of the network.

Remembering that the fees collected from the franchisees represent the entire income or revenue of the franchisor, from which s/he will have to meet his/her liabilities and still generate a profit, while the franchisee is going to resent paying fees to the franchisor and will probably always consider that the franchisor is taking too large a slice of his/her profits, the level of fees that are set have to appear to be fair and reasonable to both parties.

The franchisor will have to develop his/her business plan on the basis that s/he will know what his/her expenditure is going to be at the end of each financial period incorporating a realistic level of inflation, and set the fees at such a level that recovery of investment is achieved in a reasonable period while good profitability is attainable thereafter. The level of costs incurred and the timescale to reach breakeven are therefore significant factors in this equation, and if the fee expectation for each franchised unit is too high, it might reasonably be assumed that either the costs should be reduced or the breakeven timescale be lengthened. Alternatively, the growth of the network would need to be accelerated, but (as we have seen) this must not be done at the expense of the network's quality of support.

As the franchise system becomes more established and its reputation grows, it may be possible to increase the initial fee levels so that new franchisees and renewing existing franchisees start to pay a premium for membership of the network.

During the pilot and in the initial stages, the accountancy procedures the franchisor needs to have in place are minimally the amount of business in cash terms that the franchise is conducting, so that fees can be calculated, and the number of customers, so that an average order value can be calculated. Unless there is a strong argument for additional expenditure, such as an electronic point of sale (EPoS) system for stock control, manual accounting initially lends itself to tweaking without the complexities of having to rewrite computer programs.

Some franchisors undertake the accounting and record-keeping role for their individual franchisees, and while this is an effective control measure, many franchisees resent 'big brother' constantly monitoring their accounts and performance. This accountancy role is beyond the traditional relationship, and franchisees are still legally responsible for their own accurate book-keeping and accounting procedures – even if the franchisor is dealing with the accounting for the franchise; if the VAT does not get paid, it is the franchisee that is liable, not the franchisor! Consequently, if the franchisor does undertake some of the administrative and accounting duties, the responsibility for communication effectively shifts in this area from the franchisee-to-franchisor model, to the franchisor-to-franchisee model. Nevertheless, there are significant advantages for the franchisee of the franchisor running the franchisee's accounts; not least (as we have seen) it enables the franchisee to focus on business development without getting sidetracked by chasing bad debts or worrying unduly about the imminent tax return.

If the franchisee is to remain responsible for the franchise's accounts, the franchisor will expect to see regular reports on gross income, which will be used to calculate the fees payable. Some franchisors expect fees to be paid weekly, others monthly, still others quarterly, and whichever cycle applies to a given franchise will be detailed in the franchise agreement. If a franchisee has weak finances, then the problem will be evident more quickly if weekly fee payments are expected, as undoubtedly some weeks the payment will be late; at the same time, quarterly fees help the franchise's cash flow.

Fees are calculated by taking the franchise's gross revenues, less VAT, and the fee percentage is then applied. If there is a marketing surcharge, this too will be applied separately to the franchise's gross turnover, less VAT. This will give the franchisee a total of the fees due, to which VAT should be applied and a cheque sent to the franchisor or payment made by whatever means the franchisor prefers.

Typically, franchisors also expect to see profit and loss (P&L) statements, as these enable the early detection of margin erosion, and again the more frequent the reporting or the shorter the reporting cycle, the more benefit the information is to the franchisor's analysis. If credit is given, as is usual in B2B operations, then regular monitoring of payments is essential; nothing eats away at margins more quickly than a bad payer! There is an adage that ought to be drummed into the head of every business person: *'A sale is but a gift until it is paid for!'*

When the franchisor receives a P&L statement from the franchisee, s/he will examine the details to ascertain whether the actual performance varies from the projected performance based on experience, and if any variances are identified, closer analysis will reveal the likely cause. If the data collected is published to the other franchisees on a collated weekly or monthly basis, the franchisees will be able to judge for themselves how efficiently they are running their own businesses.

Budgeting is an area where the franchisor can offer a huge amount of help to his/her franchisees. Asking franchisees to provide budgets on a monthly basis will enable franchisors to identify whether individual franchisees are being extravagant in purchasing a better lifestyle prematurely! Budgets, together with the P&L account, will give a pretty good indication of the financial health of the franchise unit, and will help to ensure the long-term viability of the franchisee.

If the franchisor is not providing an integrated accountancy package in which all the information for both financial and management accounting is collated and generated into reports, with a payroll package attached so that franchisees can quickly produce wage slips, then guidance must be given to the franchisees in how to complete the statutory forms and returns for the various official bodies requiring regular submissions. The tendency is for a new franchisee who has never run a business previously, to look rather simplistically at what has been taken over a given period, subtract the expenditure incurred, and call the rest earnings. This naïve approach to accounting is a recipe for disaster, and it is important that the franchisor ensures that all the hard work invested in developing a nascent franchise unit is not laid waste by the taxman taking a punitive sledgehammer to the franchisee's business.

The franchisee's bank will offer some degree of assistance, and many banks nowadays offer a basic business accounting programme as part of their account incentives. Nevertheless, there is a strong and extremely valid argument for the franchisor who does not want to run the accounts of the franchisee in-house, to spend that little bit extra and offer his/her franchise network a fully integrated financial and stock control software package that will enable franchisees to run their businesses effectively with the minimum amount of time being spent on administrative duties. This also gives the individual franchisee the security of being able to establish the financial health of his business at a click of a button, or at least by the pressing of a few computer keys.

The franchisee

From the franchisee's point of view, finances are extremely important, as very few will be able to reach into their bank accounts and be able to afford the initial purchase price of the franchise, so somebody, somewhere is going to be lending them a large slice of the buy-in cost and will probably also be assisting them with ongoing working capital.

It is quite common when visiting franchise exhibitions to see franchisors advertising 'Initial Investment only £9,500' and 'Reduced Buy-In' and other such sales puffs to attract potential franchisees, and wise prospects might wonder whether these 'bargains' were really all that they purported to be. Look closely at precisely what is included in the 'bargain' price: does the franchise need a specific type of premises to operate from; or a particular type of vehicle? What about stock; is that chargeable as a separate item?

Many of these so-called 'bargain' franchises talk only about the cost of buying into the system, and not the actual cost of setting up the franchise as a working business. It is not unusual for the 'bargain' price to escalate two- or threefold, or by an even greater multiplier by the time all costs are factored into the equation. Undoubtedly, the financier will still fund 50–70 per cent of the costs, but the initial capital input by the franchisee will have grown accordingly.

Another scenario could be that the franchise offering is a new business and relatively untried; the franchisor is trying to expand the network quickly so that greater brand recognition and business awareness is achieved, and this is being done by offering a lower initial buy-in. The danger here is that the ongoing fees may be higher, but with a reduced earning capacity, or that the system may prove to be unworkable.

In the north of England there is a saying: 'Tha can't get owt fer nowt' meaning that one will not get anything for nothing, and this is very true of franchising – if it seems too good a bargain, then it probably is too good to be true! Caveat emptor or 'Let the buyer beware' is the order of the day, and remember it is the salesman's job to sell.

Responsible franchisors will be totally open and honest about the amount of money a prospective franchisee will have to invest in order to buy into their brand, the costs will all be laid out and be fully explained, as will any credit facilities that may be arranged through the franchisor's preferred bankers, which will always be subject to the prospective franchisee meeting the bank's criteria for the business development loan.

In the same way that it would almost be unethical for a franchisor to lend the money to a prospective franchisee to buy into the system, because to do so would certainly muddy the waters of the franchisor/franchisee relationship, neither will any responsible franchisor accept any franchisee who has to borrow 100 per cent of the initial investment. There has to be clear water between the businesses of the franchisor and the franchisee, and the latter must make some commitment and take responsibility for investing in his/her own business.

However, in saying this, banks do like franchises, as they have shown over many years that they are by far a safer investment for banks. Often banks will match the level of investment that a small businessperson invests in his/her own stand-alone business, but with franchising it is not unusual for banks to lend between 60 per cent and 80 per cent of the necessary funding, based on the creditworthiness of the candidate and the track record of the franchisor.

Franchisees should remember, though, that any loan taken out will have to be repaid, the loan is the responsibility of the franchisee, and neither the franchisor nor the bank will give any guarantee of success. The success or failure of the franchise unit is wholly in the hands of the franchisee, and if it all goes wrong, then it is likely that the blame will lie with something the franchisee has not done, or something s/he has done badly.

When buying a franchise, the franchisee is entering the world of business and the self-employed, and a significant element of that world is risk. No franchisee should even contemplate the move into this world without fully assessing the risks involved. There is a chance that the franchisee will lose everything, but that risk is substantially reduced compared to setting up a stand-alone business, because the franchise system is a tried and tested route to running a successful business, and it is a well-recorded fact that failures among franchises are significantly lower than for those running independent businesses.

WHAT DO YOU THINK?

Are the rules and regulations surrounding franchising and the need to have such a strict and 'one-sided' contract really necessary? Or would the industry benefit from more freedom to operate in a less restricted manner?

Do you feel that financial matters in franchising could be simplified? If so, how?

Further reading

Baldi, Roberto, *Distributorship, Franchising, Agency* (Springer 1988).

Jarkina, Viktorija, *Franchising in Theory and Practice: A Franchise Agreement in the Framework of Civil Law* (LAP LAMBERT Academic Publishing 2010).

Mendelsohn, Martin, *Franchising Law*, 2nd edn (Richmond Law & Tax Ltd 2004).

Schneider, Jeffrey A., *Business Franchise Law: Cases and Materials* (Carolina Academic Press Law Casebook Series) (Carolina Academic Press 2003).

10 DEVELOPING THE BUSINESS

INTRODUCTION AND LEARNING OBJECTIVES

Any business that hopes to survive in a rapidly changing marketplace must develop and move forward. If businesses stand still, they effectively move backwards as competitors develop and seize their market share. This phenomenon is also the case in franchising. This chapter looks at how franchised businesses can develop; how franchisees can focus their business to be more effective and to grow with the help of their franchisor; and what franchisors might consider when looking at expanding their business into new markets overseas.

The reader will be able to:

- Understand the need for growth and business expansion.
- Appreciate the levels of assistance that franchisees look for when seeking to grow their business.
- Comprehend the advantages and disadvantages to expanding a franchise internationally.

Developing the business is an important concern for both franchisor and franchisee; it is merely the scale of the expansion that differs. The franchisee may be looking at developing his/her business by becoming a multi-unit owner; while the franchisor will be looking for new markets and this might involve expansion into other countries.

First, we shall consider expanding the business with the assistance of the franchisor, so this is really targeted at the franchisee reader.

> Many franchisors like ambitious franchisees – it reduces training expenses if an existing franchisee grows his/her business by buying another area.

EXPANDING THE FRANCHISEE'S BUSINESS

The franchisee has built a successful business and now has itchy feet to try to expand the operation; s/he feels that this is the right time to take his/her franchise to the next level. Is there anything that the franchisor can do to help with these plans for expansion?

The first point the franchisee must appreciate is that s/he has signed a franchise agreement with their franchisor, and they cannot expect anything more (or less) than is included in that document. The franchisor is usually not in any way obligated to assist a franchisee expand his/her business, unless there is a clause included that gives the franchisee 'first refusal rights' in respect of adjacent franchise outlets. If there is such a clause, then the franchisor may be expected to give the franchisee a reasonable amount of assistance in developing the business.

In saying this, there are good and sound reasons why a responsible franchisor would *want* to help a franchisee expand his/her number of outlets; if for no other reason than that an existing franchisee would need minimal training and support in getting a new outlet opened, and the turnaround time would generally be considerably less. One common reason why franchisors have gone into franchising is because they want to develop their brand and exposure more rapidly than they would be able to through in-house expansion, so franchisors that aspire to growth, will typically understand that their greatest asset is the network of dedicated franchisees that operate the business. Consequently, providing support to an ambitious franchisee, beyond the terms of the agreement, is a way of reinvesting in the system.

This is the difference between a 'good' franchisor and an 'excellent' one. Qualifications for the second category include:

- Providing a highly trained support network comprising both backroom staff and field agents who can assist franchisees with all the operational aspects of the business, from marketing and functioning procedures to legal and financial concerns.
- Creating a communications network that is both free and comprehensive so that franchisees can pool resources about what is actually happening in the market and offer suggestions regarding keeping one step ahead of the game.
- Understanding what is happening with the competition and looking constantly for ways and means to improve the product offering through modifications and the lowering of costs.

This last point needs to be expanded upon, because any business can only be truly successful if the people running it completely understand what is happening among the competition. This is not something that can be left to the franchisor; the individual franchisee needs to know what is happening with the local competition if there is to be any hope of growth or expansion.

It is crucial that every business knows everything possible about the competition, from how rival companies brand their business, what their marketing techniques are, how employees are treated and paid, even how the business is managed. Any competitor worth his/her salt is assessing your business in a similar way and doing it all the time, because circumstances change and businesses evolve, so it becomes an almost constant obsession with successful franchisees that they are always up-to-date with what is happening among their competitors; so don't feel as though it is sneaky or underhand – it's how business stays one step ahead of the game.

Of course, the law would frown upon any franchisee who bugs their competitor's business premises, or who stalks them with a tape-recorder hidden under their overcoat; but typically franchisees can find out all they need through regular commercial channels, without breaking the law.

Here are ten pointers that franchisees need to implement to understand their competitors:

1 *Who is the competition?* Sounds a silly suggestion, but many franchisees can tell you who in their area is selling similar products, but very few are able to list competitors who fulfil the same consumer need. When the local supermarket starts selling Mexican food, it is easy for the local Mexican restaurant to think that the customer bases are different; they are not. Both are offering the same products, Mexican food, but not the same service. Nevertheless, both businesses have the same target customers – people who like Mexican food.

2 *What is the corporate culture?* Every business, whether large or small, has a corporate culture, and understanding what that culture is can help the successful franchisee to compete against it. Try to mix socially with the competition and always listen more than talk, that way you are more likely to learn something! The corporate culture is a bit like a person's personality, and once that has been identified the savvy franchisee can see if there is something that can be transposed into his/her own culture to make his/her business more competitive.

3 *Build a competitor inventory.* The successful franchisee will always try to identify exactly what is in a competitor's product mix, and then try to spot gaps in the market that can be recommended to the franchisor as additional products to supplement the current offering; this will differentiate the franchised business from the competition.

4 *Reputation.* Any business will succeed or fail through their reputation, and if something bad is happening with the competition, it can bring down other businesses in the same field – remember the cautionary

tale of how franchising was adversely affected by the rise of pyramid selling. Of course, if something good is happening with the competitors, the successful franchisee will try to see if there is a way that some of the kudos can rub off on them.

5   *Becoming a customer.* One of the best ways to get a complete picture of the competition is to become a customer; this is sometimes associated with 'market research' and as such is a legitimate ploy. There is no suggestion that the franchisee should go and spend money with the competitor (although that may be necessary) but much can be achieved without spending money with them. The wise franchisee would search the competitor's website, read their sales brochures, join their blog if they have one, and take note of everything that would encourage him/her to become a customer. There might just be a useful element that can be incorporated into the franchisee's own business without breaching his/her franchise agreement.

6   *Employee relations.* Any business should regard its employees as one of its greatest assets, but some are better than others at retaining staff. What benefits do one's competitors offer their staff that could be incorporated into the franchisee's business?

7   *Spotting trends.* Many franchisees gain a good understanding of what is happening with the competition when s/he buys his/her franchise, but only the most successful make it part of their routine to watch the trends of what is happening with competitors in the local area. A good example would be when the local licensing laws are relaxed to allow for longer opening times of bars; an observant fast-food franchise might choose to modify its closing times to allow customers from the bar to buy their products after the bar has closed.

8   *Price watching.* Many franchisees have limited scope to vary the cost of their product offering, but price is only one element that consumers use to identify their choice of purchases. The shrewd franchisee will take time to understand not just what the competition charge for their products, but also why. Because the local competition is charging less for their products or services, does not automatically mean that the franchisee will go out of business through not being competitive; developing additional value-added features to the product offering may mean that the franchisee in fact outsells the local competition. It is only a fool who considers that price is the be-all and end-all of the product offering, and even in the limited scope for product differentiation within franchising there are usually opportunities to enhance the customer experience to give the business a competitive edge.

9   *Social media.* Not so long ago, it was merely necessary for a franchisee to maintain a watching brief over competitors' websites, but nowadays businesses use Facebook, YouTube, Twitter and a whole host of other social media presences to promote their businesses. It's highly likely

that franchisors will also use these media to promote their businesses nationally, but there is seldom anything wrong with franchisees also spinning off these presences to promote their businesses at the local level.

10 *Market share.* The astute franchisee will know where s/he stands in relation to the market share locally, and understanding the market share of competitors will help the franchisee put into perspective his/her own position. Ironically, actual market share does not affect how much business the franchise will conduct; however, perceived market share, which is how large a market share your customers believe a franchise holds, will often improve the chances of expanding the business.

Nevertheless, if a franchisee feels that s/he is not getting the support s/he had expected from the franchisor, the first step is to make sure that his/her own actions are beyond reproach; franchisors are often unwilling to help franchisees who are either not performing to the level expected, or who have otherwise damaged their relationship. Franchisors are unlikely to provide all the assistance needed, however; sometimes the franchisee has to take the initiative and look for assistance outside the network – through lawyers, accountants, consultants, trade associations, or even going back to college to get some qualifications.

If the franchisee feels as though s/he is controlling his/her own destiny, but is still not getting the expected support, then s/he needs to let the franchisor know that expectations are not being met, and if talking to field support gets nowhere, the franchisee needs to start going up the chain of command. Eventually, it is hoped, the franchisee will attract the franchisor's attention.

Discussing expansion with the franchisor is the first step that any ambitious franchisee must undertake, and both must be open and completely above board when sharing information. No franchisor is going to want to take an effective franchisee and run the risk of them becoming less effective by loading them with problems they cannot handle. The franchisor is the guardian of the system and has responsibilities to each and every franchisee to ensure that all parties benefit to the optimal extent.

Even if the franchisee is merely seeking to increase turnover in a single unit outlet, the franchisor will usually be only too willing to help, provided the franchisee is not becoming confrontational, and is being completely sincere when discussing the business. It is, after all, in the franchisor's best interest to ensure that each outlet is operating to maximum capacity – remember, they usually derive their income from turnover.

Development of the franchisee's business can only occur if there is a good relationship between the parties; franchisors appreciate franchisees who work the system in the way they have been trained, and are usually willing to go that extra mile to help those they consider to be 'good' franchisees.

DEVELOPING A FRANCHISE OVERSEAS

Expanding businesses overseas is always going to be a strategic decision that can be fraught with dangers and difficulties, and one that has seen the downfall of many a successful business, whether involved in franchising or not.

The decision to expand operations to another country should be taken for sound economic and practical reasons, and generally there are three good reasons why businesses choose to move into the international marketplace rather than stay in the relative comfort of their domestic market, and at least one other.

The first reason, and which is most probably the main reason, is that the domestic market is becoming saturated. Either the franchise has sufficient outlets to meet the needs of the available market, or competition in the marketplace has become too intense and the franchise is starting to lose market share.

The second reason is that the business is beginning to settle into a rut, starting to languish in past glories, and needs a fresh impetus to drive it forward. The thinking is that new ideas generated by careful overseas expansion would give the domestic business a little bit of a boost that would ensure the competitive advantage remains intact.

The third, and possibly the least rational, motive is that of a tempting untapped market, though it is worth remembering that just because the market is untapped, it does not follow that there is a market to be tapped! Careful and unbiased independent research is needed before following the heart into international expansion if the only justification is that there is a virgin market just waiting for an enterprising business to 'fill the gap'.

The most foolish justification for international expansion by a successful domestic franchisor seems to be rooted in the dark and sinister world of megalomania: the franchise is extremely successful in the domestic market and the franchisor is convinced that the entire world is conquerable in the same manner. It is a fact that history is littered with the corpses of failed megalomaniacs, so one would have thought that the lesson had been learnt, but seemingly not.

Without a doubt, the franchisor must have a sound domestic business that is financially stable before even considering overseas expansion, because it will not be an inexpensive option. At all times, it must be remembered that the proposed growth is almost capricious, it is something that is not needed, but it might be beneficial in the long term; and if the core domestic business is not financially sound enough to sustain the growth, it could damage the domestic business irreparably.

At the same time, the franchise needs to have home-grown personnel who can be diverted to international operations without damage to the core business; many times key personnel have been reallocated to head an overseas division and have failed miserably, or the core business has suffered as their business acumen has been lost to the dream of globalization.

The easiest way to expand overseas is through a partnership arrangement, but with the right partner, who shares the ideals and vision of the main company, the choice of partner can make or break the venture.

At the same time, and considering the macro environment, it should be obvious that the higher the level of political stability in the target country, the greater the chances of success; however, if a country is politically unstable, at best the franchise will have a difficult time, and at worst, its entire operation will be lost.

Most franchises work in areas where income is derived from people having a high discretionary spending power; that is, they can use a high portion of their salaries to fund image enhancement, or to make 'luxury' purchases. Low discretionary spending power often means that there is a limited market, but it may still be worthwhile seeking a share of it. The foray of McDonald's into the Russian market just post-*perestroika* is a good example of a risky expansion into a country where the price of a Big Mac equalled many people's weekly wage, but such was the company's reputation that massive queues formed even before it opened it's doors for business! Nowadays, you can hardly turn a corner in downtown Moscow without tripping over the infamous golden arches.

> The attitude of the government in the target country towards franchising is often the difference between success and failure.

To say that a new company seeking to internationalize its operations should try to understand its new market might seem to be stating the obvious, but surprisingly, many companies fail to do exactly that – they seek to take their domestic culture and philosophy, and impose it on the target country. When one has a global brand such as Coca-Cola or McDonald's, one might get away with it, but if your business is the 'highly insignificant upstart franchise company', one ought not be surprised if the target country is less than impressed. Commercial colonialism is a thing of the past in today's globalized business world – unless, of course, one has a brand that is already globally recognized.

> Empire building is the worst reason to expand internationally, and many franchisors who try it will fail.

First, franchisors need to understand the territorial government's attitude towards franchising in the target country: some have a liberal attitude, some less so, and some just simply don't understand it. However, there might be incentive schemes available for certain types of industry, or in depressed areas, or for businesses seeking to expand into the country. A good first contact will be the commercial attaché at the target country's embassy.

The franchisor also needs to understand the nature of the target market – how does it differ from the market back home? Are there local laws in place to govern certain types of business activity? How much discretionary income does the average potential customer have at his/her disposal?

What's the competition like? Who else sells similar products in the target country, and how successful are they? What share of the market do they hold? What is the close competition like? Is it more popular than the direct competition? How many changes will need to be made to a franchise's offering, to suit the target market? Then there is the cultural and social structure of the market – how will the franchise adapt its business to be a 'good neighbour'?

Obviously, it might be better to be internationalizing in countries that have a similar culture to the franchise's domestic market: UK and the Irish Republic; the USA and Canada; France and Belgium; Belgium and the Netherlands; Germany and Austria; Australia and New Zealand and so on.

However, there is the irresistible draw of the emerging market, this vast vacuum of potential new customers just waiting for a franchisor to open up in their market so that they may stampede their way to do business with the latest franchise offering. Cynicism aside, following the expansion into culturally similar markets, Western franchisors are beginning to appreciate that opportunities are diminishing, and that the emerging markets may offer greater development opportunities.

Let us not forget that 80 per cent of the world's population lives in emerging economies, and some experts predict that over 70 per cent of the expansion in world trade over the next couple of decades will originate in developing countries, especially those big emerging markets in which half the world's population is resident, but which currently contribute less than a quarter of the world's gross domestic product (GDP). It is true that these markets have huge potential, but it is equally true that trading conditions are invariably vastly different from the closely parallel trading conditions that franchisor's enjoy in the developed markets of the world, from where they derive much of their experience.

To prioritize emerging markets to target, franchisors need to identify the best method for entering the market, and then calculate an appropriate fee structure so that all parties will benefit from the proposed expansion. It is worth pointing out that, whereas the fee structure within a market needs to be identical for all franchisees, it does not follow automatically that the fee structure for the whole company needs to be the same; varying market conditions in different parts of the world will advocate a fair level of fees for any individual and unique market, which is likely to be different from other markets where the franchisor operates.

There are many factors that need to be considered before deciding on a proposed expansion target, but the three main factors that need to be analysed are the growth rate of the market's economy; the level of population in the target market; and the GDP per capita mediated by purchasing parity.

Studies clearly show that *the* most important factor in deciding whether a market is conducive to franchise development is the emergence of a middle class in society. The development of a structured middle class indicates that there will be a developing demand for Western goods; additionally, there is likely to be less social discontent and the political risk is likely to be diminishing in such a market.

Whereas the GDP per capita is an important figure to consider, to gain a fuller picture of the market's potential, this must be weighed against the purchasing power of the population, and ironically one of the indices that is most recognized in this field is that generated by *The Economist* and features one of the big names in franchising: the Big Mac Index (see Figure 10.1). Should a franchisor not offset purchasing parity against GDP per capita, a distorted picture may be generated, because the cost of living and input prices are not included in the GDP figures. Consequently, the purchasing parity of the population may be higher than the official, but unadjusted, GDP figures might indicate.

Source: © *The Economist*

Figure 10.1   The Big Mac Index

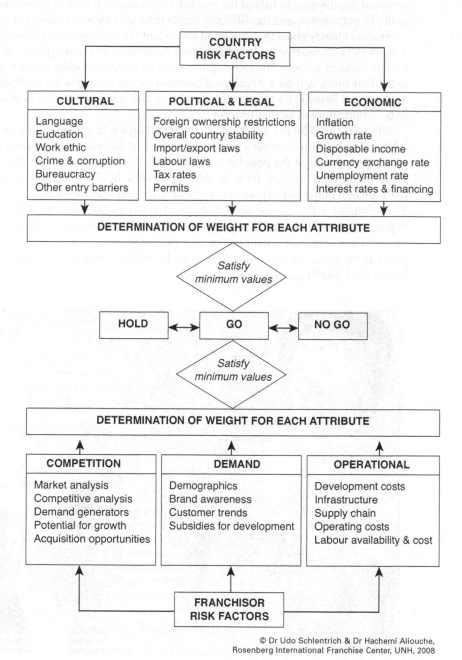

Figure 10.2 International franchising risk assessment model

Having established which country or countries will be the target of the budding global franchised business, the franchisor must make the decision as to the *manner* in which this expansion will be achieved, and the advantages and disadvantages carefully assessed and analysed (see Figure 10.2).

There are five common methods whereby franchisors seek to expand overseas, and over the next few pages I shall highlight some of the positives and negatives of each.

COMPANY EXPANSION

In this format, the franchisor will set up and run a subsidiary company in the target country. This may, or may not, be run as a strategic business unit (SBU) and will probably enjoy some degree of autonomy from the main franchisor – but the business will be wholly owned by the franchisor and will be run by appointed specialists who have both local knowledge and company allegiance.

Of all the options available to a serious franchisor, it is a highly effective and credible way to penetrate a country, but it is also the most expensive. Nevertheless, it does announce to all and sundry that the franchisor is a serious player and is intending to be in the target country for a considerable time.

It is worth remembering that even though the franchisor has run a successful pilot operation in his/her domestic market, expansion into a new country with a company-owned operation is likely to require another pilot operation to be carried out in order to justify to the local prospective franchisees that the business format works in their country as well as in the franchisor's domestic market.

Apart from needing the capital to set up what is effectively a new-start business, and support it during the pilot and growth phases, the franchisor will almost certainly also need local expertise – and the key personnel will not be head-office flunkies sent to oversee the operations; the people who are recruited will need to truly understand both the market and the franchising industry, and be able to drive the venture to success.

One significant disadvantage to this method of expansion is that it rather restricts the number of countries which can be targeted at any one time, as few franchises have the financial gravitas to be able to support expansion into too many countries at a time. Though this method means slow expansion and growth, which will undoubtedly be more thorough, it might just possibly prove to be more financially beneficial in the long term. See Figure 10.3, which illustrates five different overseas expansion models.

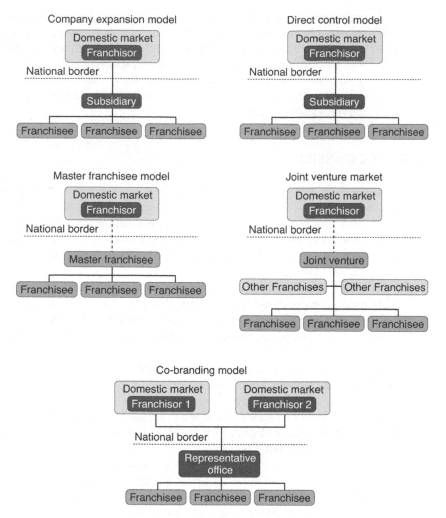

Figure 10.3 Overseas expansion models

DIRECT CONTROL MODEL

A slightly watered-down version of the Company Expansion model is the Direct Control format (sometimes called cross-border franchising), except with direct franchising the franchisor does not open up a subsidiary company, but operates the entire business from its domestic base. Perhaps this is really only viable where cultures are very similar and where there are no physical borders – such as with Belgium and the Netherlands, or Austria and Germany. Having a physical barrier between the countries, even as small as the Irish Sea, could possibly indicate that control would be too distant to make it a viable proposition.

The Direct Control method involves having the right level of support available at head office to sustain the increase in franchises that expansion will generate, and this may involve the recruitment of new personnel, which might tip the balance of viability for the cost-conscious franchisor. A hybrid of the Direct Control option allows for direct control to be retained over a smaller number of new franchises, but still allows for maximum market penetration by the creation of almost 'super-franchises' under a regional development scheme.

Let us imagine a scenario. A successful franchisor wants to expand into a neighbouring country which has similar markets and a similar demographic. Market research has shown that the two countries will stand a total of, say, 250 new franchise outlets. The franchisor calculates that, to be able to control 250 new franchisees, s/he would need a 50 per cent increase in support staff, which would increase his/her investment to a level with which s/he is uncomfortable.

The franchisor looks at Regional Development and estimates that, by appointing 25 'super franchisees', who would each be responsible for opening and developing 10 outlets, the franchisor is effectively achieving the level of market penetration that is desired, but is only increasing the franchisee base by 25, which is likely to be achievable with minimal head office expansion.

Of course, it is easier to maintain control over an increased network of fewer franchisees, but these 'super franchisees' will have more power, which can be wielded with a greater degree of force if there is discontent. At the same time, by devolving power to the Regional Development franchises, the franchisor can reasonably expect that the 'super franchisee' will expect a larger share of the profits, if only because s/he has to set up some sort of administrative structure to support the mini-network, so the franchisor will also be devolving profit ... but at the same time, s/he is buying more rapid market penetration and (possibly) fewer headaches, as low-level problems will be dealt with lower down the chain.

MASTER FRANCHISING

Master franchising is probably the most common method of expanding into new international markets. Effectively, the franchisor will recruit a master franchisor to take on the development of a large (typically national) market – so, it is comparable to the creation of Regional Developers, but on a grander scale.

Again, the master franchisee will be an independent business operation, but run with a similar level of control as a 'super franchise' within the existing network, except that the franchisor will be devolving responsibility for the localization of business, quality control, administration and so on, on a much larger scale.

This method will undoubtedly bring with it a whole raft of new problems: for a start, identifying and recruiting the right person to act as master franchisee will not be an easy task – there are many people out there who would love to take on the national franchising of McDonald's, say, in the recently declared independent state of Insignificance, but are they right for the brand?

The franchisor will need a strong and profitable domestic business to sustain the features that a new and fledgling master franchise operation will demand, and will probably need to divert key personnel, at least in the short term, to help the new master franchisee build up his/her business. How will this impact on the franchisor's domestic business? Remember Murphy's Law – it always takes more people than anticipated; it always costs more than was budgeted; and it always takes longer than planned!

CASE STUDY 10.1

McDonald's grew by catering to Indian tastes

" Global fast food major McDonald's says it survived and expanded in India by developing innovative menus to cater to the Indian taste bud, something it has not done anywhere else in the world.

As it completes 10 years of serving burgers, wraps and French fries in India, initially against opposition from nationalists, the firm has major growth plans, to double its turnover every three years in the next decade.

Two joint ventures, Connaught Plaza Restaurants Pvt Ltd, which is responsible for northern India, and Hard Castle Restaurant Pvt Ltd, which oversees the western region, manage the company in India.

Both partners have so far invested around Rs.9 billion ($193.23 million).

The decade's experience in India has witnessed an international food company developing menus that Indians would relish.

'Initially we were here just like any other part of the world. It's after a year of business we realized that we have to change if we have to survive,' Vikram Bakshi, managing director at McDonald's India, told IANS.

'Seventy per cent of our products have been developed to suit the Indian taste, something that happened for the first time in the company's 51-year history,' said Bakshi, 52.

→

CASE STUDY 10.1 *continued*

'In India we have been extra careful not to offer beef or pork items keeping in view the country's cultural sensitivity.'

The biggest challenge the American franchise faced in India was how to reach the large vegetarian population of India for which it had to re-engineer its products and yet maintain international brand value.

So in 1999 it came up with 'McAloo Tikki Burger' – a burger unheard of anywhere else.

'Today the McAloo Tikki Burger is the single highest selling product and is one of the first products to be exported to the Middle East due to high demand,' said Bakshi, speaking at his corporate office in Jor Bagh.

The McAloo Tikki has indeed won over numerous Indians.

Said Sulakshana Monga, a New Delhi-based fashion designer: 'I just love biting into Veg Surprise, and McAloo Tikki is my all-time favorite. They are the best.'

McDonald's now exports the Veg Burger and Pizza Mcpuff to the Middle East as well.

In India the company's sales have grown at the rate of 40 per cent. It has entered into three alliances with the Bharat Petroleum Corp Ltd (BPCL) to open outlets in its fuel stations.

'In India we constantly strive to do something new to maintain brand sustainability,' said Bakshi.

McDonald's has plans to open 20–22 new outlets, including one in Kolkata, which will be its first outlet in the eastern region.

'We are expected to invest around Rs.4 billion ($85.88 million). We hope to double our turnover every three years for at least a decade,' Bakshi said.

As part of its innovative marketing strategies, the company celebrated 2002–03 as the 'Year of Taste' in which the fast food chain brought out an entire range of unique items like Paneer Salsa Wrap, Chicken Mexican Wrap and McCurry Pan to cater to the Indian palate.

'For our young customers we brought out Happy Meals, which is a huge success.'

According to Bakshi, kids prefer to dine in McDonald's to any other place.

Nine-year-old Rajeshwari Dutta agreed: 'I love McDonald's as I can place orders on my own, not follow any table manners. And the best part is the outlet always gifts me a balloon.'

© *Indo-Asian News Service*, 29 August 2006

JOINT VENTURES

In franchising, so-called joint ventures are equally a blessing and a curse, and it might even be argued that they never really exist. Any agreement with a joint venture partner must, to some extent, reduce that partner to the level of master franchisee, inasmuch as the partner must buy into the concept and philosophy of the system. It is true to say that, in many ways, the joint venture agreement *is* structured in a similar manner to master franchising, in that the partner develops a country for the franchisor, and sets up and runs the individual franchisee network. So where does the difference lie?

Generally, in a joint venture partnership, the partner is an established business operating in a similar environment, who is seeking to diversify or to complement his/her 'stable' of brands. The joint venture partner has the advantage of already being aware of the machinations of the market, and will invariably already have an administrative function in place.

Throughout this book we have acknowledged that franchise agreements are somewhat skewed in favour of the franchisor, but a joint venture agreement is generally more evenly balanced, which tends to derogate the franchisor's control of his/her own business, and might even make it almost impossible to divest him/herself of an established joint venture partner.

Nevertheless, in some countries – India, Russia and China, for example – it is the only realistic method of market entry.

CO-BRANDING

Without a doubt, overseas expansion is very expensive. Consequently, mutual development of a territory through co-branding is starting to prove a very popular option and it would work in the following way.

A fast-food franchise and an ice-cream parlour franchise, say, seek to expand into the same target country at about the same time, so they join forces and set up one master franchise agreement, or one joint venture to run both franchises in tandem, perhaps even retailing through the same network of outlets.

Alternatively, the fast-food franchise seeks to expand into the target country at about the same time as a complementary franchise established in the target country seeks to expand into the domestic territory of the fast-food franchise. A co-branding agreement is set up whereby the fast-food chain markets the complementary products in their outlets and the complementary franchise markets the fast-food products through their existing outlets in their domestic market.

Or two franchises agree that, wherever else in the world they expand, they will do so together, under a co-branding agreement.

The possibilities are endless, but so are the potential problems, as there has to be a huge degree of trust between the two (or more) businesses, and the branding of common areas has to be conducive to both/all parties; but, most important, there must be common standards across the entire network. Getting it right might be a whole lot more difficult than getting it hopelessly wrong – and that might be disastrous for the parties to the co-branding agreement.

As franchises expand globally, so does the need for close supervision become increasingly important, and this presents an entirely new series of potential problems for the globalizing franchisor, especially with time differences and potentially vast distances separating the satellites from the locus of control. At some point, franchisors will need to consider some element of regional representation, and this is often achieved through so-called 'representative' offices.

These representative offices will seek to administer local agreements across large regions. It is likely that the rep office will not even be involved in the day-to-day operation of the core business, and it is likely that their role would be to act as the administrative hub of the overseas operation and to ensure that the standards set down by the corporate head office are maintained across the whole global network. They are the eyes and ears of the franchisor in another part of the world, policing the business to ensure compliance with standardized corporate principles and values.

It is another tier of the business that has been implanted to ensure the smooth operation of the sub-franchisees across the global field of operation, and will possibly be funded by a percentage cut of their ongoing fees – but it should be accepted more as a cost centre rather than one that generates profit.

WHAT DO YOU THINK?

As an ambitious franchisee, evaluate the pros and cons of growing your business by expanding through acquisition of additional territories with your franchisor. What would you expect in the way of 'discounts' to assist the expansion?

Analyse the options that a franchisor needs to understand before overseas expansion and apply the criteria to a domestic franchise operation that you know; how could the business be expanded most successfully?

Further reading

Alon, Ilan, *International Franchising in Emerging Markets: China and Other Asian Countries* (CCH, Inc. 2005).

Duggan, Ann, *Franchising 101: The Complete Guide to Evaluating, Buying and Growing Your Franchise Business* (Kaplan Publishing 1998).

Hero, Marco, *International Franchising: A Practitioner's Guide* (Globe Law & Business 2010).

Hoy, Frank, *Franchising: An International Perspective* (Routledge 2002).

Mendelsohn, Martin, *The Guide to Franchising*, 7th edn (Cengage Learning EMEA 2004).

11

EXIT STRATEGIES

INTRODUCTION AND LEARNING OBJECTIVES

In the excitement of starting a business, very few business owners would ever consider the day when their company is no longer viable, or even that one day they will want to walk away from it and take up more leisurely activities such as golf or fishing. In this chapter we consider the importance of 'exit strategies' to franchisees, as they are typically working towards a fixed timescale laid down in their franchise agreement, so part of the franchise owner's strategy must be to develop the business so that it is a saleable asset at the end of the contractual term. We also consider what happens when a franchisor decides that it is time to move on.

The reader will be able to:

- Recognize the importance of developing an exit strategy at the time the business is set up.
- Consider what the exit strategy will be for their business.
- Maximize the value of the asset.

As company owners start to plan their new businesses, very few actually consider what they are going to do when it is time to leave. There seems to be a bit of a mental dilemma when, just as their enthusiasm is running on overdrive, their mentor is suggesting that they consider how they are going to walk away from their new business. Many, if not most, have not given their exit strategy a second thought; and most are extremely reluctant to start talking about that future day when it is best for all concerned that they move on.

Of course, in an ideal world all business exits will be planned and instigated by the business owner, but sadly, and possibly increasingly, this is not always the case; many exits are forced and in these situations the exit strategy is little more than a damage limitation exercise. How does the entrepreneur or business owner walk away from the failed business with their dignity intact? Many fail to read the warnings that are written in bright red capital letters and believe that they can still save their 'baby' from drowning in a sea of insolvency; some even throw their hard-earned cash at the problem, hoping that injecting new funds will reinvigorate the company's flagging fortunes – they cannot accept the inevitable.

There is a valid school of thought that believes businesses are not 'surrogate children' that the owners have brought into the world. There is a legitimate belief that, if the parent company feels it has an undying responsibility to the familial business and a 'we must all sink or swim together' mentality exists, it is likely to lead to financial disaster. There are some businesses destined never to survive, and once failure is apparent, it is far better for all if the company is put out of its misery. Nevertheless, there still exist those business owners who assume 'parental' responsibility for their creation and disappear into the mists of oblivion uttering such platitudes as 'I did my best ...'.

So why do business owners need exit strategies? The fact is, that if you are establishing a new business you should really have a clear vision of what you want to achieve from it. In order for the business owner to maximize the value s/he gets from the business it is essential to think about how you will leave it at the appropriate time.

By structuring the exit from the business carefully, the business owner is able to ensure that:

- The right people are developed from within the business to take up the reins of the business; this applies equally to so-called 'family' businesses, where a descendant is groomed to take over, as it does to a company that is looking towards a member of the management team to assume full responsibility when the owner leaves.
- The business is shaped and crafted to the chosen exit strategy, which allows the business owner to maximize the value of the business when it is time to walk away. Whether it is a straight sale or some interest is being retained, building the worth of the business will ensure that the owner has achieved the maximum value for the future.
- The owner will be able to leave the company at his/her choice of time; when the business is booming and when market conditions are optimal.

Some would argue that an exit strategy should be incorporated into a business plan right at the start of the company. Not only does it show investors the timescale during which the business owner has planned to be involved, but also that the entrepreneur has thought about generating optimal value for the business within a finite timeframe. Of course, business plans can be reviewed and reworked (and should be on a regular basis) to reflect ongoing market conditions, and they often do need refining after the business has started trading, but setting an exit strategy at the start of the business is all about setting targets, and this gives the owner and investor a clear indication of the direction in which the business will be steered in order to achieve the exit strategy chosen.

Franchising, from the franchisee's viewpoint, will often have the exit framework already in place under the terms of the franchise agreement. In every franchise arrangement there will be a fixed term, which may (or may not) be renewable, and this timeframe is pretty much set in stone. Therefore, for a franchisee, one of the parameters has already been set, and all the potential franchisee has to do is to convince the investor that the plan that is proposed will achieve sufficient value to enable optimal returns for all parties. It is true that, in most cases, the franchisee already has a plan in place for what will happen to the franchised business after s/he leaves; most will want to sell their asset for as much as they can – but formalizing the strategy into the business plan will often bring clarity and focus to how best to achieve maximum value for the business.

From the franchisor's point of view, having an exit strategy is potentially more important, because s/he has responsibilities to the network as well as to the traditional investors. It is highly important that the franchisees are protected when the concept originator decides that s/he has had enough, and that it is time to leave the business.

The first stage in crafting the exit strategy is much more personal than merely considering any commercial factors. Look inwards and decide what is desired personally; the reason for considering starting a business and the type of business that is started will impact on this desire and this will, in turn, affect the exit options.

Let us examine the four main reasons why some people have a wish to become a business owner and operator:

- The potential business owner is pretty much fed up with being a 'wage-slave'.
- An opportunity has been recognized to generate capital growth by building up a business and then selling it on at a later date.
- There is a desire to create a business that can be passed on to the owner's children or other family members.
- The business owner has invented something and needs a vehicle to get it to market. Once established and the invention is proven, the business can be sold and even, perhaps, some level of royalty payment retained.

From the franchisee's standpoint, franchising will traditionally fit the first two of these options and may even fit with the third if the franchisor is comfortable with dynastic franchise ownership, but viewed from a franchisor's perspective any (or even all) of the options may apply.

Identifying the reasons why the business owner is taking the step to run his/her own company is the first step on the path to identifying the right exit strategy that needs to be built into the business plan. It is easy to forget that decisions taken at the launch of the business can often have ramifications at a later date, when it is time for the exit strategy to be implemented.

A good example of decisions made at the front end that will affect the exit is how the business is formulated. If it is set up as a 'sole-trader', there is little more that the businessperson needs to do than to decide when the time is right, pay all his/her creditors and shut up shop. However, if the business is set up as a limited liability company, which has a separate legal personality, there is likely to be considerably more that needs to be done to wind up the business. In saying this, a potential purchaser is likely to be considerably more interested in buying a limited liability company than they would a sole trader company; and this is not even starting to consider the legal ramifications of unwinding a partnership.

Understanding the various options available to the business owner, be they a franchisee or franchisor, right from the start might make the decision easier as to which path to follow. A diagrammatic flowchart of planning an exit strategy is shown in Figure 11.1.

RUNNING A LIFESTYLE BUSINESS

Many franchises, though few franchisors' companies, are run as so-called 'lifestyle' businesses. Lifestyle businesses are set up to provide a comfortable lifestyle for the business owners; undoubtedly, they know for how long the business is going to exist, and milk the business dry over the operating period. The business owners pay themselves huge salaries, massive bonuses and may even create a special type of share that pays inordinately high levels of dividend. The business owners do not really care what happens to the business in the future, it is not their 'surrogate child' and is purely a vehicle to make as much money as possible for them. If the owners can make more at the end of the franchise agreement by selling it on, then that would be a bonus, but the purpose of the business is to make as much as possible while the owners are involved.

> **Lifestyle businesses** *are all about providing franchisees with the maximum flexibility to enable them to live their lives as they wish.*

Naturally, this style of operation is likely to get the owners into all sorts of legal difficulties if it is applied to a publicly listed company, but in reality it is a perfectly sound business strategy in a privately owned business.

The purpose of the business is to fund the extravagant lifestyle of the business owners; however, a word of caution is appropriate, because if a business owner takes too much out of the business, then the company may not be able to weather a market downturn and the golden goose will, effectively, be strangled.

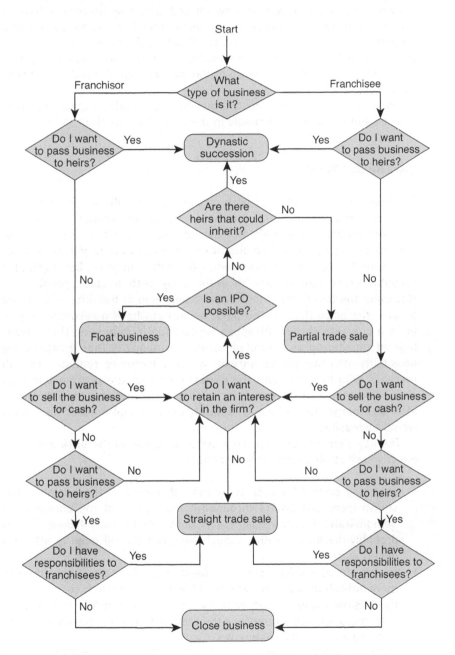

Figure 11.1 Exit strategy flow chart

From a franchising point of view, the franchisor typically monitors the performance of the franchise network and s/he may become extremely concerned about a franchisee who is milking his/her business too much; remember, the franchisor has a responsibility to the network and a duty of protection to the brand, so the ramifications of a franchisee living too highly off the profits of his/her franchise outlet may damage the system if it runs out of control.

As an exit strategy, the 'lifestyle business' is a realistic option for franchisees, but would be unworkable in the case of a franchisor.

SELLING THE BUSINESS

The most common option in both circumstances will be the sale of the business, and the eventual purchaser could be another business, a competitor business or even an existing employee. Generally speaking, the most likely suitor will be another business; not only will this probably secure the selling business owner the optimum price, but it will also probably allow him or her to walk away with a clear conscience. Naturally, the better condition the business is in at the time of sale, the greater the price that will be paid, so owners have a responsibility to build a business that is attractive to potential purchasers. One advantage of registering as a limited liability company is that it makes the possibility of a merger as an exit strategy far more realistic, though mergers tend to come with the expectation that the retiring business owner will stay with the company in some capacity for a period of time after the merger take place; it is highly unlikely that a quick walk away would be feasible.

The key elements of securing a successful sale of the business as an effective exit strategy are likely to include:

- *Increased profitability over every year of trading.* If the business has shown increased profits throughout the course of the operation, it demonstrates that the business is both solvent and efficient. This is probably the most positive aspect the business will need to attract a generous suitor.
- *Have a strong and loyal customer base.* It would make it considerably more difficult for a purchaser if they had to generate new customers for the business after it has been taken over or merged. Having loyal customers will help to convince the purchaser that the business is both a strong and sound investment.
- *Have a great team already on board.* The last thing a purchaser will want to do is to start a root-and-branch reorganization of the company's personnel. Remember, businesses are only as good as the personnel

they employ, and having a strong team underlines how substantial and worthy is the target company.

- *A quality product or service that is industry recognized.* This is probably the main aspect of the business that has attracted the suitor. If it is a weak product/service, the purchaser will have to spend time and money redeveloping the product or service to fit his/her existing product offering; and much less time will be needed to absorb the product or service if it is already highly regarded.
- *Maintaining assets in good order.* Companies that are seeking new acquisitions will almost certainly look at the assets the company holds and consider the condition in which they have been maintained. Assets are the bedrock of the business; poorly maintained assets give a pretty good indication that the rest of the business will also have been poorly maintained.

By carrying out a regular 'health check' of the business and making sure that the points above are covered may not be a guarantee of a good and profitable sale, but they will ensure that it will be more difficult for the seller to be savaged by a potential purchasing shark! Sharks, like other predators, tend to exist by attacking the weakest targets, and if the seller ensures that the business is not a weak target, this will usually be sufficient for the shark to swim off to other waters and seek easier prey!

As mentioned, the eventual purchaser may not come from outside the business, but may be an existing employee or group of employees who are keen extend their stake in the business. Whereas technically this does fall into the sphere of a 'sale', it really ought to have its own section. Traditionally, this type of sale is called a 'management buy-out' (MBO for short) and while in this case the timescale for the sale to be concluded may be substantially reduced, it may also lead to a lower sale price and/or payments extended over several months/years. Not only that, but the break may not always be clean. Sometimes selling owners are almost expected to be unpaid consultants as the business re-establishes itself under the new ownership team.

> *Because of the fixed term of a franchise agreement, it might be difficult to create a 'dynastic' business, unless it is as a franchisor.*

DYNASTIC SUCCESSION

As mentioned earlier, if the franchisor is comfortable with the notion of extending the franchise agreement to the sons or daughters of existing franchisees, this can be a highly effective method of passing control of the operation of the franchise to others, but still retaining an interest in the business at the time of franchise renewal. However, many franchisors will often desire a clean break from the existing franchisee and will not accept a renewal from a close family member. The reason, often cited by franchisors, is that franchisees become 'stale', becoming less dynamic and possibly less effective as the franchise term progresses and complacency sets in. Complacency and exit strategies are incompatible bedfellows, and to generate and implement an effective exit strategy, complacency cannot be allowed to take hold in the business. Consequently, a franchisor will often need a fair amount of convincing before renewing a franchise agreement in which s/he cannot be certain that the existing franchisee will not effectively still be controlling the franchise.

Dynastic succession is much easier to effect if the business is a franchisor, and having the benefit of the retiring business owner in the background to act as wise counsel can be highly advantageous. Moreover, it allows the retiring business owner to retain an interest, while also capitalizing on his/her asset by passing it on to his/her heirs.

If the plan is to pass on the business to the owner's heirs, then it is crucial that they become involved in the running of the business at the first opportunity; this allows for a thorough grounding in the business, so that when they take over control, the heirs are fully conversant with all aspects of the way that the business operates. However, in saying this, it is also beneficial to allow the heirs to work in other similar businesses to enable them to gain an insight into how other businesses operate. This might give a clearer appreciation of how the business they are inheriting operates, and may even bring a renewed strategic viewpoint to the company.

It can be hugely disappointing, however, and can significantly derail the exit strategy, if the chosen heirs decide that they do not want to work in the business and have ideas of their own. There is no real answer to this phenomenon, but getting the heirs involved as soon as possible and encouraging them to be active in the business and in this way developing a keen interest in the company might reduce the likelihood of their pursuing different options in the interim period between the present and the time in the future the business is handed on – perhaps as long as 20 years in the future.

One successful dynastic succession in the franchise industry saw the future business owner being 'given' a franchise outlet as a birthday present. The prospective heir was not treated any differently from any other franchisee, and was expected to develop the outlet in accordance with the overall franchise plan. The path was not an easy one to follow; the heir quickly identified what he thought were better ways to run the franchise outlet and often went head-to-head with the business owner over the strategic direction of the business. At first, the business owner was encouraged that the heir was 'thinking outside the box', but as the ideas became more and more hare-brained, the business owner started to despair and even thought at one time about cancelling the plans for the family succession and considering a straight trade sale. Luckily, as time progressed, the heir realized that many of the so-called improvements would have driven the business into the ground and he started to moderate his thoughts and actually start to learn the business. When the succession eventually took place, the company had a huge advantage over many of their competitors; they had a CEO who understood the business from the point of view of a franchisee, the business was being perceived from a wholly different perspective, and the result was a more dynamic business that developed in ways that the retired business owner had not even dreamt of – moreover, it developed successfully. It is not uncommon for successful franchisees to acquire new outlets and place close family members into the business as sub-franchisees and, as the business expands, there is almost a dynasty being formed within the franchise operation.

The one concern about dynastic succession is that emotion can often cloud reality, and taking the advice of a specialist consultant could help answer some key concerns:

* No business is worth damaging family relations for, so will the proposed succession damage relationships and generate conflict within the family? If so, is it worth the risk? Or how can this be minimized?
* Nobody likes to give any more than necessary to the government in taxation, so will the proposals be tax efficient?
* How will the succession affect the potential inheritance tax liability of the chosen successor?
* Will the restructuring ensure that the retiring business owner has a future that is sufficiently financially secure?
* Are there other options that will maximize the retiring business owner's capital return on his/her business, while not affecting the desire to pass on the business to his/her heir?

CLOSING THE BUSINESS

Shutting up shop is not necessarily a 'doomsday' scenario for some businesses; it might be the kindest way to get out, but in the case of a franchisee it is unlikely to be an option that their franchisor would welcome, and for the franchisee it effectively denies them the option of recovering some of the investment that s/he has made in his/her franchised business.

From a franchisor's perspective, shutting up shop is not really an option, as they have ongoing responsibilities to the franchise network, and pulling the plug on the business will leave the network unacceptably exposed.

So, simply closing the doors on the business in franchising will typically always be the consequence of a catastrophic event, the 'doomsday' scenario mentioned above, which usually comes into effect through a decision taken by others who are not involved in the everyday running of the business, or an external agency.

The decision to cease trading will have ramifications for others, no matter which side of the franchisee/franchisor divide the business resides, and it is usually stipulated clearly in the franchise agreement what will happen in either case. As a worst case situation, if the franchisor ceases trading, the individual franchisees may well still have stand-alone businesses that can continue to trade, but without the support of the franchise network. If a franchisee goes out of business, then the franchisor will be forced to replace the unit ahead of schedule – which may cause a hiatus in the franchisor's business in relation to that franchisee's territory and may cause the franchisor some additional expense in recruiting a new franchisee, but a franchisee ceasing to trade is unlikely to be terminal for the entire franchise network.

Whichever situation applies, the other party should take professional advice, from both a legal and financial perspective.

CASE STUDY 11.1

Exiting: Papa Antonio's story

Antonio Morinelli was a second-generation Italian émigré. Though he was born in London, he felt a great affinity for his father's Italian home city of Naples, and his family roots were very much a part of Antonio's character. Whenever the family went on holiday to visit relatives in Italy, Antonio was struck by how strong the family ties were, and how even distant aunts, uncles and cousins gathered together for a family meal to celebrate their arrival in the 'home' country. Antonio was also struck by how different female cousins were presented to him each time he visited, right from his early teens, and it soon became clear that Antonio was being groomed to marry into his father's family. Shortly after his twenty-third birthday, just after he graduated from university with a first-class honours degree in Business Administration, Antonio fell in love with Adriana, who was a distant relative, and they got married and moved to London.

Antonio was, at the time, working as a manager of a branch of a large chain of pizza restaurants. Though English was his native language, Antonio was bilingual and found it easy to drop into the dialect of his roots, and his ability to talk to customers with a strong Italian accent made him very popular with his customers. Soon Antonio found himself being promoted through the management structure of the business, and by the time he was thirty was earning a considerable salary as an executive who was destined to be offered a position on the board of directors as soon as a vacancy arose.

→

CASE STUDY 11.1 *continued*

The shock came when it was announced that a major drinks chain had bought the company, and in the manner of such takeovers, was keen to install its own management team, so Antonio found himself redundant. His severance package was extremely generous, but with a large mortgage and two young children at a private preparatory school and another baby on the way, finding himself out of work was a significant, life-changing moment for Antonio.

He decided that he should capitalize on his skills – he had been a very successful middle-ranking executive in the catering industry and had the natural background of being Italian. For many years, one of Antonio's pet hates was that the pizzas his former employer made in their restaurants were not at all authentic; they were manufactured for Anglo-American tastes and even the salami they used was sourced from Hungary. Antonio reckoned it was about time he set up a 'real' pizzeria and introduced the wondrous tastes and delicacies he had enjoyed when visiting his 'nonna' and 'nonno' back in Italy when he was a child.

When Antonio's first pizzeria opened its doors in a semi-fashionable suburb of London, the food was received with great acclaim: 'wonderfully authentic' and 'a true taste of Italy' were among the accolades that the hard-bitten restaurant critics gave in the first week of opening, though the traditional 'trattoria'-style decor was criticized as being a bit passé.

Over the next five years, Antonio's business went from strength to strength, and the single pizzeria had developed into a chain of five strategically placed restaurants throughout the capital, all of which were out-performing the local competition; in fact, when it was known that Antonio was planning to open a new outlet in a certain area, local competitors started to panic!

But, despite being a very successful restaurant owner, Antonio wanted greater challenges.

After a visit to a franchise exhibition, Antonio started to plan the expansion of his chain into the provinces by means of franchising. He selected one of his middle-performing restaurants and talked to Luigi, the manager, about becoming the first franchisee of the business expansion, running the pilot operation as a fully-fledged franchise.

Working closely with a reputable franchise consultant and a competent specialist lawyer, the guidelines for the business development were established, and eight months after their initial chat, Luigi signed the very first franchise agreement for the company and the die was cast.

One slight surprise that Antonio received early in the negotiations with the franchise consultant was being asked what he wanted to

→

CASE STUDY 11.1 *continued*

achieve with the business, and when he was planning to leave it – in other words, what was his exit strategy. Antonio had no more thought of leaving the business than he had of walking on the moon, but the thought of spending more time with his beloved Adriana and (he hoped) his grandchildren was quite attractive. So, at the tender age of 42, Antonio started to plan his retirement.

Completely without their knowledge, Antonio started to make plans for his two sons and daughter, Marco, Roberto and Elisa, to join the business and gradually take over control, thus allowing Antonio to retire from the business when he was about 57 years old. Antonio and Adriana began to structure their children's education so that they would have good skills to bring into the business. Marco was a natural entrepreneur, already at the age of ten he had developed a small trading business that enabled him to earn sufficient money to buy the new racing bicycle that he wanted. Elisa was the one with a head for figures, so she would be guided to become an accountant, and the youngest, Roberto, always had his head stuck in a book, so perhaps he would become a lawyer. Marco began spending more time with Antonio, visiting the restaurants, and he started to understand the business.

The launch of the franchise business after successful piloting was a huge success, and within six years of opening the first pilot franchise, there were already 15 franchised outlets throughout the UK; this may not sound many, but Antonio was extremely careful as to who was recruited, and the high purchase price of a fully-fitted outlet often deterred the less committed applicants.

At about this time, Adriana contracted terminal cancer and was given less than a year to live. Marco was just starting his 'A' levels at school and was devastated by the news that his mother would soon not be around, and as a result he totally flunked his exams. Antonio decided it was better to take Marco into the business immediately so that he could focus on something constructive; after all, there was plenty of time for Marco to understand how to run the business before Antonio planned to retire.

Elisa graduated from high school and (as predicted) studied for her accountancy qualifications, but little Roberto lost interest in studying when his mother died and took up acting, which meant that he had plenty of time to work as a waiter in one of Antonio's restaurants, but he did not show any interest in running the business.

On graduation from university with a first-class degree in accountancy and finance, Elisa was quickly snapped up by a major accountancy practice and it soon became clear that she was being fast-tracked to an early partnership, especially as she developed a romantic attachment to the son of the managing partner. She announced during

→

CASE STUDY 11.1 *continued*

one Sunday lunch, as the family gathered for the traditional weekly meal, that she was being offered a junior partnership with the firm and she would not be joining the family business. Antonio was both extremely proud and a little disappointed that his daughter would not be joining the business.

Roberto, was starting to get bigger and bigger parts in the acting profession, probably as a result of his relationship with Stephen, who was a producer working with the BBC. Though Antonio disapproved, he was glad that his youngest son was happy.

That left Marco, and Antonio was starting to come to the conclusion that his eldest son was 'not the sharpest knife in the drawer'. He seemed to lack the drive to be fully committed to the business and was more interested in 'get-rich-quick' schemes, many of which were moderately successful but these were outweighed by those that delivered spectacular losses. Antonio quickly realized that, if left to Marco, the business would be gambled away and there was the ultimate responsibility to the franchisees who had invested in the system.

The plans that Antonio and Adriana had for the successful development of the children into the family business were unravelling rapidly, and Antonio realized that he would have to modify his planned exit strategy radically. Antonio set up a meeting with his original franchise consultant to discuss the options available, and was surprised to learn that his focal point when deciding how best to proceed was not to be his own financial security, but the continued viability of the (now) 28 franchisees who were part of the system.

In exploring the options available, it was decided that a flotation on the stock market was an unrealistic option, as was a straight trade sale, as this option was unlikely to offer the guarantees needed to protect the network franchisees. It was at this point that a slight twist occurred. Luigi, who had opened the original pilot franchise and subsequently purchased two further outlets, indicated that he would like to become more involved with the day-to-day running of the business. He would be able to raise sufficient money to buy out about 80 per cent of Antonio's shareholding from the sale of his existing franchises, but it was conditional on Antonio staying involved for a period of two years in a consultative capacity, after which Luigi would buy out Antonio's remaining shareholding at the market rate.

What had started as being an opportunity for Antonio to provide a successful business for his children had developed into a successful MBO. Antonio was able to take his retirement earlier than he had planned, and to spend time with his grandchildren, though he was saddened that he could not share this time with his Adriana. The business went from strength to strength under the management of an

→

> **CASE STUDY 11.1** *continued*
>
> invigorated Luigi and the new management team, all under the watchful eye of Papa Antonio, as he was affectionately known throughout the business.
>
> *While this case study is based on a true story, the names of the unlucky franchisor and the industry in which he operated have been changed for legal reasons. The Papa Antonio franchise used for this illustration is a fictitious business and does not reflect on any existing business, whether franchised or otherwise.*

THE STOCK MARKET FLOTATION

The final option that could be considered is the stock market flotation and obviously, this is going to be more appropriate for the franchisor than the individual franchisee.

Whereas a flotation can be extremely rewarding as it gives the retiring business owner the opportunity to sell some or all of his/her shares to the general public through the stock market, it also is likely that the owner's planned retirement will be partial, or at least staged, as the new investors will be extremely nervous of an investment opportunity where the business owners are placing all their shares on the market in a single tranche.

It should also be borne in mind that any potential flotation will need the agreement of all the existing shareholders and current investors, many of which will hold rights that could easily prevent any flotation from happening if they are not satisfied with the plans to float.

In reality, floating a business purely as an exit strategy is going to be fraught with difficulties; it needs to be coupled with an expansion plan or some development in the business which needs the additional funds that a flotation would attract. It could work tremendously well if a retiring business owner has already groomed his/her successor, and the new CEO goes to the market with plans for a major development in the business (perhaps expansion overseas, or the development of a secondary franchise offering in a complementary market). Flotations must have a positive spin, not a negative one, and the planned retirement of the business brain that has led the business to the success it enjoys is hardly inspiring for future investors.

> *Flotation on the stock market may not be a true 'exit strategy' but perhaps more an opportunity to fund a change in lifestyle?*

Before taking the potential flotation to market, a revised structured business plan, prospectus and specific accounts will need to be generated. The business will need to have achieved high growth and profitability over several years, and the plan will show how this will be consolidated and developed as a result of the flotation.

The stages a business will need to follow for a successful flotation will probably follow these guidelines:

- Having in place a strong, dependable and credible management team that will inspire confidence in future investors.
- Long-term growth and high profitability to give the new investors confidence that they will receive an above-average return on their investment.
- The appointment of high-profile and competent financial advisers whom the market trusts to give an honest appraisal in respect of the company's potential, and who will guide the company through the jungle of legal requirements of offering shares to the general public.
- Development of sound financial, operational and management structures that are strong enough to handle the growth planned as a result of the flotation.

Most businesses, it should be remembered, are not suited to public flotation, and therefore exiting business owners should be extremely confident that the business is a sound enough proposition before committing it to this course of action. If the business fails as a publicly listed business, not only will the owner lose the value of their shareholding as it becomes worthless, but s/he may even face enquiries in front of and instigated by the appropriate financial authorities that could lead to legal action being brought against him/her through the courts.

Therefore, while the potential rewards may seem irresistible to business owners seeking to maximize the potential of their shareholding, the consequences of getting it wrong are immense, and it may well be felt that the options listed earlier in the chapter offer more realistic and financially sound opportunities to obtain a realistic return on their investment.

> **WHAT DO YOU THINK?**
>
> Planning a dignified exit from a franchise might seem a peculiar thing to do when the excitement of buying a business is paramount, but what advantages does forward planning bring to the shrewd franchisee?
> What differences exist for franchisors planning their exit strategy?

Further reading

Murphy, Kevin B., *The Franchise Handbook: A Complete Guide to All Aspects of Buying, Selling or Investing in a Franchise* (Atlantic Publishing Company 2006).

Norman, Jan, *What No One Ever Tells You About Franchising: Real-Life Franchising Advice from 101 Successful Franchisors and Franchisees* (Kaplan Publishing 2006).

12 DEVELOPING THE FUTURE OF FRANCHISING

INTRODUCTION AND LEARNING OUTCOMES

This chapter considers how the face of franchising has changed in recent years, and looks at trying to identify the direction in which the industry will move in the near future. Initially, we consider how technology is smoothing the opportunities for franchisor and franchisee alike, and then we move on to consider how being 'green' is likely to give a franchise a competitive edge that will ensure success.

The reader will be able to:

- Recognize that franchising is a dynamic industry that welcomes change.
- Understand that enhancements in technology are there to improve systems, not to create further barriers.
- Appreciate that retaining a competitive edge is crucial.
- Realize why long-term social issues can be a good reason to establish new franchising systems.

THE DEVELOPMENT OF INFORMATION TECHNOLOGY

Whenever most people start reading a chapter entitled 'The Development of Information Technology', their minds seem to gravitate to the notion that it is going to be another opportunity to sing the praises of the Internet, written by a geek whose whole life is dedicated to the promotion of the World Wide Web. Even respected authors who write on the subject focus narrowly on this aspect of technology.

The reader may be relieved to hear that this chapter is not going to become all technical about new technology or try to unravel the complex legal elements of e-commerce law, or attempt to analyse the thought processes of governing bodies who seek, almost with a Luddite approach to technology, to restrict the benefits of electronic trade.

The phrase 'information technology (IT)' relates to any mechanical equipment that can be used to manipulate the data that a company generates so that the business operates more smoothly and efficiently. This can range from the humble typewriter right through to complicated computer programs, and from the humble telephone through to sophisticated satellite-generated remote reporting technology. Most important, it is a tool that can be used to benefit a business; but it is not some minor deity, at the altar of which business owners need to pay homage!

Even in the early days of franchising, basic information technology was used by franchisees when reporting or communicating with franchisors. Undoubtedly the pioneers working for Singer or McCormick harvesting machinery would have communicated with head office by telegraph or the infernal Bell telephonic apparatus, so the implementation of new information technology is not something to which the franchising industry is a stranger; as each new improvement has been introduced, franchising has been at the vanguard of businesses seeking to adopt it.

The difficulty in today's world is that the speed by which new forms of information technology are introduced is gathering momentum, and the latest piece of technology that has been adopted by business is generally almost obsolete by the time the wrapper has been taken off the box in which it was delivered.

Whereas in the 1960s a new typewriter might reasonably have been expected to have a useful working life of over ten years, computer systems that are central to modern business need constant nurturing and enhancing with updates and variations. This, in itself, is no bad thing, but it has put additional stresses and strains on an industry that relies on being highly efficient in the way it conducts business, and often franchisors are running to stand still in the race for improved business technology.

A British Franchise Association (BFA)/NatWest survey of 2002 reported that 91 per cent of all franchisors had a website, and 41 per cent an intranet site; 70% of franchisees used a computer on a daily basis and 86% used one at some point in their business; 88 per cent used computers for email communication; and 78 per cent for maintaining a database of customers. It may be argued that the reason why, in the UK, the BFA/NatWest survey no longer reports updates on IT usage is that 100 per cent has been achieved across the board!

As it would be almost impossible to run a modern-day franchise operation with the technology that existed in the pioneer days, so in 100 years' time, franchisors will undoubtedly wonder that life could have been maintained with such primitive equipment. Consequently, franchisors need to look to the future and adopt the latest technology as it becomes available and, as the speed of adoption and/or availability varies, they must be prepared to invest more of their capital budget to ensure that they are reasonably up-to-date with the technology available.

Having preached enough on the subject of the industry's involvement with information technology, we shall now consider ways in which IT has benefited industry so far, and will then try to look at where this fascinating topic might potentially lead in the future.

To deal with the obvious aspects first, just about every franchise that exists, except perhaps in the developing world, will have a web presence of some description. Most will use it as a means of advertising their products or services to their customers, and it has to be said that money spent on this form of advertising represents a good investment – pound-for-pound it is good value for money.

According to the BFA/NatWest survey, as recently as 2002 less than 10 per cent of all franchisors used their website as a means of selling their products or services over the Internet. This figure will have increased substantially as greater security in the handling of sensitive data, such as payment information, has reduced the wariness of customers about buying online. The greater availability and accessibility has brought about another challenge whereby franchisors are almost tempted to compete with the franchisee network by having a direct sales operation online, and this raises all sorts of ethical and legal questions. If franchisors generated online sales on behalf of the franchisees there would be few qualms from disgruntled franchisees, but there have been occasions where franchisors sell directly (and possibly under a different brand name) at Internet discounted prices at which it would be uneconomic for franchisees to trade. This false competition is one of the negative aspects of increased IT accessibility, and has even been a reason for franchisors to withdraw from the industry to concentrate on their more lucrative online sales.

There is a valid adage in the world of Sales that states unequivocally 'Never sell on price, because in a price war the only way to go is down!' To run any successful sales business, you do not have to be the cheapest, but you must offer the best value. Franchising adds value, because there is a franchisee who wants to give his/her customers the personal service they expect and, as franchises generally have lower overheads, they can pitch

> *Price is a poor battleground on which to fight a war of competitiveness; value is a far better arena!*

their prices at a level that makes them good value; they will seldom be the cheapest, but equally neither will they be the most expensive.

Discount operators come and go, as they are invariably in business for a 'quick buck', but franchising builds relationships that expect to exist for many years, so it is false economy for franchisors to turn their backs on a tried and tested business model to opt for a quick profit.

An intranet is another aspect of web-based IT that will play an important part in the future of franchising, as being able to communicate information directly to the franchisor in a speedy and standardized format enables greater efficiencies to be applied throughout the business. Centralized customer databases have twofold benefits to a franchised business. First, they allow for lead generation to other franchisees who may have a branch of a 'happy customer' in their territory, and enable fast dissemination of sales intelligence across the network; and second, it means that the customer list is retained in the event of a franchisee leaving the business and taking his/her better clients along with him/her.

This second point goes to the heart of the question of to whom do customers belong – the franchisee or the franchisor? Generally, the answer lies in the franchise agreement, and usually customers of the franchise are the assets of the franchisor, but form part of the 'goodwill' of the franchise outlet. Nevertheless, if a franchisee leaves the system to go it alone, or to join a rival operation as the result of a forced franchise relinquishment, it is not unusual for him/her to try and take some of the better customers to build a foundation for his/her continuation business; retaining the information centrally maintains the benefit for both the franchisor and the replacement franchisee.

STOCK CONTROL

Holding high stock levels can affect the viability of any business, but it can certainly affect franchisees, who are typically working to tight margins. In the pioneer days of franchising, franchisees had to hold minimum stock levels of parts and accessories to meet customer needs, as ordering and delivery times were extended. Nowadays, however, modern stock control and EPoS (electronic point of sale) technology has substantially reduced the need to hold undue amounts of stock, especially with 'sell-by' and 'use-by' dates being applied to all manner of consumable products.

There is a story about strawberries and a grocery franchise. The season for the delectable fruit has just arrived, the grocery store has just received its first consignment of the year and the franchisee lovingly puts his new product line in pride of place in his store. The first customer arrives and selects a pack of fruit, which is taken to the cash desk to be paid for. In doing so, the customer fires the gun on a whole welter of IT data application.

As the shop assistant scans the pack of strawberries across the EPoS reader, the computer technology wakes up and registers the fact that a pack of strawberries has been sold. The information on the number of packs sold by the store that day is collated and sent by means of the intranet to the central database at the franchisor's head office, at a set time after the store has closed. The information as to the number of packs sold by every outlet in the region is assembled by the franchisor's central computer and a purchase order is sent out by the computer to the preferred supplier, who picks some more strawberries and packs them up ready for dispatch that night to the franchisor's distribution warehouse. On delivery, they are sent on to the various stores that have sold strawberries the previous day to replenish the stocks.

The pack of strawberries purchased on day one has been replaced on the second or third day after the sale. This 'just in time' stock control method means that customers are offered a full range of products that are fresher and of higher quality, more convenient and at a better price, because storage charges have all but been eliminated from the cost.

However, it does not stop there. The frequency of purchase of packs of strawberries at the store is also recorded, and this information is used to plot a store demographic of the purchasing profile of the average core customer. This enables the franchisor to plot buying habits so that the right stock mix is available to customers shopping in different stores, thus enhancing the customers' buying experience and regulating stock efficiency to ensure that turnover is optimally calculated. Even the placement of the stock within the store can be tested by means of the EPoS calculations, as different positioning will attract greater or fewer sales of certain product lines.

If loyalty cards are used, they enable each customer's buying profile to be recorded to allow for targeted marketing to incentivize greater purchasing from the store, or promotional activity on lines by which the customer might be tempted. Even if loyalty cards are not used by the franchisor, general promotional activity can be better focused at the store customer demographic profile, enabling a less general and more refined or targeted local advertising campaign to be implemented, either by the franchisee or through the marketing budget of the franchisor.

Managing data efficiently within a franchised operation is crucial for the success of the individual franchise outlet to maximize the opportunity that the franchisee has bought into, and this is one of the core responsibilities of the franchisor. Consequently, the selection of any system that is to be implemented has to follow strict guidelines as to the relevance and use of the data that it retrieves, holds and disseminates. Franchisors also need to remember that any information used may be subject to data protection legislation.

The acronym used in Figure 12.1 is a good benchmark when assessing the viability of any new systems purchase.

The 'ACCURATE' mnemonic is equally useful when considering the implementation of a semi-automated or even a manual system, as it is when installing an automated or computerized data management system, and this is where I need to revert to the original point and remind the reader that information technology refers to any mechanical apparatus that can be used to manage the data that an organization creates, so that the organization operates more efficiently and smoothly. The phrase can just as easily be applied to basic IT, like a telephone system, as it can to all-encompassing and complicated business management software.

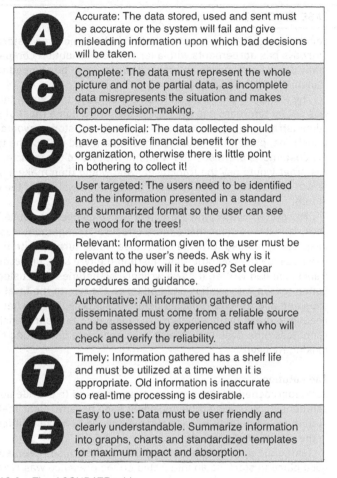

Figure 12.1 The ACCURATE table

CASE STUDY 12.1

United Tireways

United Tireways offers trade and public customers a personalized 'at own premises' tyre repair and replacement service through its liveried mobile franchised network. Its franchisees aim to give a same-day service and the company incentivizes franchisees who beat the 'average response time' to get to customers with flat tyres.

By operating out of a mobile unit, the franchisees keep their overheads to a minimum, although they do need to stock a range of the most

➔

CASE STUDY 12.1 *continued*

popular tyres; if a tyre is not available in the franchisee's stock, United Tireways has agreements with a large tyre distribution company with many depots nationwide and most tyre sizes can be shipped to the franchisee within four hours.

The Managing Director, Jack van Buren, says that when the company was set up ten years ago the franchisees were doing most of the administrative functions of the business. The customer would ring the franchisee, place the order, the franchisee would collect the tyre, go to the customer's premises and would fit the tyre to the vehicle, and the customer would pay the franchisee, who would then make a daily return to the franchisor and settle up the due royalties at the end of the month.

'The system was highly inefficient and wide open to abuse,' says Jack, 'and it was clear that a more effective arrangement was desperately needed. Often, a franchisee would turn up with the wrong tyre because the customer had misread the tyre size, or because the franchisee had written it down wrongly; sometimes the customer had gotten fed-up with waiting and had taken the tyre to the local repair shop and had the tyre replaced before our guy could even get there. We needed to make the business more efficient so that our franchisees spent less time dealing with problems and more time fitting tyres (and making money)!'

The solution
Jack approached a local company that promised to provide automated solutions to business problems, and it soon became clear that the system would need to be radically redesigned to make it fit for purpose in the twenty-first century.

Taking the initial contact away from the franchisee seemed like a good place to start, so an integrated online presence was created whereby the customer entered their details, and as soon as the zip-code was inputted the system automatically allocated the job to the nearest franchisee. It was even possible to include a 'preferred appointment time' to allow the customer to book the appointment – this actually gave the franchisee a greater leeway to complete the job, as many customers elected an appointment that was not time critical; it also meant that response times to 'urgent' jobs fell radically.

Next came the tyre identification, so the customer would enter the make, model and year of the vehicle and a range of applicable tyre sizes would enable the customer to choose which was required and this was followed by a choice of manufacturers. After the customer made the choice, the system would check the stock of the local franchisee, and if stock were unavailable it was automatically ordered at the nearest distribution centre, which would deliver to the franchisee within

→

CASE STUDY 12.1 *continued*

the four-hour timeframe, or the franchisee could collect if more convenient.

Finally, the site collected the full charge from the customer's credit card, which all but cancelled out the lost jobs.

The online ordering system was backed up by a contracted-out, 24-hour call-centre operation that seeks to resolve customer problems and concerns immediately, with much of the cost of this side of the business being offset by using chargeable 'premium-rate' numbers.

When the online order had been completed, it was flashed through to a printer in the franchisee's van and was scheduled on a virtual diary in the cab. The full charge for the job was credited to the franchisee's account and a monthly statement showed total jobs completed and their value, minus the cost of materials and the management service fee.

'This new system cost a whole packet,' says Jack van Buren, 'but our franchisees have seen an upswing in business of about 20% just by freeing up their time by taking away much of the administrative side of running their business, so it has proved to be highly cost effective – it might cost our guys a little more, but they're doing a whole heap more work; and our customers get faster, more convenient turnaround times and better customer service, all at a better price!'

Again, although this case study is based upon a true story, names have been changed for legal reasons. The United Tireways franchise used for this illustration is a fictitious business and does not reflect on any existing business, whether franchised or otherwise.

GREEN FRANCHISING

In the past, the only time the word 'environment' arose in a business setting was when commentators talked of the 'business environment', the 'corporate environment', or the 'economic environment', but now things are changing. Mention the word 'environment' to business owners nowadays and their minds immediately leap to the worry that they are not being as environmentally friendly as they might, and in franchising this is doubly the case. Nobody likes to be considered a social pariah and this is certainly the case in franchising, where franchisees actively want to be good neighbours in the locality in which they operate so often it is the franchisee that is driving attempts at greener business.

The fact is that it is not possible to run any business without leaving some mark on the environment. All businesses consume energy, buy in unprocessed materials and generate waste that requires disposal;

the cost of a buoyant economy is to some extent a degradation of the environment.

Many franchised businesses are taking radical action to ensure that the ecological impact of their commercial activity is minimized. In Finland, every McDonald's outlet has solar power to help run the restaurant and to reduce the need for traditionally sourced carbon-positive energy; and this is Finland which spends half of the year in perpetual darkness!

A recent television programme on the environment interviewed a businessman who was trumpeting his company's eco-friendliness, and was then seen leaving the interview in his six-litre, gas-guzzling, chauffeur-driven limousine! This cynicism is the root of the problem that many business owners pay lip service at the altar of environmentalism to convince the world of their eco-friendliness and gain the commercial and economic advantages of being seen to be environmentally responsible, whilst actually doing very little to reduce the impact of their businesses on the environment.

Government ministers, keen to be seen as eco warriors, litter legislation with environment-friendly legislation and forcing businesses to comply, but it is a trait of human nature that legislation is complied with reluctantly, whereas encouragement achieves a more willing response. Reinforcing the message that 'being green is good for the bottom line' will achieve more, more quickly and more enthusiastically than trying to compel businesses through forced legislation. The Finnish McDonald's outlets achieve a 25 per cent reduction in their energy usage by embracing solar power; but even changing to low-energy light bulbs will have a positive impact on the profitability of a business. Combine these measures with waste reduction techniques, and soon the average franchised business will begin to see very positive results.

One of the huge advantages for computerization was to be the creation of a 'paperless' office, but of course that has never been achieved; indeed the opposite is true, as we now generate more paper in our 'paperless' Utopia than we ever did when things were done manually. The economics are not rocket-science: generate less waste and companies will reduce the raw material cost, and reduce any disposal charges they may have to pay; in other words, taking a sensible approach to environmental matters is a good thing both morally and ethically, and it also improves profitability.

It is proven statistically that waste costs businesses about 4 per cent of turnover on average, and accepting that a business will never entirely eradicate waste, even a reduction of 50 per cent will increase profits by a substantial amount. In franchising, as we have seen, the franchisee fee is invariably calculated on the turnover figure, so a reduction of 2 per cent of turnover could easily translate to a real increase in profits of 5 per cent, which is worth fighting for. This is why profit-conscious franchisees are driving franchisors to be more environmentally aware.

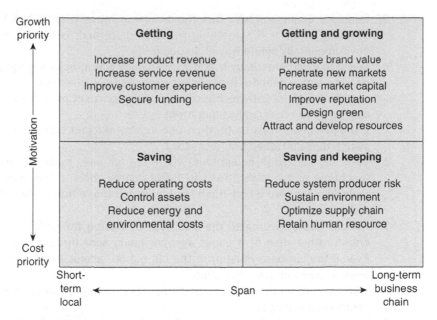

Figure 12.2 Green franchise matrix

Looking at the green franchise matrix in Figure 12.2, it can be seen that the benefits to business are wide-ranging and pretty much all-encompassing, but even though implementation would have a positive effect on the environment, it is arguably almost as a by-product; but it does illustrate the point that measures taken to make a company 'greener' do provide a financial payback.

The fact is that designing companies to be eco-friendly actually costs very little, but the ongoing benefits can be tremendous, which is why many new franchisors are adopting the 'eco warrior' mantle and developing their businesses to be 'seen to be green', but many more are trying their best to adapt in order to benefit from the green revolution.

There are twelve ways listed below showing how to become more environmentally responsible, and these apply to franchised businesses as much as they apply to other firms:

1   Carry out a green audit. There are many companies and agencies who will conduct these for businesses, some make a charge, but others such as those offered in the UK by the Carbon Trust, are free.
2   Appoint a 'green champion'. Someone who will monitor the company's progress towards eco-friendliness. Directors, managers and franchisees must be encouraged to take it seriously and get involved, but it must not detract from the company's main goal of generating profits.

3 Consider quality control. Can the business reuse what it has been throwing away, or if something must be discarded, is there a more environmentally sound way of disposal?

4 Invest in environmentally friendly technology when replacing lighting, heating and insulation. It may cost more initially, but many schemes are offered to incentivize businesses with tax relief or grants when upgrading to eco-friendly equipment.

5 If the premises must be lit, then use energy efficient bulbs, but even switch these off when not necessary.

6 Turn off electrical equipment when not in use, such as during lunchtime or overnight; this will halve energy costs. If the company toilets do not have a half-flush facility, install those that do to reduce water usage.

7 Reduce paper income to the business by having the utilities billed online rather than by a paper account being sent through the post. Even if the business must print the bill out on receipt, there will have been a saving on transportation.

8 Instead of flying or driving to that important meeting, consider video conferencing instead.

9 Look at ways of using more sustainable energy in the business. It costs very little to install solar panels, but they will reduce long-term costs and eventually be extremely cost efficient.

10 Replace non-fuel-efficient vehicles in the company's fleet with more efficient ones and target mileage reductions year-on-year. Incentivize employees to ride a bike to work rather than drive.

11 Target carbon-neutral status in order to win new business from socially responsible companies.

12 Shout about it! If the business is turning green, turn it into positive PR and make sure that staff, clients, customers, franchisees, investors and suppliers know about it. It may even make a few of them go green as well, and not just from envy!

One notable franchisor has developed a 'Green Team' headed by a senior executive and including managers and staff, but mainly comprises franchisees and their staff. The group meets physically on a monthly basis, but recently the meeting has been carried out using video conferencing to save group members having to travel. Meetings are scheduled to last for four hours and some franchisees were travelling three hours each way to attend, which effectively took the franchisee and key staff members away from the business for ten hours, whereas by scheduling a video conference meeting, the franchisee saved six hours of his/her time, which s/he then spent being productive in his/her business.

Apart from the video conference meeting savings, other ideas that have been implemented is to shred waste paper and use it to replace expensive (and non-eco-friendly) polystyrene chip packaging; to reduce the size of packaging (which also reduces shipping costs); recycling plastic bottles and cans; using passive infra-red motion detectors to switch off lights when offices are not in use; replacing the fleet of vans with more fuel-efficient and lower CO_2 emitting vehicles (which also reduces vehicle tax liability); greening the supply chain; and before anything new is bought for the business, either as capital or operating expenditure, a mini eco-audit is conducted to ascertain whether the company is buying the most ecologically friendly product, or whether there is a comparable product available that is more environmentally friendly.

On every computer terminal in the business there is now a 'Think! Can I be switched off?' label, staff are actively encouraged to use public transport or bicycles to get to work and are actively incentivized to do so, and on every piece of company stationery and promotional material there appears the company's 'We're going green' logo.

The company's MD is justifiably proud of their goal to achieve a zero carbon footprint, but he also recognized that this was going to take a good deal of time and be hard work; nevertheless, the whole company was committed to the aim. The MD stated that the average franchise unit had achieved cost savings of 17.3 per cent, which had translated directly into the profit account of the franchisee; head office cost savings were running at about 9.6 per cent and the promise was to pass 50 per cent of those cost savings back to the franchisee network in the form of incentive payments and interest free loans to install solar energy and/or small wind turbines to reduce energy consumption and reduce utility costs to the individual franchised businesses.

With a strong commitment to generating a brand that is synonymous with environment-friendly business practices, the company aims to increase sales by 17.5 per cent in the coming twelve months, and that is despite facing the worst recession the world has experienced since the 1930s!

Nevertheless, there is still some way to go to maximize the eco-friendliness of franchising, though it is encouraging to see that in theBFA/NatWest Survey in the UK (2011), two whole paragraphs have been dedicated to the fact that 32 per cent of UK franchises are taking measures to reduce their carbon footprint, which is up from a mere 10 per cent in 2006.

CASE STUDY 12.2

Greening up with franchising

Franchisees are seeking to clean up by teaming up with franchisors that have well-established 'green' credentials. In recent years many franchisors have modelled their franchised businesses on being more environmentally friendly than the industry 'norm' and there is strong evidence that they are influencing their industries.

Take, for instance, the growth in printer cartridge recycling. It has been estimated that one printer cartridge is thrown away every eight seconds of every day and each ink-jet printer cartridge takes about 430-years to degrade in a landfill; laser printer cartridges can take up to 1,000 years to break down! Quite apart from the actual cost of replacing printer cartridges with original replacements from the printer manufacturers, that is a frightening legacy that consumers are leaving for the future.

One of the better-known cartridge recycling brands is Cartridge World, which was founded as a franchised business in Australia by Bryan Stokes and Paul Wheeler in 1992. Bryan had an established business in refilling laser printer cartridges and Paul had an outstanding reputation in franchising and business; together they have built a multinational business with over 1600 outlets in 52 countries.

One might believe that companies like Cartridge World would be welcomed with open arms by an industry seeking to clean up its act, but, no, printer manufacturers go out of their way to develop technology that specifically seeks to thwart the efforts of the refilling businesses and thereby force consumers to throw away their old cartridges and buy over-priced original equipment manufacturer replacements. The reason? Printers are sold so cheaply nowadays in a highly competitive market that manufacturers rely on the sales of consumables to generate profits – even though their actions risk damaging the environment irreparably.

Another easily franchised industry that has an unenviable reputation for harming the ecology is the dry-cleaning industry. The active ingredient in many traditional dry-cleaning operations is a chemical called perchlorethylene, otherwise known as PERC, which has been linked with both asthma and cancer.

A leading specialist in the industry sums it up nicely when saying, 'Perchlorethylene is not a human-friendly chemical. Even short-term contact with the substance has been known to cause headaches, dizziness, loss of memory, nose and throat inflammation, dermatitis and severe depression of the nervous system; and if there is prolonged exposure then it contributes to various cancers and can damage major

→

CASE STUDY 12.2 *continued*

organs of the body like the kidneys and liver. This is not scaremongering by the green lobby, these facts have been borne out in many studies by both the World Health Organization and the American National Institute of Environmental Health.'

Perhaps the catalyst to changing the universal standard of dry cleaning with perchlorethylene came when the State of California banned its use in 2007, and this effectively forced all dry-cleaners in the state to find an alternative method of cleaning garments.

One of the leading companies in alternative dry-cleaning is Green-Earth Cleaning of Kansas City, Missouri. Green-Earth have developed a method of cleaning fabrics effectively and efficiently by using liquid silicone as a replacement for the harsh and damaging chemicals. Liquid silicone is derived from silica, or sand, and is one of the world's most abundant and safe materials.

Green-Earth Cleaning now has a presence in over twenty-four countries worldwide and its international affiliates have won an enormous number of world-renowned awards for environmental leadership.

These are examples of franchised or franchisable businesses that have seized the 'green' challenge and have become global market leaders in their fields specifically because of their commitment to the environment; but every franchise can make a difference.

Going green is good for the bottom line! Using energy efficiently reduces the size of gas and power bills; creating less waste not only cuts down on raw materials spending but also reduces any landfill charge that businesses have to pay. It is clear that taking a sensible attitude to environmental issues is not only a good thing to do from an ethical and moral viewpoint; it also makes sound business sense.

The Chartered Institute of Purchasing and Supply in the UK asserts that the actual cost to businesses of waste is not purely the cost of unused and thrown-away product, but includes wasteful use of raw materials, needless use of energy and water, faulty products, disposal of unnecessary by-products, waste management and wasted man hours. The actual cost of 'waste' for companies can be quantified as being typically 4–5% of turnover, and can be as high as 10%.

Even the most conservative estimation of 4% would have a significantly positive effect on the viability of a franchised business ... So the slogan 'Get Keen – Go Green' is most apt in franchising!

THE FUTURE IS ALL ABOUT CHANGE

There is an old adage that says if something isn't broken then don't fix it, and to some extent that is true, except that markets constantly change and offerings do need to change to reflect the current market. I am old enough to remember the Wimpy Burger chain in their glory days of the early 1960s after J. Lyons and Co. rolled the concept out across the whole of the UK; the latest fast-food craze to arrive from America, this strange food called a 'hamburger' that was not made with ham, but with beef. Moreover, they created a 'Hawaiian Burger' that was truly exotic, a hamburger with a canned pineapple ring stuck on top, with a cherry in the hole where the pineapple core used to be. It was a whole meal in a bun, savoury and sweet at the same time – incredible!

But Wimpy failed to change their product offering and their outlets started to look tatty and stuck in a 1950s time warp and by the time, in the early 1970s, that McDonald's moved to the UK, Wimpy almost disappeared. They have started to make a bit of a comeback in recent years, but the original market leader in burger fast food has about as much chance of regaining the number one spot as a hamburger has in hell!

Change happens, and any franchisor needs to change with the market trends to stay ahead of the game. Ask any franchisor whether the market for their product or service has changed over the past 10 years and be extremely circumspect about any that answer in the negative. As a follow-up question, ask whether their business has evolved in terms of product and service, and be even more circumspect about any that answer in the negative. But one wonders how many franchisors are still profiling their ideal franchisee in the same way as they did 10 years ago? Surely, if the market has changed and the products/services have been developed to suit the changed market, then is it not reasonable to expect that the franchisee profile will also have changed to reflect the evolution of the business?

Over the past 10 or 20 years, not only has the marketplace changed but the workforce has also altered. The skilled worker of today is of a diverse background: minorities, women and people with disabilities have become educated, established and highly successful. The diversity of the workforce is reflected in the demands placed on businesses, because there is an expectation that the businesses they frequent reflect their cultures and ethnicities. This diversity in the marketplace is also reflected in the pool of investors who are ready to invest in small businesses, and they too expect that the businesses they support reflect diversity.

The franchises that will be successful in the future must embrace change, not merely accept it. Change is not something that should scare the enterprising franchisor or franchisee; they ought to be excited by it – because out of change comes progress, and a progressive business is one that is more likely to succeed than not.

THE FUTURE OF THE INDUSTRY

The future of franchising is healthy, largely because of the undeniable sense of the fundamental concept. Franchising undoubtedly offers ambitious, new business owners the highest probability of success with the lowest risk. Analysts predict that, in less than a decade, franchising will account for over 50 per cent of the retail economy, will employ many millions of people, and will enable thousands of aspiring business owners to realize their ultimate dream of success. As the world economies recover from the world economic crisis that began around 2007, and they expand with ever-growing populations, together with the move towards free market economies in new markets, innovative franchise concepts will be introduced and those existing, well-managed and proven franchise companies will continue to grow.

Better protection of franchisee rights will undoubtedly have to evolve, and as time progresses, increasing numbers of franchisors will see the benefit of shaping the relationships with their franchisees to achieve a better balance of accountability, and it may even see a move away from the imbalanced franchise contracts that exist in the current market.

Without a doubt, franchising as a concept and an industry is evolving. Never before in the field of franchising have the opportunities been greater for wealth creation and growth.

Consequently, budding business owners, or those who have an existing business that they want to grow should seriously consider whether franchising could be the method that will enable personal or corporate dreams to be realized in the twenty-first century.

WHAT DO YOU THINK?

How might franchising evolve in the future? Will the challenges and opportunities of information technology make life easier for either the franchisee or the franchisor? How can the industry best maximize its impact on the world of business in the coming years?

Further reading

Duckett, Brian, *How to Turn Your Business into the Next Global Brand: Creating and Managing a Franchised Network* (How to Books 2008).

Gitman, Lawrence J., *The Future of Business: The Essentials (with Building Your Career Booklet)* 4th edn (South-Western College Publishers 2008).

Sitkin, Alan, *International Business: Challenges and Choices* (Oxford University Press, New York 2010).

APPENDIX 1: EUROPEAN FRANCHISE FEDERATION CODE OF ETHICS

European Code of Ethics for Franchising
Part I – Introduction

I – THE EFF REPRESENTS EUROPEAN FRANCHISING

The European Franchise Federation is an international non-profit Association, constituted in 1972. Its members are national Franchise Associations or Federations established in Europe.

The European Franchise Federation also accepts Associate members who are non European Franchise Associations or Federations.

II – THE AIMS OF THE EFF

1) The promotion of Franchising in Europe.

2) Protecting the Franchise Industry by promoting the European Code of Ethics.

3) Influencing and encouraging the development of Franchising in Europe.

4) Representing the interests of the Franchise industry to international organizations such as the European Commission and the European Parliament.

5) The promotion and representation of the European Franchise industry and its members world-wide.

6) The exchange of information and documentation between national Associations or Federations in Europe and in the world.

7) Serving the Member Associations.

III – CONDITIONS FOR MEMBERSHIP

All representative national Associations or Federations established in Europe can apply for membership of the Federation. MEMBERS are subject to the following conditions:

a) members of the national Associations or Federations must be Franchise networks comprising Franchisors and their Franchisees, their governing body primarily composed of Franchisors elected by accredited Franchisor members. Furthermore, the Chairman of the Association or Federation must be a Franchisor and national Board member.

b) acceptance without reservation of the Articles of the FEDERATION and the rules and regulations drawn up in accordance with the Articles.

In particular, member Associations or Federations must require their member Franchisors to accept and comply with the European Code of Ethics on Franchising.

c) each member Association or Federation must operate an accreditation scheme with positive checks to ensure that it's voting Franchisor members comply with the European Code of Ethics on Franchising

d) acceptance by the Board of Directors of the FEDERATION

e) payment of the dues fixed by the Board of Directors of the FEDERATION. The Federation will also admit to Associate membership on terms to be agreed by the Board of Directors, national Franchise Associations who, whilst they do not meet the above conditions, commit to and are demonstrably working towards meeting those conditions.

Part II – The Text of the Code

(last amended on December 5th, 2003)

IV – EUROPEAN CODE OF ETHICS FOR FRANCHISING

This European Code of Ethics is the up-to-date version of the Code first elaborated in 1972 by the European Franchise Federation (EFF).

Each National Association or Federation member of the EFF has participated in its writing and will ensure its promotions, interpretation and adaptation in its own country. Proposed adaptations by Member Associations may come as complements to the basic Code, without altering it, and must be approved by the EFF's governing bodies before being implemented.

This Code of Ethics is meant to be a practical ensemble of essential provisions of fair behavior for Franchise practitioners in Europe.

1. DEFINITION OF FRANCHISING

Franchising is a system of marketing goods and/or services and/or technology, which is based upon a close and ongoing collaboration between legally and financially separate and independent undertakings, the Franchisor and its individual Franchisees, whereby the Franchisor grants its individual Franchisee the right, and imposes the obligation, to conduct a business in accordance with the Franchisor's concept.

The right entitles and compels the individual Franchisee, in exchange for a direct or indirect financial consideration, to use the Franchisor's trade name, and/or trade mark and /or service mark, *know-how*, business and technical methods, procedural system, and other industrial and /or intellectual property rights, supported by continuing provision of commercial and technical assistance, within

the framework and for the term of a written franchise agreement, concluded between parties for this purpose.

"Know-how" means a body of non-patented practical information, resulting from experience and testing by the Franchisor, which is secret, substantial and identified;

▶ "secret" means that the know-how, as a body or in the precise configuration and assembly of its components, is not generally known or easily accessible; it is not limited in the narrow sense that each individual component of the know-how should be totally unknown or unobtainable outside the Franchisor's business;

▶ "substantial" means that the know-how includes information which is indispensable to the Franchisee for the use, sale or resale of the contract goods or services, in particular for the presentation of goods for sale, the processing of goods in connection with the provision of services, methods of dealing with customers, and administration and financial management; the know-how must be useful for the Franchisee by being capable, at the date of conclusion of the agreement, of improving the competitive position of the Franchisee, in particular by improving the Franchisee's performance or helping it to enter a new market;

▶ "identified" means that the know-how must be described in a sufficiently comprehensive manner so as to make it possible to verify that it fulfills the criteria of secrecy and substantiality; the description of the know-how can either be set out in the franchise agreement or in a separate document or recorded in any other appropriate form.

2. GUIDING PRINCIPLES

2.1 The Franchisor is the initiator of a franchise network, composed of itself and its individual Franchisees, of which the Franchisor is the long-term guardian.

2.2 The obligations of the Franchisor: The Franchisor shall

▶ have operated a business concept with success, for a reasonable time and in at least one pilot unit before starting its franchise network,

▶ be the owner, or have legal rights to the use, of its network's trade name, trade mark or other distinguishing identification,

▶ provide the Individual Franchisee with initial training and continuing commercial and/or technical assistance during the entire life of the agreement.

2.3 The obligations of the Individual Franchisee:

The Individual Franchisee shall

▶ devote its best endeavors to the growth of the franchise business and to the maintenance of the common identity and reputation of the franchise network,

▶ supply the Franchisor with verifiable operating data to facilitate the determination of performance and the financial statements necessary for effective management guidance, and allow the Franchisor, and /or its agents, to have access to the individual Franchisee's premises and records at the Franchisor's request and at reasonable times,

▶ not disclose to third parties the know-how provided by the Franchisor, neither during nor after termination of the agreement.

2.4 The ongoing obligations of both parties

Parties shall exercise fairness in their dealings with each other. The Franchisor shall give written notice to its Individual Franchisees of any contractual breach and, where appropriate, grant reasonable time to remedy default;

Parties should resolve complaints, grievances and disputes with good faith and goodwill through fair and reasonable direct communication and negotiation.

3. RECRUITMENT, ADVERTISING AND DISCLOSURE

3.1 Advertising for the recruitment of Individual Franchisees shall be free of ambiguity and misleading statements.

3.2 Any recruitment, advertising and publicity material, containing direct or indirect references to future possible results, figures or earnings to be expected by Individual Franchisees, shall be objective and shall not be misleading.

3.3 In order to allow prospective Individual Franchisees to enter into any binding document with full knowledge, they shall be given a copy of the present Code of Ethics as well as full and accurate written disclosure of all information material to the franchise relationship, within a reasonable time prior to the execution of these binding documents.

3.4 If a Franchisor imposes a Pre-contract on a candidate Individual Franchisee, the following principles should be respected:

▶ prior to the signing of any Pre-contract, the candidate Individual Franchisee should be given written information on its purpose and on any consideration he may be required to pay to the Franchisor to cover the latter's actual expenses, incurred during and with respect to the Pre-contract phase; if the agreement is executed, the said consideration should be reimbursed by the Franchisor or set off against a possible entry fee to be paid by the Individual Franchisee;

▶ the Pre-contract shall define its term and include a termination clause;

▶ the Franchisor can impose non-competition and/or secrecy clauses to protect its know-how and identity.

4. SELECTION OF INDIVIDUAL FRANCHISEES

A Franchisor should select and accept as Individual Franchisees only those who, upon reasonable investigation, appear to possess the basic skills, education, personal qualities and financial resources sufficient to carry on the franchised business.

5. THE FRANCHISE AGREEMENT

5.1 The Franchise agreement shall comply with the National law, European community law and this Code of Ethics and any national Extensions thereto.

5.2 The agreement shall reflect the interests of the members of the franchised network in protecting the Franchisor's industrial and intellectual property rights and in maintaining the common identity and reputation of the franchised network. All agreements and all contractual arrangements in connection with the franchise relationship shall be written in or translated by a sworn translator into the official language of the country the Individual Franchisee is established in, and signed agreements shall be given immediately to the Individual Franchisee.

5.3 The Franchise agreement shall set forth without ambiguity, the respective obligations and responsibilities of the parties and all other material terms of the relationship.

5.4 The essential minimum terms of the agreement shall be the following

- ▶ the rights granted to the Franchisor
- ▶ the rights granted to the Individual Franchisee
- ▶ the goods and/or services to be provided to the Individual Franchisee
- ▶ the obligations of the Franchisor
- ▶ the obligations of the Individual Franchisee
- ▶ the terms of payment by the Individual Franchisee
- ▶ the duration of the agreement which should be long enough to allow Individual Franchisees to amortize their initial investments specific to the franchise
- ▶ the basis for any renewal of the agreement
- ▶ the terms upon which the Individual Franchisee may sell or transfer the franchised business and the Franchisor's possible pre-emption rights in this respect
- ▶ provisions relevant to the use by the Individual Franchisee of the Franchisor's distinctive signs, trade name, trademark, service mark, store sign, logo or other distinguishing identification
- ▶ the Franchisor's right to adapt the franchise system to new or changed methods
- ▶ provisions for termination of the agreement
- ▶ provisions for surrendering promptly upon termination of the franchise agreement any tangible and intangible property belonging to the Franchisor or other owner thereof.

6. THE CODE OF ETHICS AND THE MASTER-FRANCHISE SYSTEM

This Code of Ethics shall apply to the relationship between the Franchisor and its Individual Franchisees and equally between the Master Franchisee and its Individual Franchisees. It shall not apply to the relationship between the Franchisor and its Master Franchisees.

APPENDIX 2: THE WORLD FRANCHISE COUNCIL'S PRINCIPLES OF ETHICS

I - PREAMBLE

▶ These principles are based on the common principles and experience of 34 countries representing the 5 countries;

▶ Each of the World Franchise Council's national franchise associations or federations has contributed to its formulation, and ensures its promotion and specific interpretation in their respective countries;

▶ These principles are not intended to be a law. They describe good professional conduct amongst the actors in franchising around the world.

II - INTRODUCTION

▶ Franchising is a commercial development strategy based on an interdependent partnership between independent commercial entities, the franchisor and the franchisees;

▶ The franchisor and the franchisee commit themselves reciprocally in view of their common and mutual success;

▶ To attain this objective, the commitments of both parties, throughout their relationship, are based on fundamental ethical principles;

▶ These principles apply to the relationship between franchisor and franchisee, as well as to the relationship between master-franchisee and sub-franchisee.

III - ACQUISITION OF THE FRANCHISE

▶ The franchisor must communicate to the prospective franchisee all the information necessary for the franchisee to engage himself in the franchise relationship in full knowledge of his commitments and responsibilities. This information must be provided within a reasonable delay before the signing of the contract, delay which cannot be less than 7 days;

▶ The information provided must be objective, verifiable and devoid of delusion or deceit;

▶ The contract must be communicated to the prospective franchisee as well as a copy of the national Code of Ethics, both in language in which the franchisee is competent;

▶ The franchisor selects franchisees with the aim of achieving their common and mutual success. The franchisor's choice is not based on discrimination relating to race, religion, gender, etc ...;

▶ The prospective franchisee must be open and honest in the information he provides to his future franchisor on his experience, financial means, training, etc. in view of being selected as a franchisee;

▶ The franchisor encourages the prospective franchisee to seek professional advice before signing the franchise contract;

▶ The franchisor encourages the prospective franchisee to make contact and talk to the franchisees of the franchise network he is seeking to join;

▶ In case franchisor and prospective franchisee sign a "contract of reservation" before the franchise contract, the franchisor must specify the conditions under which he will reimburse the prospective franchisee's guarantee payment, if any;

▶ During the negotiation phase, the franchisor may ask the prospective franchisee to sign a legally binding "statement of confidentiality".

IV – CONDUCT OF THE FRANCHISE

The franchisor's general commitments:

▶ The franchisors develop and maintain the commercial and technical know-how that supports the franchise network and favors a permanent and structured dialogue with the franchisees to aid the protection and development of the franchisor's know-how;

▶ In case of non respect of the concept by the franchisee, the franchisor must allow when appropriate the franchisee a reasonable delay to conform to his obligations, after due notification;

▶ The franchisor must ensure that each franchisee respects their obligations and commitments for the general interest of the network.

The franchisee's general commitments:

▶ The franchisee takes an active part in the life of the network and contributes to safeguarding its interests;

▶ The franchisee cannot compete with the network, in particular by appropriating or diverting the know-how transmitted by the franchisor;

▶ The franchisee provides the franchisor with the operational information concerning his franchise business;

▶ The franchisee has a duty of confidentiality during and after the franchise contract.

Commitments common to franchisor and franchisee:

▶ Franchisor and franchisee co-operate in all loyalty and in respect of their mutual obligations and commitments;

▶ In case of litigation, the franchisor and/or the franchisee will seek, when appropriate, to resolve the conflict through mediation;

▶ Franchisor and franchisees commit themselves according to their responsibilities to protect the interests of the consumer.

The franchise contract:
▶ The contract defines the respective rights and obligations of the parties;

▶ The provisions of the contract must be equitable for both of the parties;

▶ The term of the contract must allow a return on investment for the franchisee;

▶ The contract must specify the conditions of sales or transfer of the franchisee's business;

▶ The contract must specify the conditions for any renewal and for termination;

▶ The franchisor must not impose clauses which are not necessary to the protection of the concept;

▶ The contract will be written in the language of the country in which it is to be applied.

V – TERMINATION OF THE FRANCHISE

The termination provisions should protect the franchisor's know-how through appropriate non compete restrictions on the franchisees.

APPENDIX 3: THE INTERNATIONAL FRANCHISE ASSOCIATION CODE OF ETHICS

PREFACE:

The International Franchise Association Code of Ethics is intended to establish a framework for the implementation of best practices in the franchise relationships of IFA members. The Code represents the ideals to which all IFA members agree to subscribe in their franchise relationships. The Code is one component of the IFA's self-regulation program, which also includes the IFA Ombudsman and revisions to the IFA bylaws that will streamline the enforcement mechanism for the Code. The Code is not intended to anticipate the solution to every challenge that may arise in a franchise relationship, but rather to provide a set of core values that are the basis for the resolution of the challenges that may arise in franchise relationships. Also the Code is not intended to establish standards to be applied by third parties, such as the courts, but to create a framework under which IFA and its members will govern themselves. The IFA's members believe that adherence to the values expressed in the IFA Code will result in healthy, productive, and mutually beneficial franchise relationships. The Code, like franchising, is dynamic and may be revised to reflect the most current developments in structuring and maintaining franchise relationships.

TRUST, TRUTH, AND HONESTY:

Foundations of Franchising

Every franchise relationship is founded on the mutual commitment of both parties to fulfill their obligations under the franchise agreement. Each party will fulfill its obligations, will act consistent with the interests of the brand and will not act so as to harm the brand and system. This willing interdependence between Franchisors and Franchisees, and the trust and honesty upon which it is founded, has made franchising a worldwide success as a strategy for business growth.

Honesty embodies openness, candor, and truthfulness. Franchisees and franchisors commit to sharing ideas and information and to facing challenges in clear and direct terms. IFA members will be sincere in word, act, and character — reputable and without deception.

The public image and reputation of the franchise system is one of its most valuable and enduring assets. A positive image and reputation will create value for franchisors and franchisees, attract investment in existing and new outlets from franchisees and from new franchise operators, help capture additional market share, and enhance consumer loyalty and satisfaction. This can only be achieved with trust, truth, and honesty between franchisors and franchisees.

MUTUAL RESPECT AND REWARD:

Winning together, as a team

The success of franchise systems depends upon both franchisors and franchisees attaining their goals. The IFA's members believe that franchisors cannot be successful unless their franchisees are also successful, and conversely, that franchisees will not succeed unless their franchisor is also successful. IFA members believe that a franchise system should be committed to help its franchisees succeed, and that such efforts are likely to create value for the system and attract new investment in the system.

IFA's members are committed to showing respect and consideration for each other and to those with whom they do business. Mutual respect includes recognizing and honoring extraordinary achievement and exemplary commitment to the system. IFA members believe that franchisors and franchisees share the responsibility for improving their franchise system in a manner that rewards both franchisors and franchisees.

OPEN AND FT COMMUNICATION:

Successful franchise systems thrive on it

IFA's members believe that franchising is a unique form of business relationship. Nowhere else in the world does there exist a business relationship that embodies such a significant degree of mutual interdependence. IFA members believe that to be successful, this unique relationship requires continual and effective communication between franchisees and franchisors.

IFA's members recognize that misunderstanding and loss of trust and consensus on the direction of a franchise system can develop when franchisors and franchisees fail to communicate effectively. Effective communication requires openness, candor, and trust and is an integral component of a successful franchise system. Effective communication is an essential predicate for consensus and collaboration, the resolution of differences, progress, and innovation.

To foster franchising as a unique and enormously successful relationship, IFA's members commit to establishing and maintaining programs that promote effective communication within franchise systems. These programs should be widely publicized within systems, available to all members of the franchise system, and should facilitate frequent dialogue within franchise systems. IFA members are encouraged to also utilize the IFA Ombudsman to assist in enhancing communication and collaboration about issues affecting the franchise system.

OBEY THE LAW:

A responsibility to preserve the promise of franchising

> IFA's members enthusiastically support full compliance with, and vigorous enforcement of, all applicable federal and state franchise regulations. This commitment is fundamental to enhancing and safeguarding the business environment for franchising. IFA's members believe that the information provided during the presale disclosure process is the cornerstone of a positive business climate for franchising, and is the basis for successful and mutually beneficial franchise relationships.

CONFLICT RESOLUTION:

> IFA's members are realistic about franchise relationships, and recognize that from time to time disputes will arise in those relationships. IFA's members are committed to the amicable and prompt resolution of these disputes. IFA members believe that franchise systems should establish a method for internal dispute resolution and should publicize and encourage use of such dispute resolution mechanisms. For these reasons, the IFA has created the IFA Ombudsman program, an independent third-party who can assist franchisors and franchisees by facilitating dialogue to avoid disputes and to work together to resolve disputes. The IFA also strongly recommends the use of the National Franchise Mediation Program (NFMP) when a more structured mediation service is needed to help resolve differences.

Support of IFA and the Member Code of Ethics

> Franchisees and franchisors have a responsibility to voice their concerns and offer suggestions on how the Code and the International Franchise Association can best meet the needs of its members. Franchisors and franchisees commit to supporting and promoting the initiatives of the IFA and advocating adherence to the letter and spirit of the Member Code of Ethics. Members who feel that another member has violated the Code in their U.S. operations may file a formal written complaint with the President of the IFA.

APPENDIX 4: NATIONAL FRANCHISING ASSOCIATIONS

Country	Association name	Website address
Argentina	Asociacion Argentina de Franchising	www.aafranchising.com
Australia	Franchise Council of Australia	www.franchise.org.au
Austria	Österreichischer Franchise-Verband	www.franchise.at
Belgium	Fédération Belge de la Franchise	www.fbf-bff.be
Brazil	Associação Brasileira de Franchising	www.abf.com.br
Canada	Canadian Franchise Association	www.cfa.ca
China	China Chain Store & Franchise Assn	http://www.chinaretail.org
Czech Republic	Česká asociace franchisingu	www.czech-franchise.cz
Denmark	Dansk Franchise Forening	www.franchise foreningen.dk
Egypt	Egyptian Franchise Development Association	www.efda.org.eg
Finland	Suomen Franchising Yhdistys ry	www.franchising.fi
France	Fédération française de la franchise	www.franchise-fff.com
Germany	Deutscher Franchise Verband e.v.	www.franchiseverband.com
Greece	Greek Franchise Association	www.franchising.gr
Hong Kong	Hong Kong Franchise Association	www.franchise.org.hk
Hungary	Magyar Franchise Szövetség	www.franchise.hu
India	Indian Franchise Association	www.franchiseindia.org
Italy	L'Associazione Italiana del Franchising	www.assofranchising.it
Japan	Japan Franchise Association	www.jfa-fc.or.jp
Kazakhstan	Kazakhstan Franchise Association	(Unknown)
Malaysia	Malaysian Franchise Association	www.mfa.org.my
Mexico	Asociación Mexicana de Franquicias	www.franquiciasde mexico.org

Netherlands	Nederlands Franchise Vereniging	www.nfv.nl
New Zealand	Franchise Association of New Zealand	www.franchise.co.nz
Philippines	Philippine Franchise Association	www.pfa.org.ph
Portugal	Associação Portuguesa da Franchise	www.apfranchise.org
Russian Federation	Russian Franchise Association	www.ru.rusfranch.ru
Singapore	Franchising and Licensing Association (Singapore)	www.flasingapore.org
Slovenia	Slovenian Franchise Association	www.franchise-slovenia.net
South Africa	Franchise Association of South Africa	www.fasa.co.za
Sweden	Svenska Franchiseföreningen	www.franchise foreningen.se
Switzerland	Schweizer Franchise Verband	www.franchise verband.ch
Taiwan (PoC)	Taiwan Chain Store and Franchise Association	www.tfca.org.tw
Turkey	Türkiye Franchising Derneği - UFRAD	http://www.world franchisecouncil.org/ control/www.ufrad.org.tr
United Kingdom	British Franchise Association	www.thebfa.org
USA	International Franchise Association	www.franchise.org

BIBLIOGRAPHY

BOOKS

Adams, John (2006) *Franchising: Practice and Precedents in Business Format Franchising*, 5th edn (Tottel Publishing).

Atlantic Publishing Company (2006) *The Franchise Handbook: A Complete Guide to All Aspects of Buying, Selling or Investing in a Franchise* (Atlantic Publishing Company).

Baldi, Roberto (1988) *Distributorship, Franchising, Agency: Community and National Laws and Practice in the EEC* (Springer).

Barkoff, Rupert M. (2004) *Fundamentals of Franchising*, 2nd edn (American Bar Association).

Bennett, Julie with Babcock, Cheryl (2008) *Franchise Times Guide to Selecting, Buying & Owning a Franchise* (Sterling Press).

Birkeland, Peter M. (2004) *Franchising Dreams: The Lure of Entrepreneurship in America* (University of Chicago Press).

Bisio, R. and Kohler, W. M. (2008) *The Educated Franchisee: The How-To Book for Choosing a Winning Franchise* (Bascom Hill Publishing Group).

Blair, Roger D. (2005) *The Economics of Franchising* (Cambridge University Press).

Bradach, Jeffrey L. (1998) *Franchise Organizations* (Harvard Business Review Press).

Clifton, Daphne (2008) *Franchising: Making Franchising Work for You Without Breaking the Bank (Business on a Shoestring)* (A & C Black).

Diaz, Odavia Bueno (2008) *Franchising in European Contract Law: A Comparison between the Main Obligations of the Contracting Parties in the Principles of European Law on Commercial Agency, Franchise and Distribution* (Sellier European Law Publishers).

Dicke, Thomas S. (2010) *Franchising in America: The Development of a Business Method, 1840–1980* (University of North Carolina Press).

Foster, D. L. (2008) *Franchising: The Inside Story* (CreateSpace).

Hero, Marco (2010) *International Franchising: A Practitioner's Guide* (Globe Law and Business).

Hoy, Frank (2002) *Franchising: An International Perspective* (Routledge).

Icon Group (2008) *The 2009–2014 World Outlook for Franchising* (ICON Group International, Inc.).

Illetschko, Kurt (2010) *Get Started in Franchising (Teach Yourself)* (Hodder & Stoughton).

Jarkina, Viktorija (2010) *Franchising in Theory and Practice: A Franchise Agreement in the Framework of Civil Law* (LAP LAMBERT Academic Publishing).

Judd, R. J. and Justis, R. T. (2007) *Franchising* (Custom Publishing).

Keup, Erwin (2007) *Franchise Bible: How to Buy a Franchise or Franchise Your Own Business*, 6th edn (Entrepreneur Press).

Kinch, J. E. and Hayes, J. P. (1988) *Franchising: The Inside Story – How to Start Your Own Business and Succeed!* (HarperCollins).

Lafontaine, Francine (2005) *Franchise Contracting and Organization (Business Economics)* (Edward Elgar).

Levonsky, Rieva (2004) *Ultimate Book of Franchises* (Entrepreneur Press).

Maitland, Iain (2000) *Franchising* (Management Books 2000 Ltd).

Massetti, R., Jr. (2007) *Is Your Business Right for Franchising?* (Lulu).

Mendelsohn, Martin (2004a) *Franchising Law*, 2nd edn (Richmond Law & Tax Ltd).

Mendelsohn, Martin (2004b) *The Guide to Franchising*, 7th edn (Cengage Learning EMEA).

Murray, Iain (2006) *Franchising Handbook* (Kogan Page).

Olson, S. (2008) *Grow to Greatness: How to Build a World-Class Franchise System*, 2nd edn (Franchise Update Media Group).

Palmer, Andrew P. (2007) *The Seven Pillars of Franchising Success* (Xlibris Corporation).

Parker, Philip M. (2006) *The 2007 Report on Franchising: World Market Segmentation by City* (ICON Group International, Inc.).

Parker, Philip M. (2007) *Franchising in Finland: A Strategic Reference, 2006* (ICON Group International, Inc.).

Pratt, John H. (2006) *The Franchisor's Handbook: Your Duties, Responsibilities and Liabilities* (About Face).

Purvin, R. L., Jr. (2008) *The Franchise Fraud: How to Protect Yourself Before and After You Invest* (BookSurge).

Ritzer, G. (2012) *The McDonaldization of Society: 20th Anniversary Edition* (Sage).

Shane, Scott A. (2005) *From Ice Cream to the Internet: Using Franchising to Drive the Growth and Profits of Your Company* (FT Press).

Sherman, Andrew J. (2011) *Franchising & Licensing: Two Powerful Ways to Grow Your Business in Any Economy*, 4th edn (AMACOM).

Shook, Carrie (1993) *Franchising: The Business Strategy That Changed the World* (Prentice Hall Trade).

Spinelli, Stephen, Jr. (2003) *Franchising: Pathway to Wealth Creation* (FT Press).

Stanworth, John (1991) *The Barclays Guide to Franchising for the Small Business (Barclays Small Business Series)* (Blackwell).

Sugars, Bradley (2005) *Successful Franchising (Instant Success Series)* (McGraw-Hill).

Sun, S. (2011) *Grow Smart, Risk Less: A Low-Capital Path to Multiplying Your Business Through Franchising* (Greenleaf Book Group Press).

Worth, Sophie (2008) *Key Note Market Report 2008 Franchising* (Key Note Limited).

PAPERS

Aliouche, E. H. and Schlentrich, U. (2010) The Franchise Ownership Structure Puzzle, in *Proceedings of the 24th Annual International Society of Franchising Conference*.

Azevedo, P. F. and Silva, V. L. S. (2003) Food Franchising and Backward Coordination: An Empirical Analysis of Brazilian Firms, *Journal on Chain and Network Science*, 3(1): 33–44.

Baker, G. (2006) Sharon Kenny on Franchising, *NZ Business*, 20(7): 38–9.

Baroncelli, A. (1997) Franchising as a Form of Divestment: An Italian Study, *Industrial Marketing Management*, 26(3): 223–35.

Barroso, J. M. D. (2009) Putting Corporate Social Responsibility at the Heart of our Vision, *CSR Europe*: 1.

Bates, T. (1998) Survival Patterns Among Newcomers to Franchising, *Journal of Business Venturing*, 13(2): 113–30.

Boyle, E. (2002) The Failure of Business Format Franchising in British Forecourt Retailing: A Case Study of the Rebranding of Shell Retail's Forecourts, *International Journal of Retail Distribution Management*, 30(5): 251–63.

Brickley, J. A. and Dark, F. H. (1987) The Choice of Organizational Form: The Case of Franchising, *Journal of Financial Economics*, 18(2): 401–20.

Brodie, S., Stanworth, J. and Wotruba, T. R. (2002) Direct Sales Franchises in the UK: A Self-Employment Grey Area, *National Small Firms Policy and Research Conference*, 2: 977–1000.

Castrogiovanni, G. J., Combs, J. G. and Justis, R. T. (2004) Views on Franchising, *Management* (1968): 1–7.

Chan, P. S. and Justis, R. T. (1993) To Franchise or Not to Franchise?, *Management Decision*, 31(5): 22–6.

Charnes, A., Huang, Z. M. and Mahajan, V. (1995) Franchising Coordination with Brand Name Considerations, *Research in Marketing*, 12: 1–47.

Chow, L. and Frazer, L. (2003) Servicing Customers Directly: Mobile Franchising Arrangements in Australia, *European Journal of Marketing*, 37(3/4): 594–613.

Cochet, O. and Garg, V. K. (2008) How Do Franchise Contracts Evolve? A Study of Three German SMEs, *Journal of Small Business Management*, 46(1): 134–51.

Colomb, G. G. (2010) Franchising the Future, *College Composition and Communication*, 62(1): 11–30.

Combs, J. G. and Ketchen, D. J. (2003) Why Do Firms Use Franchising as an Entrepreneurial Strategy? A Meta-analysis, *Journal of Management*, 29(3): 443–65.

Dant, R. P., Brush, C. G. and Iniesta, F. P. (1996) Participation Patterns of Women in Franchising, *Journal of Small Business Management*, 34(2): 14–28.

Dant, R. P., Perrigot, R. and Cliquet, G. (2008) A Cross-Cultural Comparison of the Plural Forms in Franchise Networks: United States, France, and Brazil, *Journal of Small Business Management*, 46(2): 286–311.

De Azevedo, P. F. (2009) Allocation of Authority in Franchise Chains, *International Studies of Management and Organization*, 39(4): 31–42.

Dickey, M. H., McKnight, D. H. and George, J. F. (2007) The Role of Trust in Franchise Organizations, *International Journal of Organizational Analysis*, 15(3): 251–82.

Dittman, D. A. (1996) Franchise Relations, *Cornell Hospitality Quarterly*, 37(3): 2.

Doherty, A. M. and Alexander, N. S. (2006) Power and Control in International Retail Franchising, *European Journal of Marketing*, 40(11/12): 1292–316.

Eroglu, S. (1992) The Internationalization Process of Franchising, *International Management Review*, 9(5): 19–30.

Fladmoe-Lindquist, K. (1996) International Franchising: Capabilities and Development, *Journal of Business Venturing*, 11(5): 419–38.

Frazer, L. (2001) Causes of Disruption to Franchise Operations, *Journal of Business Research*, 54(3): 227–34.

Gale, D., Des, H. and Aug, P. (2008) Franchising Stays Strong in Tough Times, *Hotels*, 42.

Gallini, N. T. and Lutz, N. A. (1992) Dual Distribution and Royalty Fees in Franchising, *Journal of Law Economics and Organization*, 8(3): 471–501.

Gilbert, G. R., Veloutsou, C., Goode, M. M. H. and Moutinho, L. (2004) Measuring Customer Satisfaction in the Fast Food Industry: A Cross-National Approach, *Journal of Services Marketing*, 18(5): 371–83.

Hadfield, G. K. (1990) Problematic Relations: Franchising and the Law of Incomplete Contracts, *Stanford Law Review*, 42(4): 927–92.

Holme, R. and Watts, P. (2000) Corporate Social Responsibility: Making Good Business Sense, *World Business Council for Sustainable Development*: 8.

Hoy, F. and Shane, S. (1998) Franchising as an Entrepreneurial Venture Form, *Journal of Business Venturing*, 13(2): 91–4.

Huang, Z. (1997) Bargaining, Risk and Franchising Coordination, *Computers & Operations Research*, 24(1): 73–83.

Hunt, S. D. and Nevin, J. R. (1975) Tying Agreements in Franchising, *Journal of Marketing*, 39(3): 20–6.

Huszagh, S. M. (1992) International Franchising, *International Management Review*, 9(5): 5–18.

Inma, C., Shurville, S, and Williams, J. (2005) Purposeful Franchising: Re-Thinking of the Franchising Rationale, Singapore *Management Review*: 3031.

Isakson, B. M. M. and Clean, A. S. (2005) The Characteristics of a Leader in Franchising, *Franchising World* (January): 26–8.

Johnson, B. D. (2007) Franchising Expansion Fueled by Industry Entrepreneurs, *Franchising World* (December): 2005–7.

Kaufmann, P. (1999a) Franchising and the Domain of Entrepreneurship Research, *Journal of Business Venturing*, 14(1): 5–16.

Kaufmann, P. (1999b) Standardization and Adaptation in Business Format Franchising, *Journal of Business Venturing*, 14(1): 69–85.

Kaufmann, P. J. (1999) Franchising and the Choice of Self Employment, *Journal of Business Venturing*, 14(4): 345–62.

Kaufmann, P. J. and Kim, S .H. (1995) Master Franchising and System Growth Rates, *Journal of Marketing Channels*, 4(1): 49–64.

King, D. (2004) Selecting a Franchise for a Business Enterprise, *Real Estate Finance*: 18–22.

Kirby, D. and Watson, A. (1999) Franchising as a Small Business Development Strategy: A Qualitative Study of Operational and 'Failed' Franchisors in the UK, *Journal of Small Business and Enterprise Development*, 6(4): 341–9.

Klein, B. (1995) The Economics of Franchise Contracts, *Journal of Corporate Finance*, 2(1–2): 9–37.

Klein, B. and Saft, L. F. (1985) The Law and Economics of Franchise Tying Contracts, *Journal of Law and Economics*, 28(2): 345–61.

Kunitomo, R. (1997) Seven-Eleven Is Revolutionising Grocery Distribution in Japan, *Long Range Planning*, 30(6): 877–89.

Lafontaine, F. (1992) Agency Theory and Franchising: Some Empirical Results, *The RAND Journal of Economics*, 23(2) (Summer): 263–83.

Lafontaine, F. (1995) Pricing Decisions in Franchised Chains: A Look at the Restaurant and Fast-Food Industry, National Bureau of Economic Research Working Paper Series, No. 5247.

Lafontaine, F. and Bhattacharyya, S. (1995) The Role of Risk in Franchising, *Journal of Corporate Finance*, 2(1–2): 39–74.

Lafontaine, F. and Slade, M. E. (2002) Incentive Contracting and the Franchise Decision, National Bureau of Economic Research Working Paper Series, No. 6544(1978): 133–88.

Lashley, C. and Morrison, A. J. (2003) A Franchise: A Resource-rich Small Service Firm?, *Service Industries Journal*, 23(4): 135–49.

Lavonen, R. (2010) Franchising as a Potential Growth Strategy for a Small Enterprise, *Business management thesis*, Mikkeli University of Applied Sciences, Finland.

Leblebici, H. and Shalley, C. E. (1996) The Organization of Relational Contracts: The Allocation of Rights in Franchising, *Journal of Business Venturing*, 11(5): 403–18.

Leibowitz, L. (1997) Franchise Margins and the Sales-Driven Franchise Value, *Financial Analysts Journal*, 53(6): 43–53.

Lindblom, A. and Tikkanen, H. (2010) Knowledge Creation and Business Format Franchising, *Management Decision*, 48(2): 179–88.

López, B., González-Busto, B. and Álvarez, Y. (2000) The Dynamics of Franchising Agreements, *Proceedings of the 18th International Conference of the System Dynamics Society*: 131.

Lutz, N. A. (1995) Ownership Rights and Incentives in Franchising, *Journal of Corporate Finance*, 2(1–2): 103–31.

Mariz-Pérez, R. and García-Álvarez, T. (2009) The Internationalization Strategy of Spanish Indigenous Franchised Chains: A Resource-Based View, *Journal of Small Business Management*, 47(4): 514–30.

McIntyre, F. S. and Huszagh, S. M. (1995) Internationalization of Franchise Systems, *Journal of International Marketing*, 3(4): 39–56.

Michael, S. C. (1999) The Elasticity of Franchising, *Small Business Economics*, 12(4): 313–20.

Michael, S. C. (2003) First Mover Advantage Through Franchising, *Journal of Business Venturing*, 18(1): 61–80.

Michael, S. C. and Bercovitz, J. E. L. (2009) A Strategic Look at the Organizational Form of Franchising, *Advances in Strategic Management*, 26(2009): 193–220.

Mumdžiev, N. and Windsperger, J. (2011) The Structure of Decision Rights in Franchising Networks: A Property Rights Perspective, *Entrepreneurship: Theory and Practice*, 35(3): 449–65.

Nyadzayo, M. W., Matanda, M. J. and Ewing, M. T. (2011) Brand Relationships and Brand Equity in Franchising, *Industrial Marketing Management*, 40(7): 1103–15.

Oxenfeldt, A. R. and Thompson, D. (1969) Franchising in Perspective, *Journal of Retailing*, 44(4): 3–13.

Paswan, A. K. and Wittmann, C. M. (2009) Knowledge Management and Franchise Systems, *Industrial Marketing Management*, 38(2): 173–80.

Peretiako, R. (2009) Franchising in Ukraine, *European Journal of Marketing*, 43(1–2): 21.

Perrigot, R. (2006) Services vs Retail Chains: Are There Any Differences? Evidence from the French Franchising Industry, *International Journal of Retail Distribution Management*, 34(12): 918–30.

Petersen, B. and Welch, L. S. (2000) International Retailing Operations: Downstream Entry and Expansion via Franchising, *International Business Review*, 9(4): 479–96.

Prager, R. (1990) Firm Behavior in Franchise Monopoly Markets, *The Rand Journal of Economics*, 21(2): 211–25.

Roh, Y. S. and Andrew, W. P. (1997) Sub-Franchising: A Multi-Unit Alternative to Traditional Restaurant Franchising, *Cornell Hospitality Quarterly*, 38(6): 39.

Rothenberg, A. M. (1967) A Fresh Look at Franchising, *The Journal of Marketing*, 31(3): 52–4.

Rubin, P. H. (1978) The Theory of the Firm and the Structure of the Franchise Contract, *Journal of Law and Economics*, 21(1): 223–33.

Sanghavi, N. (1998) Franchising as a Tool for Small Medium Sized Enterprises (SME) Development In Transitional Economies – The Case of Central European Countries, *Management Research News*, 21(11): 35–44.

Shane, S. and Spell, C. (1998) Factors for New Franchise Success, *Sloan Management Review*, 39(3): 43–50.

Shane, S. A. and Hoy, F. (1996) Franchising: A Gateway to Cooperative Entrepreneurship, *Journal of Business Venturing*, 11(5): 325–7.

Shay, B. M. (2007) The Brain Behind Franchising – Branding, *Franchising World* (May).

Sigué, S. P. and Chintagunta, P. (2009) Advertising Strategies in a Franchise System, *European Journal of Operational Research*, 198(2): 655–65.

Stanworth, J. and Curran, J. (1999) Colas, Burgers, Shakes and Shirkers: Towards a Sociological Model of Franchising in the Market Economy, *Journal of Business Venturing*, 14(4): 323–44.

Stanworth, J., Purdy, D., Price, S. and Zafiris, N. (1998) Franchise Versus Conventional Small Business Failure Rates in the US and UK: More Similarities than Differences, *International Small Business Journal*, 16(3): 56–69.

Stern, P. and Stanworth, J. (1994) Improving Small Business Survival Rates via Franchising: The Role of the Banks in Europe, *International Small Business Journal*, 12(2): 15–25.

Storholm, G. and Scheuing, E. E. (1994) Ethical Implications of Business Format Franchising, *Journal of Business Ethics*, 13(3): 181–8.

Tuunanen, M. (2001) Entrepreneurial Paradoxes in Business Format Franchising: An Empirical Survey of Finnish Franchisees, *International Small Business Journal*, 19(4): 47–62.

Vaughn, C. L. (1974) International Franchising, *Cornell Hotel and Restaurant Administration Quarterly*, 14(4): 103–10.

Wallace, J. E. (1999) Franchise Law Firms and the Transformation of Personal Legal Services, *The American Journal of Sociology*, 104(4): 1218–20.

Watson, A. (2008) Small Business Growth Through Franchising, *Journal of Marketing Channels*, 15(1): 3–21.

Weaven, S. and Frazer, L. (2004) Multi Unit Franchising: Australian Revelations, in *Proceedings of the 18th International Society of Franchising Conference*.

Weaven, S., Isaac, J. and Herrington, C. (2007) Franchising as a Path to Self-Employment for Australian Female Entrepreneurs, *Organization*: 345–65.

Windsperger, J. (2003) Complementarities and Substitutabilities in Franchise Contracting: Some Results from the German Franchise Sector, *Journal of Management and Governance*, 7(3): 291–313.

Wright, O. and Frazer, L. (2007) A Multiple Case Analysis of Franchised Co-branding, *Australasian Marketing Journal*, 15(2): 68–80.

Wright, O., Frazer, L. and Merrilees, B. (2007) McCafe: The McDonald's Co-branding Experience, *Journal of Brand Management*, 14(6): 442–57.

Zanarone, G. (2009) Vertical Restraints and the Law: Evidence from Automobile Franchising, *Journal of Law and Economics*, 52: 691–700.

ELECTRONIC REFERENCES

AccessMyLibrary (2010) Franchising World article archives from May 2009. Available at: http://www.accessmylibrary.com/archive/6114-franchising-world/may-2009.html.

AllBusiness.com (2010) Franchising: Business solutions. Available at: http://www.allbusiness.com/small-business-franchising/15613700-1.html.

Business Link (2010) Turn Your Business into a Franchise. Available at: http://www.businesslink.gov.uk/bdotg/action/layer?topicId=1077055924.

The Franchise Magazine online (2010). Business franchise opportunities and UK franchise information. Available at: http://www.thefranchisemagazine.net/.

The Franchisor magazine (2010) News, information and special offers for UK franchisors. Available at: http://www.thefranchisor.co.uk/.

University of New Hampshire, Whittemore School of Business and Economics (2010) Rosenberg International Franchise Center. Available at: http://www.wsbe.unh.edu/william-rosenberg-center-international-franchising.

Which Franchise (2010) Franchise opportunities and best business franchises for sale in the UK. Available at: http://www.whichfranchise.com/.

INDEX